Praise for *Time and* [...]

'I love James Wallman's principles for spending your time wisely. This isn't just a book about how to be more productive, it's a guidebook for living an awesome life!'

– Nir Eyal, bestselling author of *Hooked* and *Indistractable*

'A perfect combination of engaging, profound, and instructive. It's changed how I think of and spend my own personal time. The time you spend reading *Time and How to Spend It* will reward you a hundredfold with weeks, months, and years better spent.'

– Adam Alter, Professor of Marketing and Psychology, New York University, *New York Times* bestselling author of *Irresistible* and *Drunk Tank Pink*

'If you're one of those people who feels they aren't taking a big enough bite out of life, you're likely to find the perfect antidote in this easy-to-read tour of the academic literature on happiness and well-being.'

– Tom Gilovich, Professor of Psychology, Cornell University

'The puzzle we all face today is how to best to spend our time. This book provides an entertaining and insightful guide for how to spend our weekends, vacations, and life. It's definitely worth your time!'

– Cassie Mogilner Holmes, Associate Professor of Marketing and Behavioural Decision Making, UCLA

'Follow James Wallman's advice, and we will change our days, and in turn, our lives. For once, this book deserves the description "life-changing".'

– Rachel Kelly, author of *Black Rainbow* and *Walking on Sunshine*

'Our modern lives whizz by in a digital din of pings and dings leaving us frazzled and short of time. James's entertaining and brilliant book helps us get much more from our most precious resource, time. A timeless classic for navigating 21st century life.'

– Michael Acton Smith OBE, author of *Calm*

'James Wallman is the Malcolm Gladwell of today's Experience Economy. He brings together the best of social science research with insights and stories relayed with wit and verve.'

– B. Joseph Pine II, co-author of *The Experience Economy: Competing for Customer Time, Attentions, and Money*

'Unlike money, time must be spent: 24 hours of it, every day. James Wallman distills behavioural science into a set of actionable guidelines to help us make the most of the time we have to spend.'

– Michael Norton, Professor of Business Administration at Harvard Business School, and co-author of *Happy Money*

'Our happiness is determined by how we choose to spend our time. This book is an inspiring call for us to prioritise experiences over things and focus on what really matters.'

– Dr Mark Williamson, Director of Action for Happiness

'James Wallman's treatise on time contains some awesome solutions for the ancient conundrum of what it means to live a good life. Drop what you're doing right now and read this book.'

– Scott Carney, *New York Times* bestselling author of *What Doesn't Kill Us*

'Fresh, fun, provocative and practical. James Wallman gets you thinking, deciding and acting. Reading *Time and How to Spend It* is time very well spent.'

– Julia Hobsbawm, Honorary Visiting Professor at Cass Business School and author of *Fully Connected*

'One of those rare books that can make you think seriously about how you could live a better life – not one that's superficially appealing and Instagram-worthy, but one filled with satisfaction, joy, and yes, time well spent.'

– Alex Soojung-Kim Pang, author of *Rest*

'If there's one book to read to make sense of today's "I can't put my phone down" culture (and how to live better in it) – this is it. Smart, well-researched and very readable. I didn't want to put it down.'

– Marianne Cantwell, author of *Be a Free Range Human*

TIME
AND HOW TO
SPEND IT

THE 7 RULES FOR RICHER, HAPPIER DAYS

JAMES WALLMAN

1 3 5 7 9 10 8 6 4 2

WH Allen, an imprint of Ebury Publishing,
20 Vauxhall Bridge Road,
London SW1V 2SA

WH Allen is part of the Penguin Random House group of companies
whose addresses can be found at global.penguinrandomhouse.com

Penguin
Random House
UK

Copyright © James Wallman 2019

Excerpt from 'Do not go gentle into that good night',
copyright © The Dylan Thomas Trust.

James Wallman has asserted his right to be identified as the author of this
Work in accordance with the Copyright, Designs and Patents Act 1988

First published in the United Kingdom by WH Allen in 2019

www.penguin.co.uk

A CIP catalogue record for this book is available from the British Library

ISBN 9780753552650

Illustrations by Greg Stevenson

Typeset in 10.25/13.5 pts Sabon LT Std
by Integra Software Services Pvt. Ltd, Pondicherry

Printed and bound in Great Britain by Clays Ltd, Elcograf S.p.A.

Penguin Random House is committed to a sustainable future for our
business, our readers and our planet. This book is made from
Forest Stewardship Council® certified paper.

For Jenny and Alan,
for showing me how to spend time.

'How we spend our days is, of course, how we spend our lives.'

Annie Dillard

CONTENTS

Eternal Sunshine for Your Spotless Mind

'Time is what we want most, but what we use worst.'

WILLIAM PENN

O nce upon a time there was a girl who moaned so much about a one-night stand she inspired a movie that won an Oscar. This was more than two decades ago now, and the details about the girl – her name, the colour of her hair, and what she looked like – have faded like the colours on an old T-shirt. They haven't been deliberately erased, just, like so many memories, forgotten.

But the night she'd rather forget will live on – because it sparked a thought that would grow wings and carry her friend all the way from France, across the Atlantic, to the USA: to 6801 Hollywood Boulevard, Hollywood, California, and on to the stage at the Kodak Theatre on 27 February 2005, to accept an Academy Award for Best Original Screenplay.

There's a far more important outcome than her friend winning an Oscar, though. Details like the colour of her hair may have faded, but that's nothing compared to the tangerine-bright, vital question she raised.

The girl's friend, the one she was complaining to, is a man by the name of Pierre Bismuth. Bismuth is an artist. Born in France in 1963, he looks like a stockier version of the comedian Omid Djalili: balding with glasses and a bushy, salt-and-pepper beard.

'She'd just had sex with some guy two nights before, and she was a little ashamed,' Bismuth says now, a typical French air in his accent, remembering fragments from that conversation in the mid-1990s. 'I wanted to torture her a little, you know. To show that it was impossible to resolve this problem simply by erasing the memory.'

So, when the girl kept moaning, and said, 'I wish I could just forget it ever happened,' Bismuth had an idea.

'If you were able,' he said, curious, 'to wipe this "adventure" from your memory, would you do it?'

What would you have said? You've probably done something you've regretted in the past. Perhaps you said something, did something. We all have, haven't we? We all make mistakes. Things go wrong. Bad things happen, even to good people like you and me and Bismuth's friend. We have to just shrug – 'c'est la vie' – and move on.

But what if we didn't? What if you could not only sweep your bad memory into a corner, but clear it out completely? We tidy up our homes and our lives. We discard things as we outgrow or lose interest in them. Why not clean up your past too? Why not wipe your memory, and make your past pristine?

When Bismuth asked his friend if she'd like to do this, she said, without hesitation, 'Yes!' As she did that, though she wouldn't have had any idea at the time, she lit a fuse in Bismuth's curious, creative mind.

What would that mean? What would erasing a memory look like? Could it be done? If not today, surely it would be possible at some point in the future. And if it could be done, Bismuth wondered, 'What situations would arise as a result and how would you deal with those possibilities?'

One situation that did arise in the real world was Bismuth talking about the idea with another friend of his, a fellow Frenchman and film director named Michel Gondry. They took it to an American screenwriter named Charlie Kaufman. And he wrote the script for the Oscar-winning movie *Eternal Sunshine of the Spotless Mind*.

There are two stars in the movie. Kate Winslet plays Clementine, a mixed-up twenty-something girl who dyes her hair blue, green and tangerine orange. One windy, lonely, grey day at the beach, Clementine meets a mixed-up twenty-something boy called Joel, played by Jim Carrey. They're drawn together, they fall in love. But they have one of those rocky, up-down relationships. After one break-up, they both decide to erase their memories of each other.

So we watch as the people at the memory-deletion firm scan Joel's mind, looking for memories of Clementine to scrub. They delete arguments, bust-ups, those boring dinners when they'd run out of things to say to each other. But then they begin to delete the good times too.

That's when Joel realises, and when we, in the audience, realise too, that you can't just airbrush the past to perfection. Bad experiences aren't islands, set adrift from the rest of our lives. They're not like clothes in your wardrobe. If you throw a memory out, you lose more than just that one memory. The bad are usually connected to the good, and to something else besides: lessons we've learned, who we were, who we are, who we want to be. Rummage around in your treasure chest of memories for a moment. If you were to toss out some of those bad, boring or ugly experiences you wish hadn't happened, what else would you lose?

The question here – the one that Bismuth's friend prompted, that Bismuth asked, and that became the central idea of *Eternal Sunshine of the Spotless Mind* – reminds me of a classic thought experiment called the Experience Machine.

The idea of the Experience Machine was introduced by an American philosopher named Robert Nozick in 1974.

It's a sort of sci-fi flotation tank, designed to give people the ultimate experience for the rest of their natural lives. To plug in, you get inside, lie back, attach some electrodes into your brain, like you'd install a set of speakers, and you're off, guaranteed to have the best possible experience of life.

The Experience Machine doesn't just offer a 'cupcakes-and-rainbows', happy-ever-after version of life. The life you'd experience if you plugged in would include just the right amount of challenge and hardship and interest value necessary to give you the best, happiest experience of life. For instance, as Nozick wrote, 'Superduper neuropsychologists could stimulate your brain so that you would think and feel you were writing a great novel, or making a friend, or reading an interesting book.'

After describing his sci-fi idea, Nozick asked a simple question: 'Should you plug into this machine for life, preprogramming your life's experiences?'

I want to ask you the same question: to plug in, or not to plug in?

Introducing a Real-World Experience Machine for Time-Rich People Like You

Before you answer, think back to the idea in *Eternal Sunshine of the Spotless Mind* – and you'll see that Nozick's Experience Machine asks almost the same thing.

The question in the film is: would you like to airbrush the life you've lived so far, to create a perfect past? The Experience Machine asks us: would you sign up for a perfect future?

Our reactions to both reveal so much about what we want and who we are. Our instant, gut reaction is, 'Yes!' –

because we want as much happiness as possible. We want to cram as many amazing experiences into these too-short lives of ours as we can. We're afraid of missing out. We're scared of uncertainty. We live our lives, ever so slightly, on a precipice. We don't know what's going to happen next. We don't know if something will be worth our time, or a waste of time. That's why people wonder if they should go to the cinema tonight: the movie better be good, because you'll never get those two hours back. That's why we holiday in places we've been to before, hang out with old friends, and order the same food in the same restaurants. You know what you're going to get. It's safe. No wonder, then, as the happiness- and certainty-craving creatures we are, our first response is, 'Yes!'

But our almost instantaneous follow-on reaction to the Experience Machine is, 'No!' – because we want our happiness to be real, to be ours. We don't want pre-packaged perfect experiences. We don't think happiness is something you can just pick off a shelf and wolf down in a minute, just like that. We believe, in some way, that happiness has to be earned. Life is a meal whose flavours require much more chewing to get all the good stuff, a dish whose nutrients are released over time.

What if I told you I've come across a real-world Experience Machine? Not a thought experiment based on some futuristic sci-fi tech that removes you from real life, but a practical tool for your life today, based on a mix of ancient wisdom and some of the most intriguing, counter-intuitive recent discoveries about how to achieve health, wealth and happiness – from scientists at universities like Cambridge, Cornell, Harvard, Stanford and the London School of Economics.

What if I told you I've distilled the practical wisdom those philosophers, psychologists and economists have unearthed into a set of principles for everyday living, and I've crafted them into a seven-point checklist that you'll find easy to *remember and use* in your actual life – this year, next weekend, tonight?

What if I reminded you that time is the most valuable asset you possess, and that while you probably think you have very little, the stark, shocking truth is – you have loads? We all do. We have more leisure time today than ever. More than five hours a day! On average, Americans get five hours and fourteen minutes, and Britons get five hours and forty-nine minutes. Sure, no one's exactly average, and most days aren't either. There are times when you really have to put the hours in at work. And we get less free time during the week, and more at weekends. But still, this means we typically have something like thirty-six to forty hours of disposable time every week to spend however we want. So there's no way anyone should call us time-poor today. We're rich, you and me – time-rich.

So how come so many of us don't feel time-rich? Economists and sociologists have been puzzling over this for some time. They've identified seven reasons that explain why the relationship we have with time has soured in recent years.

One, we earn more, so time feels more expensive and scarce. If you make £5 an hour, then sixty minutes watching your kids play sport is no big deal. But if you could earn £100 in that hour, that game doesn't sound quite so appealing. Can't someone else go?

Two, we've come to believe that busyness is a status symbol. Important people are busy, so we want to be busy too. The conspicuous consumption of leisure has been replaced by conspicuous busyness. Instead of long lunches, golf and five-day cricket matches, people send emails at midnight, at 5.45 a.m. and on a Sunday.

Three, there's the flood of incoming emails, texts, tweets and twenty-four-hour news and gossip updates.

Four, there's an endless ocean of possibilities, both digital and in the real world. Just as there's always something new to read or watch online, so there are more things than ever to keep up with and visit and try out – new festivals, restaurants, pop-up bars, and cities that are now only a short flight away. The comparison between what we can do and what others are doing, versus what we are doing, is making us anxious. This anxiety is often called FOMO – fear of missing out.

Five, we try to push back the tide and keep up by multitasking. This fools us into thinking we're being more productive and efficient with our work time, so we start to multitask in our leisure time too. When we're playing with our kids in the park, we check Facebook and the football scores. When we're hanging out with one group of friends, we post pictures to show another. But multitasking doesn't do any good for your free time either. It makes it worse. Sociologists even have a nasty name for the thing you get if you multitask: 'contaminated time'.

Six, we're addicted to the Internet via devices like our smartphones. As recently as 2007, the amount of leisure time that we spent on them could be measured in minutes. But now it's best measured in hours: we now spend, on average, three and a half hours a day online.

Compare that with the five or so hours of disposable time we have every day: we're spending way more than half of it glued to our screens. Once we've unhooked from our devices, we've only got about two hours of leisure time left.

No wonder we feel so time-poor today. No wonder people say they're too busy to make friends out of work, too busy to date, too busy to sleep. No wonder eight out of ten Brits say they're too busy, even, to eat dessert, although four out of ten say dessert is better than sex – which makes me not only worry about their sex lives, but also wonder what they have for dessert.

The seventh and final reason is a problem that's hard-wired into our system. The business of capitalism is, first and foremost, business. Capitalism cares about work, productivity and GDP. So schools and universities and night-schools and online courses focus on teaching us how to be more productive and efficient at work. Too few bother to explain how we should spend our free time any more. They think that knowing how to work is essential, but knowing how to live is a frivolous luxury: the sort of thing that feckless social dilettantes, born with silver spoons in their mouths and with more time and money than sense, wasted their time on in the nineteenth century. So we all end up thinking that leisure is trivial and doesn't require any special training.

7 Reasons Why We Feel Time-Poor

WHY WE FEEL SO BUSY	EXPLANATION	EXAMPLE
1	We earn more, the cost of time is higher, time feels more scarce	You don't want to watch your kids play sports because you could be earning £££
2	We think busyness is status	Your boss sends you an email at 5.45 a.m.
3	Too much! We have too many incoming messages, too many demands on our time	You have hundreds of emails in your inbox (many of them from your boss at 5.45 a.m.)
4	Instead of helping, multitasking creates 'contaminated time'	You check your phone while playing with your kids
5	We have more opportunities than ever – endlessly scrolling online, more new places to go to and events to attend – and end up feeling FOMO (fear of missing out)	The number of festivals has doubled in recent years
6	Smartphones and all of our digital devices now eat around 60% of our leisure time	Most people check their phones before breakfast. Some check them during sex
7	Leisure isn't taught, and has become trivialised, belittled	People want an MBA or a business degree. A course in French literature, not so much

Maybe, until recently, it didn't. Maybe, when most of our lives were shorter and tougher, and we weren't blessed with so many possibilities, and before we had smartphones and tablets, we didn't need training because our skills mostly matched the challenge.

But now the challenge and the opportunity have changed. There are more demands on our attention from ever better devices, and ever more exciting choices in today's 'experience economy'. There'll be more of both in the future.

Instead of just wading in and hoping for the best, how can we make ourselves fit for today and ready for tomorrow, so that instead of feeling like we're going under, we can swim along in the flood, or, even, surf this wave of challenge and opportunity?

Or, put another way, how can we learn to spend the most valuable asset we have in a way that's more likely to lead to happiness and success?

These questions are far from trivial. Because while our lives are getting longer, they're still frustratingly short. No matter how hard you clench, you can't stop the sands of time slipping through your fingers. Time is finite in a way that money could never be. It's unquestionably our most valuable asset. As Warren Buffett, the world's third-richest man with a net worth of more than $80 billion, once said, 'I can buy anything I want, basically, but I can't buy time.'

Knowing how to spend our most precious asset strikes me as the most important practical knowledge a person could have. And that's what this book is about.

So, what if I said that, if you use the seven rules in this book, instead of drowning in the flood, you'll learn how to confidently ride the challenging, magical wave that is life in the twenty-first century?

What if I said you'll have fewer disappointing, waste-of-time experiences, and instead more of the sort of meaningful, exciting, share-worthy experiences that lead not only to more joy, but a more *enduring* sort of happiness?

What if I ended by saying that, if you apply this checklist, you'll be able to look into the future and be more certain about your life? You'll improve your odds for health, wealth and happiness. And you'll make the most of the most valuable, finite resource you have.

If I told you all that, you'd be sceptical, I hope. And look, I can't guarantee you eternal sunshine in every moment. I wouldn't want to either. If you airbrush all the clouds away, you'll have a less meaningful journey. But if you read this book, and apply this real-world version of the Experience Machine – as the science makes plain – you'll give yourself and your family, and even the rest of society, a better chance of filling life with richer, happier days.

Super, Junk and Empty: Foods We Want, Foods We Don't

Hands up if you've ever bought food because it was labelled 'superfood', or because you thought something was a superfood? If you have, you're not alone: three out of every five Brits, for instance, admit to buying food because the label said it was super.

The term was originally introduced in the early 1990s, by nutritional consultant Michael van Straten. He wrote about the 'four-star superfoods' which 'supply the vital bricks that build your body's resistance to stress, disease and infection'. He did not specifically call out kale, beetroot, blueberries, goji berries, or any of today's so-called superfoods. What he meant were simply the sort of everyday fruit and vegetables, wholegrains and nuts that we all recognise as key to a good, balanced diet.

Next, the term was adopted by journalists trying to add spice to their headlines, and marketers trying to sell more of their products. But it turns out superfoods don't really exist. Since 2007, the EU has banned anyone using the term unless they have specific evidence of health benefits. Since then, marketers have become suspiciously quiet about making superfood claims. But that hasn't dampened our enthusiasm for them. At one point, people were typing 'superfood' into Google and searching for it more than 250,000 times a month. Publishers responded with lots of books on superfoods. In recent years, they've released *Superfood Soups*, *Superfood Snacks*, *Superfood Smoothies*, *Superfood Breakfasts*, *Super Food for Superchildren*, and plain old *Superfoods*. Even Jamie Oliver has got in on the trend, with his *Everyday Super Food* and *Super Food Family Classics*.

I think the success of the idea of 'superfood' reveals two things. First, it says as much about us as it does about food. We're excited about the idea because, as we discovered when we thought about *Eternal Sunshine of the Spotless Mind* and the Experience Machine, we want to get the most out of life and, actually, everything.

When we shop, we want to make our money go as far as possible. When we invest, we want the returns to be as high as possible. When we go to the gym, we want every minute there to do as much for our health and figures as possible. And when we eat, we want as much nutritional bang as possible from every bite.

Second, while superfoods may not be able to live up to some of the claims made about them – how they can single-handedly zap diseases, slow down ageing and make us more intelligent, for instance – they do at least have nutrients in them. They're not junk food. And they're definitely not just empty calories.

An American by the name of Morgan Spurlock illustrated the problem with junk food in his documentary film *Super Size Me*. Eating nothing but food from McDonald's for thirty days, he put on weight, his body mass and his cholesterol went up, he felt depressed, fat accumulated in his liver, and he became unable to have sex.

When a Frenchman by the name of François Magendie tried a similar experiment more than two hundred years ago, he discovered the problem with empty calories. 'I took a dog of three years old, fat, and in good health,' wrote Magendie, 'and put it to feed upon sugar alone … It expired the 32nd day of the experiment.' If you stop and think, for a moment, about the time and energy and focus we put into avoiding junk foods and empty calories, and choosing better, healthier options instead, it really makes you wonder.

First, if it makes sense to put so much time and energy into what we put into our bodies, doesn't it make as much sense to think about what we do with our time? If we try to avoid junk foods and empty calories, because we know real food is better for us, shouldn't we also avoid junk and empty experiences and invest our time in 'real' and 'super' experiences instead?

Second, are there any experiences that would count as 'super' or at least healthy and good and likely to provide the vital bricks for our well-being? And are there experiences that you could call 'junk' and 'empty' – that is, that look fancy and appealing but actually aren't nurturing at all? Take watching TV, for instance. Scientists have found that as sure as sandpaper scrubs off paint, so watching too much TV erodes happiness – more of that later. Or consider spending time on social media. More on that in the *Outside & Offline* chapter, and the *Intensity* chapter too.

Third, just as our modern capitalist system has evolved to cajole us into eating junk foods and empty calories, do you think it might have done that with how we spend our time too?

A man by the name of David Graeber thinks so. Graeber, a professor of anthropology at the London School of Economics, says modern life has thrown up all sorts of meaningless jobs, like telemarketing and a 'whole host of ancillary industries (dog-washers, all-night pizza delivery) that only exist because everyone else is spending so much of their time working in all the other ones'.

'These,' he wrote a couple of years back, 'are what I propose to call "bullshit jobs". It's as if someone were out there making up pointless jobs just for the sake of keeping us all working.'

Now, this book isn't about what you do at work. It's less time management, in which people try to get more out of less at work, and more 'playtime management', in that it's about how to get more out of your free time.

But I think Graeber has an important point that applies to the rest of our lives – that there are now people out there making up pointless experiences just to keep us all watching, clicking, spending, hooked, mindless.

At the least, these empty experiences do little more than innocently pass our time. But even that sounds like a crime to me. Innocent? They're taking the most precious thing we possess! At the worst, some of these junk experiences actively erode our happiness and health. In between are the ones that just aren't worth the time investment. What are they? Think for a moment of the things you do now that leech away your life and pay you back by leaving you feeling flat and depleted. Here's a few that scientists have shown are bad for us: watching too much TV, playing fruit machines, commuting, and spending too much time inside.

If you're one of those people who cares about what food you and your family eat, I want to ask: do you think about how you and your family spend your time? Do you know how much of it you spend on junk, empty or bullshit experiences? And how much you spend on 'super experiences', the ones that provide the vital bricks for enduring happiness and success?

If eating unhealthy food is as bad for you as Spurlock and Magendie have shown, what do you think spending your time on bad experiences does for you? Here's a few things: your weight and body mass and cholesterol will go up. You'll be more likely to get depressed. You'll have fewer friends, a less attractive partner, and less sex. And you'll be more likely to die earlier.

So, knowing the answer to this question – how should you spend your time? – strikes me as about as important as anything in our lives because, well ... *tick-tock*.

You Don't Have to Be a Time Waster

The Roman poet Catullus captured the bittersweet nature of time in a love letter to his girlfriend. In it, he complained of our *brevis lux*, our 'brief light', and that afterwards all we had to look forward to was *nox est perpetua una dormienda*, 'a night that's never ending and in which we'll always be asleep'.

Dylan Thomas had an answer: 'Rage, rage against the dying of the light.'

I don't know about you but, before the never-ending night comes, I'm intending to make the most of my brief light. If you want to make the most of yours and, even if you don't feel the need to rage against the dying of it, but at least want to hold it off for as long as possible – you'll agree that knowing how to spend time is arguably the most important skill in life.

Because you don't want to waste the short time you have on this earth gathering a set of mediocre memories.

You don't want to lie on your deathbed wondering what might have been if only you'd known better.

You may not want happiness handed to you on a plate, but you don't want to miss out on happiness you could have had. Actually, unless you're reading this on your deathbed, you don't want to miss out on happiness you could still have – do you?

That's where this book comes in. It's a guidebook for free time, informed by decades of research and practice and the latest scientific discoveries. It's constructed with help from some of the world's leading happiness researchers, people like Tom Gilovich at Cornell University; Cassie Mogilner at the University of California, Los Angeles; Amit Kumar at the University of Texas; Liz Dunn at the University of British Columbia; and Joe Gladstone at University College London. So the ideas in this guide may be revolutionary, but they stand on the shoulders of scientists.

These science-based tools will show you the sort of experiences you should aim for, to make the most of today, tomorrow, this weekend and the one after. You think those days aren't important? But they are. Because how we spend our days is how we spend our lives.'

Now, you may be wondering if you really need this guide. You might be thinking, what can these scientists tell me that I don't know already? After all, you're probably pretty confident when it comes to choosing a holiday, or deciding what to do at the weekend. Maybe your thing is going on city breaks in central Europe, riding your mountain bike through muddy puddles, discovering new writers at fringe theatres, teaching under-nines how to play cricket, moshing till 4 a.m., talking about *The Underground Railroad* with your first-Tuesday-of-the-month book club. Whatever it is, since you know the sort of things you enjoy, you quite reasonably figure that means you know how to spend your time.

Here's the psychologist Mihaly Csikszentmihalyi's take on it:

'The popular assumption is that no skills are involved in enjoying free time, and that anybody can do it. Yet the evidence suggests the opposite: free time is more difficult to enjoy than work. Having leisure at one's disposal does not improve the quality of life unless one knows how to use it effectively, and it is by no means something one learns automatically.'

We'll hear more from Csikszentmihalyi in the *Intensity* chapter. But back to you – when you're on holiday, do you ever wonder if you'd be just as happy at home? At the end of the holiday, do you ever regret what you did and vow never to go to that sort of place and do those sorts of things ever again?

Because, worryingly, scientists have found that people are often no happier after a holiday than if they hadn't taken one at all. And, frighteningly, almost all of us – 96 per cent, in fact – admit to living much of our lives on 'autopilot', doing things without even thinking about whether they'll be good or bad for us. I don't know about you but I find the idea that holidays fail to leave us feeling any happier depressing, and the thought that so many of us could be short-changing ourselves ridiculous.

And I want to do something about it.

This isn't only about holidays. Do you ever get to the end of the weekend, and wonder why you've bothered? Do you ever catch yourself at the tail end of a YouTube or Facebook binge, and wish you could get that time back? Do you worry that you're not spending your time as well as you could?

If you do, you're far from alone. Despite more free time, four out of five Americans say they don't have enough time to do what they want to do, and three out of four Britons say they're not getting the most out of their time. And when people all across Europe were asked if they were happy with how they were spending their time back in 2013 – before mobile devices had taken over so much of it – three in ten said they weren't.

What's your reaction to those statistics? Mine's shock. That's like leaving free money on the table. You wouldn't do it, would you? Or, if a holiday company offered you a stay in a room with a great view at a five-star resort on the beach, you wouldn't say, 'Thanks for the offer, but actually I'll take a room with a view of the car park at a three-star place nearby on a busy road for the same money,' would you? I'm exaggerating, but you get the point. You'd take all you could get, and rightly so. And you'd enjoy it as much as possible. This is why they say, 'Seize the day.' And why they don't say, 'Seize *some* of the day.'

And so it sounds to me like there are tens, perhaps hundreds of millions of people around the world who aren't getting the most from their time – and could really get some value out of this book. I hope you'll get at least three ideas from every chapter that make a real difference in your life.

Again, I'm not saying that you, and all those millions of others, don't already have a reasonably good sense of what you like. But just as the wine connoisseur might not only think about the grape, the producer and the year, but also listen to a sommelier's opinion before choosing a bottle; and just as you might not only read some ratings and reviews, but also ask an expert friend before buying new speakers; if you want to have the finest experiences, you'll curate a better life if you refer to an expert guide.

That's what this book sets out to be. It's a bit like the mental cheat sheet a sommelier considers when helping you choose your wine, or the one a superstar DJ uses to select the next track, but for the experiences you have in your life instead.

After reading this book, as well as knowing which experiences from your past gave you the most happiness, you'll understand *why* they worked so well. With these new insights, you'll be able to plan more enjoyable, more enriching experiences for the future, and live a more satisfying, happier life.

That's how it's been working for me and my family. It's changed the way we spend our time, the way we plan our holidays, the way we think about our weekends.

By reading a ton of science papers and talking with the scientists, I feel like I've seen a ripple in the matrix, and discovered seven secrets to a more joyous and satisfying life. Now, thanks to some tips I learned while researching the *Outside & Offline* and *Relationships* chapters of this book, every weekend feels like a holiday. Inspired by some of the insights in the *Story*, *Intensity* and *Extraordinary* chapters, the holidays I take with family and friends follow a shape that delivers a mix of exhilarating experiences, calm moments and challenging times – all in the right order. And thanks to something else I took out of the *Story* chapter, I even get on better with my wife.

I don't get it right all the time, of course. But now, by using the seven rules, I've been having fewer empty, waste-of-time, junk experiences – and far more that are worth my precious time. These are the secrets I want to share with you in this book.

Time and How to Spend It — A 7-point Summary So Far

1. We have more leisure time than ever, but it doesn't feel like that.

2. We don't feel like we have much leisure time because we're misspending it.

3. We're misspending it because our society has placed a high value on work and a low value on leisure.

4. Because of this, we've been trained how to work, but haven't learned how to live.

5. Knowing how to live has become more difficult, and more important, today:
   a. because of the Internet and our always-on, always-there devices;
   b. because there are more things than ever to do in today's experience economy.

6. Misspending our time is like winning the lottery, but only taking some of the winnings.

7. If we learn how to spend our leisure time, we can use our time better, and access previously untapped reserves of happiness.

Why 'Experience Intelligence' Is Critical for the Great Life

'Life, if you know how to use it, is long.'

SENECA

The story of success, of where it comes from and how to get it, can be told, I think, in five steps:

1. the Old Testament story of Job;

2. the court of King Louis XIV;

3. the influence of John Maynard Keynes;

4. the success of Bill Clinton; and

5. the startling revelations of the past few years from social scientists like Sonja Lyubomirsky and Shawn Achor.

In Step 1, we meet Job. (In case you slept during this part of religious studies, Job doesn't rhyme with Bob. It rhymes with lobe.) Life was very good for him. He loved and worshipped God, and God showered him with success. Job had seven sons and three daughters, seven thousand sheep, three thousand camels, five hundred oxen and five hundred donkeys.

But then, one day, God pointed out Job to Satan, because He was so proud of the way Job avoided evil and worshipped Him. Satan made God doubt whether Job really was as committed as He had claimed. After all, since God had made everything so great for Job, it was easy for him to honour his maker.

So God decided to let Satan test Job. Satan began by sending some bandits to steal all of Job's donkeys and oxen, and kill all the servants looking after them – except one who miraculously survived and came and told Job exactly what had happened. Next, Satan sent a fire, and burned all of Job's sheep and the servants with them – except one who, as luck would have it, survived and came and told Job what had happened. Then, Satan sent three raiding parties to steal Job's camels, and kill all the servants with them – except one who – guess what? – escaped and came and told Job what had happened. Then, Satan sent a very large gust of wind to collapse the roof of the house where Job's seven sons and three daughters were feasting, so they all died, along once more with all the servants – except one who – you'll never guess – survived and came to deliver the news to Job.

Finally, Satan covered Job with festering boils from the top of his head to the soles of his feet. They were so itchy he scratched them with a piece of broken pottery while he lay crying on the floor.

Job wavered a little, but, amazingly, never gave up believing it was all part of God's plan. Because he remained faithful, God later rewarded him with more sheep, oxen, donkeys and camels than he had in the first place, and blessed him with seven new sons and three new daughters. And so Job thanked God and was happy.

The moral of this story is hard to fathom. Typically, it is used to illustrate that we have to accept God's ways. But it shines a huge light on how, for millennia, people made sense of the capricious nature of life and death and success. It is all, as in this story, in the lap of God or the gods. They could choose whether or not to make you successful.

While this version of success strikes me, and probably you too, as barren, and at least a little crushing, it's how most people have viewed it for much of human existence.

Fast-forward to the seventeenth century, and on to a gilded Step 2: the entrance to the magnificent, shining, golden court of Louis XIV at Versailles in France. Here you can see that success still looked similar. Except now, instead of being given or withheld directly by God, success or failure was handed out by His representative on earth – Louis, also known as the Sun King, because everything revolved around him like the sun, and as Louis the God-given, since God had given him his powers.

In the first step, the key to success was to bow down and pray to and worship a deity you couldn't see. In the second, it was to bow down and worship and get as close as possible to the living deity wearing the preposterous wig in Versailles.

It was the revolutions of the eighteenth, nineteenth and twentieth centuries that carry us forward to Step 3. In the French Revolution, the people rejected the divine right of kings. In the American Revolution, the patriots rejected the divine right of the British monarchy to tax them heavily. In the first and second Industrial Revolutions, it became clear that bowing down before a monarch was not the only route to success. Inventing new machines and new ways of doing things, from engines to management processes, offered another.

By the early twentieth century the way we thought about success had firmly changed. Rather than rely on the gods, or a god-appointed king, people began to realise that intelligence was key. Step 3's core idea was personified in the life of John Maynard Keynes, the economist from Cambridge whose ideas rescued the world from economic implosion in the 1930s and, again, after the financial crash of 2008.

This was codified, in the early twentieth century, in the concept of intelligence quotient, usually shortened to IQ, which became the standard way to determine a person's potential. In the First World War, for instance, the US army used IQ tests to work out how high up the ladder to place new recruits. Intelligence, as tested by numerous IQ tests, became the key signpost for success. The more intelligent you were, the more likely you would be accepted for a more challenging and higher paid role. The higher your IQ, the more likely your career would progress. Our schools, our jobs, a person's success was built on this.

And then, on to the marble and crimson carpeted steps of the White House for Step 4, with Bill Clinton.

Clinton is often cited as the charismatic, charming, smiling poster boy for the revolution discovered by a pair of psychologists at Yale University and the University of New Hampshire, named Peter Salovey and John Mayer, and popularised by the writer Daniel Goleman.

Up till then, as we saw a moment ago, people had believed that success was determined by what you and I think of as 'regular' intelligence – the sort that's tested in end-of-term exams – and what psychologists call 'general intelligence'. This, according to the standard definition, crafted by a psychologist named David Wechsler in 1940, is the 'capacity of the individual to act purposefully, to think rationally, and to deal effectively with [their] environment'.

But as Salovey and Mayer showed, success is also determined by what they called 'emotional intelligence'. This, as they wrote in 1990, is the 'ability to monitor one's own and others' feelings and emotions, to discriminate among them and to use this information to guide one's thinking and actions'.

Suddenly, because of the science that had emerged, instead of believing that IQ was the best route to success, we realised that emotional intelligence, often referred to as EQ, is actually essential too. And so EQ took its place alongside IQ as a key determinant of success.

Something very interesting, and largely unnoticed, has been happening in psychological studies in recent years that not only adds another element to how social scientists think about success, it also leads us on to Step 5 of this story.

Evidence has emerged – thanks to work by researchers like Sonja Lyubomirsky at the University of California, Ed Diener at the University of Illinois, Laura King at the University of Missouri, and Shawn Achor at Harvard University – that strongly suggests a causal link between happiness and success.

Of course, saying these two are linked sounds as obvious as announcing that there's blue sky on a sunny day. But what's really fascinating here is the direction of the relationship.

Most of us assume that success leads to happiness. We tend to think that once we get the dream job, home or partner, life will feel clicked into place. So, based on this, you should focus on your IQ and your EQ and then you'll be successful and happy.

But what psychologists like Lyubomirsky and Achor have now found flips this idea on its head. They have discovered that people who, in the scientific jargon, have 'emotional health' or display 'positive affect' – that is, people who you and I would just say are happy – are more likely to succeed.

Let me shine a light on why that's so interesting. This new research shows that if you want success, you should first aim to be happy. Then, there's a growing body of other research – as discovered by the likes of Tom Gilovich at Cornell University, Elizabeth Dunn at the University of British Columbia, and Mike Norton at Harvard Business School, and as I've reported for publications like *New Scientist* and the *Guardian*, and in my last book,

Stuffocation – that has shown conclusively that, if you want to be happy, you should spend more of your focus and money on experiences.

Think of these two discoveries for a moment, and a simple truth becomes clear. If we agree that if A leads to B, and B leads to C, then A leads to C, then these scientific discoveries show that if you want to have a successful life, you should focus on experiences. Here's how this would look on a blackboard:

If A ⟶ B

And B ⟶ C

Then A ⟶ C

If Experiences ⟶ Happiness

And Happiness ⟶ Success

Then Experiences ⟶ Success

Or, if you were feeling arty as well as logical:

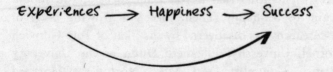

Experiences ⟶ Happiness ⟶ Success

Toughen Up, Buttercup – Your Happiness Will Last Longer

There's a further reason why a focus on experiences is more likely to lead to success: resilience. In recent years, another wave of research – from psychologists, education researchers and leading thinkers like Adam Grant at the University of Pennsylvania – has shown that being able to handle tough times and bounce back is not only essential for happiness, it's also key for success. A headline in business publication *Forbes* captures this idea: 'How successful are you? Answer: how resilient are you?'

If you read the American Psychological Association (APA) advice on the ten ways to increase your resilience – like the importance of relationships, self-discovery and moving towards your goals – they fit almost hand-in-glove with some of the key reasons why scientists say experiences are good at making us happy. Because they bring us closer to other people, for instance, because they give us a chance to define who we are, and because they challenge us.

Consider the APA's advice, and you can swiftly see how experiences – think of playing tennis, kite-surfing and even belonging to a book club – can improve our ability to bounce back from difficulties. And you can also see why experiences, because they help people develop what psychologist Ann Masten calls the 'ordinary magic' of resilience, are an ideal launch pad not only for happiness, but also for success. Again, if you were writing this on a blackboard:

If A $\longrightarrow$ B

And B $\longrightarrow$ C

Then A $\longrightarrow$ C

If Experiences ⟶ Resilience

And Resilience ⟶ Success

Then Experiences ⟶ Success

Again if you were feeling smiley:

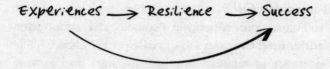

Experiences ⟶ Resilience ⟶ Success

Both these conclusions bring us back to the same answer and the same question. If you want to be successful, you should focus on experiences. But what sort of experiences, and what mix of them, should you aim for?

Say Hello to Our New Friend: The Twenty-first-Century Definition of Success

If you look again at the diagrams, you may notice something. For the sake of ease, I've called happiness and success different things, even though there's a lot of overlap. In fact, I think the modern definition of success is changing. For most people, for most of human existence, success meant what it meant for other animals: staying alive long enough to procreate and continue the species. Then, in the twentieth century, it got bound up with materialistic consumerism. If you had the big job, big house, big car and were 'living large', you were successful. Have you seen *MTV Cribs*? Society's success was measured – some would say 'mismeasured' – in terms of economic success, and defined by GDP. But in the twenty-first century, our definition, for society and individuals, is evolving. For societies, we are more interested in well-being; as individuals, in happiness. So instead of separating the two, we have to see them as intimately connected. The best sort of success, ultimate success, includes happiness. The best sort of happiness includes success.

And yet, as we saw in the story of Job, as we were reminded in the story about Clementine, things happen. The Athenian wise man Solon captured this when he said to the richest man in the world, King Croesus, 'Never call a man happy till he's dead.' Success is never sure. It comes and goes. So the best sort of happiness and success will be backed by resilience. Back to the blackboard again:

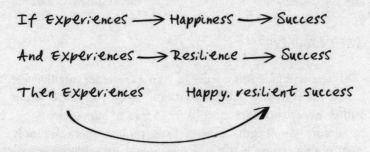

If Experiences ⟶ Happiness ⟶ Success

And Experiences ⟶ Resilience ⟶ Success

Then Experiences ⟶ Happy, resilient success

To live the best life, it's clear we require three ingredients: happiness, success and resilience. The most direct route to achieving all three is through not only experiences but the right kind of experiences – not junk, empty, bullshit ones, but healthy, nurturing, exciting ones that are more likely to supply the vital bricks for enduring happiness and success.

As science now makes clear, the ability to distinguish between these two types of experiences, to recognise them when they appear in front of us, and to plan them, and organise our lives around them, is essential.

In other words, science now strongly suggests that just as general intelligence and emotional intelligence are critical for success, so too is 'experience intelligence'. I define this as 'having the ability to recognise good and bad experiences, to discriminate among them and to use this information to effectively guide your thinking and actions'.

Or, here's a simple way to remember what science is now suggesting: if you want success, then as well as IQ and EQ, you also need a healthy dose of ExQ – 'experience quotient'.

Till now, no one has constructed a bona-fide test for ExQ, and there's nothing in the scientific literature yet. But I've discussed this idea with a number of leading social scientists, and it resonates with them. More importantly, you're probably wondering: what's your experience intelligence? Take the test on the next pages to find out.

What's Your ExQ?

This test will give you a sense of your experience intelligence.

At the end, you will find out how much you know about which experiences are most likely to lead to happiness.

Before you begin, a note. Even though there are only two options to each of these questions, you will sometimes be tempted to say, 'It depends.' But put, 'It depends,' aside a moment, and make a choice.

As you read on, you may notice there's a difference between what you think the correct answer is and what you'd do in real life. Don't worry about that. Lots of people have had the same reaction. It's got me a few times too. This is a useful way to not only test your experience intelligence level, but also see if you're actively applying the experience intelligence you already have. Write your answers down in the table on page 32.

1. Which is likely to bring more happiness?
   a. An adventure and volunteering holiday, sleeping in clean but run-down hotels.
   b. An all-inclusive beach break at a boutique five-star resort.

2. You're in Japan. Which is likely to bring more happiness?
   a. A guided walk in Yakushima forest.
   b. A guided architectural tour around Tokyo's Shibuya district.

3. Which is likely to bring more happiness?
   a. You eat an amazing meal in a new pop-up restaurant.
   b. You eat an amazing meal in a new pop-up restaurant, and share photos of the food on Instagram.

4. Which is likely to bring more happiness?
   a. You and your buddies go to a concert.
   b. On the way to the same concert, you get offered a much better ticket. You won't hang out with your friends, but you'll be much closer to the band.

5. Which is likely to bring more happiness?
   a. A week on a crewed yacht, where the staff do the route planning, sailing, etc.
   b. A week's bareboat charter, where *you* do the route planning, sailing, etc.

6. You have a day to yourself. Which is likely to bring more happiness?
   a. You stay at home and binge-watch a box set.
   b. You put your boots on and head out for a day's hiking.

7. Which is likely to bring more happiness?
   a. You spend the evening watching TV.
   b. You spend the evening reading.

8. You're feeling a bit flat. Which is likely to bring more happiness?
   a. You treat yourself really nicely. Stay in, watch TV and wait for the clouds to pass.
   b. You make yourself get up and go for a walk.

9. You're planning your summer holiday. Which is likely to bring more happiness?
   a. Two weeks staying a mile from the beach.
   b. One week staying on the beach.

10. You find £100 down the back of the sofa. Which is likely to bring more happiness?
    a. You spend it on yourself.
    b. You spend it on someone else.

QUESTION	WHAT YOU THINK IS THE CORRECT ANSWER		WHAT YOU'D DO IN REAL LIFE	
Which is likely to bring you more happiness?	Answer here	Score here	Answer here	Score here
1.				
2.				
3.				
4.				
5.				

QUESTION	WHAT YOU THINK IS THE CORRECT ANSWER		WHAT YOU'D DO IN REAL LIFE	
6.				
7.				
8.				
9.				
10.				
Total based on answers at the back. Score 1 for correct, 0 for incorrect.				

This test was constructed with assistance from Tom Gilovich.

Now, find the answers at the back of the book on page 359.

The Plane that was Too Much for One Man to Fly

By the early 1930s, top brass in the US army realised they needed to upgrade their planes. If another war did happen, the biplanes they'd used in the First World War wouldn't be much use.

By the time October 1935 rolled around, they were just about ready to make their decision. Technically, there were still three planes in the running: Martin's Model 146, Douglas's DB-1, and Boeing's Model 299. But the truth was, the decision had been all but made.

The Model 299 flew circles around the competition. It could cruise at 250 miles per hour, far faster than the other planes. It had four engines instead of two, and was the first combat aircraft that could continue its mission if one of its four engines failed, making it the most technologically sophisticated airplane of its time.

And then, you just had to look at it. With a central bomb bay and gunner stations spaced around the fuselage for defence, it had already been dubbed the Flying Fortress by one newspaperman who'd seen it.

On 30 October 1935, the army's procurement officers gathered at Wright Field, in Dayton, Ohio, to make their final decision. Covered in polished aluminium panels, the Model 299 glinted on the runway like a test pilot's smile. That day, Boeing had selected one of the most experienced aviators available, Major Ployer Peter Hill, who had been flying since he'd joined the army's aviation section in 1917, eighteen years before.

Hill gunned the engine, and the Model 299 hurtled down the runway and took off. But then, only 300 feet into the air, it banked sharply to the left, fell out of the air and landed on its nose. Hill and another crew member died instantly. Miraculously, three survived.

Onlookers were distraught. The engineers at Boeing were also confused. This was their flagship, and on previous occasions it had successfully flown for more than forty hours. How could this have happened?

When they investigated, they discovered that nothing mechanical had gone wrong. It seemed that Hill had made a simple but fatal mistake. He'd left the elevator and rudder controls locked. Why would he have done that?

The only conclusion they could think of was simple, yet strange. Hill was experienced. He'd piloted and tested nearly sixty of the army's newest aircraft. And yet, they concluded, it was 'pilot error' – even if, perhaps, that wasn't his fault.

The problem, they soon realised, was the complexity of the new aircraft. Till then, planes had been simple, just as small planes still are today. Once you're up in the air, there's a stick, and if you push it left, the plane rolls left. If you push it right, it rolls to the right. Back, and the nose goes higher. Forward, the nose goes down. There are a few instruments, like on a car, really – except there's one that tells you how far from horizontal you are, to keep you from getting disoriented – and that's it.

It isn't like that in a modern commercial airliner, and it wasn't like that in the new Model 299. It was, as a newspaper at the time put it, just 'too much plane for one man to fly'.

The plane looked like such a useful long-range bomber that the army bought some anyway, and tried to figure out a way to make this 'flying fortress' work. The solution has turned into legend.

In order to solve the complicated problem of remembering, they invented something so simple it sounds a bit silly now. Since it wasn't in the mechanics, the problem they were looking to fix was the human operator. And this wasn't a problem of knowledge or ability. It was this: how to focus someone's attention to make sure they do every last thing they're supposed to do.

The solution they came up with was something so simple it'll make you wonder why no one had thought of it before – the first safety checklist – and it worked. Using the checklist, the Flying Fortress bomber would be flown for 1.8 million miles with not a single accident from 'pilot error'. It would go on to help the Allies win the Second World War, and so protect the world from fascism.

There's a clear lesson from this story: when something simple becomes complicated, we need a new way to approach it. This new way should do two things. It should make the complex thing elementary again. And it should ensure we get the basics done right.

Or, to borrow from that newspaperman back in 1935, if something's too much plane for one person to fly, that person needs a checklist.

But isn't that how life is today? Think of the kaleidoscopic range, and bewildering number, of things we can do and places we can go nowadays. There are apps you could use, and a never-ending stream of updates you could check out right now. There are pop-ups you could eat and drink at, matches you could watch, shows you could see, and talks you could attend tonight. There are cities you could visit, festivals you could go to, escape rooms you could escape from, and box sets you could binge on this weekend. There are new careers you could follow, and other places you could live. Hell, there are different lives you could lead.

Life used to be simple, but today, with its myriad options, it has become too much plane for one person to fly. We all need a checklist.

The Snowflakes, the Snow, and the Experience Manifesto

'Aha!' you may be thinking. 'I see your point. But no.'

You probably agree that modern life is complex. You can see that checklists help when things get complicated. But, you might say, how could anyone claim to have found 'the answer' and reduced it to a simple checklist when people are so different?

Let me begin by pointing out that I'm not claiming to have found the answer. What I'm really doing is reporting the science: I have gathered and read published papers, and discussed the ideas with social scientists, in order to distil a multitude of insights into something that strikes the right balance between being scientifically correct and clear enough to be meaningful, as well as practical enough for you and me to use in our daily lives.

But, even then, there are 7 billion people on this planet. How could there possibly be one checklist that works for everybody?

After all, we're all different. Fiona loves clubbing (still!), going to Ibiza, and foodie festivals. Rakesh can't get enough of playing and watching football, and seems to go on a lads' holiday every month. And Stevie loves working out, tattoos, heavy metal, and, weirdly, rom coms.

But while, at a detailed level, we're all as individual as snowflakes, at a basic level, we're all snow. You and me and Fiona and Rakesh and Stevie, and all those millions of others, may enjoy doing all sorts of different things. But being rejected, feeling lonely, and spending too much time inside would be bad for all of us.

More important, checklists have been shown to work when dealing with something as complicated as humans – as the physician Atul Gawande makes clear in his book *The Checklist Manifesto*.

Thinking about how Boeing discovered the safety checklist in 1935, Gawande wondered whether checklists could work in hospitals too. 'Sick people,' he wrote, 'are phenomenally more various that airplanes. A study of 41,000 trauma patients in the state of Pennsylvania – just trauma patients – found that they had 1,224 different injury-related diagnoses in 32,261 unique combinations. That's like having 32,261 kinds of airplane to land.'

In 2001, a critical-care specialist named Peter Pronovost at Johns Hopkins Hospital in Baltimore, USA, decided to run a test to see if a checklist would make any difference in emergency care. The problem he wanted to check was something called 'central line infection'. Central lines are those tubes that go directly into a vein in a patient's arm or chest, making it very easy for doctors to administer medicines, fluids and nutrients. But because they bypass the body's protective outer layer, they also make it easy for bacteria and germs to get in. Every year, central line infections were adding billions of dollars of added healthcare costs, and causing thousands of deaths.

Pronovost wrote a checklist of the five simple steps that a physician should take when inserting a central line: one, wash hands with soap; two, clean skin with antiseptic; three, put sterile drapes over the entire patient; four, wear a mask, hat, sterile gown and gloves; five, put a sterile dressing on the insertion point once the line is in. The infection rate went from 11 per cent to zero.

Then he started testing checklists in more areas, and they worked too. The number of patients catching pneumonia fell by a quarter. The amount of time patients stayed in the intensive-care units dropped by a half. And twenty-one fewer patients died in the hospital, compared to the previous year.

Buoyed by these successes, Pronovost tried to get more hospitals to use checklists. He met with plenty of resistance. Some doctors were offended. Most thought they simply didn't need them. They were experts, after all. They'd spent years training. What could they possibly gain from a simple checklist?

Some pointed out that it was all well and good that these lists worked in a well-funded hospital like Johns Hopkins, but they wouldn't work in a place that was struggling. So, Pronovost found a very different type of hospital to run a trial: Michigan Health and Hospital Association, which ran more than fifty public hospitals and medical centres.

The results were even more astounding. The central line infection rate fell by 66 per cent. Before, when they didn't use the checklist, the infection rate in one of their hospitals, Sinai-Grace in inner Detroit, was worse than 75 per cent of hospitals in the US. When they did use the checklist, the infection rate across Michigan Health and Hospital Association's hospitals was better than 90 per cent of all hospitals in the US. Over an eighteen-month period, the association estimated that they saved $175 million in costs, and more than 1,500 lives.

And all because, as Gawande wrote, 'of a stupid little checklist'.

Not long afterwards, the World Health Organization in Geneva got to hear about this, and wondered if checklists could reduce avoidable deaths from surgery. By 2004, 230 million operations were being performed by surgeons every year – one for every twenty-five human beings on the planet. And those operations were leaving 7 million people disabled and 1 million dead. The WHO wanted to see if the results happening in the US would work in other places too.

They did. They created a checklist with nineteen points, one of which is that everyone has to introduce themselves to each other, and tested it out in eight different hospitals around the world, from London to New Delhi in India, Amman in Jordan, Auckland in New Zealand, and Ifakara in Tanzania. The results were no less than breathtaking. After checklists were introduced, the rate of deaths and surgical complications fell by more than a third across all eight pilot hospitals.

Since then, checklists have been tested in more countries: in Norway, Iran, Liberia, the Netherlands. And it works there too. It doesn't matter if it's a rich country or a poor one. It doesn't matter if it's a well-funded hospital, or one struggling to keep up. And it definitely doesn't matter if it offends the ego of the doctors who think they're above such a simple idea.

Checklists don't only work in airplanes and hospitals. They work in construction, in investing, in hiring. They work in any situation that's become complex. They work any time there's too much plane for one person to fly.

And the best bit of magic is this: they're free, or near as dammit. You don't need to spend money on better equipment or more training. Once you start using a checklist, even when you put the same in, you get more out.

If they work for doctors who've trained for years, and for pilots who've flown thousands of times, why wouldn't you try a checklist for life? Maybe, by using one that's based on the latest science, we can avoid the autopilot that sends us into too many negative, wasted holding patterns. Maybe we can be the active pilots in our own planes. Instead of wasting our hours, days and lives having empty, junk experiences, we can make better decisions, and live richer, happier lives – by using a checklist.

To make these insights more memorable, easier to use, and more likely to help you, I've given this cheat sheet an easy-to-remember name: I call it the STORIES guide. Each letter represents the essentials you should look for when you decide how to spend your time: Story, Transformation, Outside & Offline, Relationships, Intensity, Extraordinary and, finally, Status & Significance.

In brief:

Story – for two reasons. First, experiences give us a sense of identity that's both inward- and outward-facing. They tell each one of us who we are, and they enable us to tell others too. Second, when you have a story, you set in motion a domino line of positivity that almost inevitably leads to happiness: experiences give us stories, stories give us conversation, conversation creates connection, connection leads to relationships, and relationships, as mentioned in the chapter with that name, lead to happiness.

Transformation – because human beings, from an emotional point of view, are a bit like bicycles. If you're not heading towards something, you tip over. Growth, purpose and becoming the person you want to be are all key for happiness.

Outside & Offline – because science is now clear that spending time in nature is good for you, lowering heart rate and blood pressure, reducing stress, and improving happiness. And because in an ever more complex and demanding world of digital connections and distractions – when friends, family and your boss can get hold of you any time and everywhere – it's more important than ever that we turn off our digital devices, drop out of the never-ending social media whirl, and tune in to real life instead.

Relationships – because, as study after study has confirmed, including a eighty-year-long study at Harvard University Medical School, our friends, family, neighbours and community are key to well-being.

Intensity – because experiences that engage and challenge us give us a chance to be good at something, and get us into what psychologists call a state of 'flow' – they make us happy. Think of skiing or cycling or singing or making love. We'll also discover why flow is available to all of us – whatever our passions or age or income – because, ultimately, it isn't *what* you do, but *how* you do it that matters most.

Extraordinary – because one of the magical reasons why experiences bring us so much happiness is that we not only get to enjoy them in the moment, we also get to look forward to them and remember them afterwards. Those we're most likely to look forward to and remember feature moments that are out of the ordinary and give us a sense of awe. Think about the sunsets you saw, or a boat trip you took, on your last holiday. Or how you're more likely to remember a run along a beach or through a city on holiday than a run on a treadmill in the gym you go to every week. But, as we'll see, there's an important place for ordinary experiences too.

Status & Significance – because, although we don't like to talk about status, who we are, what we are, and where we are in society does matter. That's partly because we tend to think about status as ego-driven, selfish and empty – the sort of success that leaves you lost. The key to making status meaningful is to learn from the lives of others, and the psychological studies that show the exceptional satisfaction that comes from giving.

TIME and how to spend it CHECKLIST

- Story ☐
- Transformation ☐
- Outside and offline ☐
- Relationships ☐
- Intensity ☐
- Extraordinary (and ordinary) ☐
- Status and significance ☐

How to Use the 7 Rules

You shouldn't think of this STORIES guide like a set of train tracks. It's not a straitjacket. It's a tool, designed to help you get the basics right.

I think of the STORIES checklist a bit like the rules of grammar, or the basics of tennis. You can break the rules of grammar. Once you know what they are. And you can develop your own way of playing tennis, but it's useful to know what the lines on the court mean, how to hold the racket right, when to play a cross-court shot, and when to send the ball down the line.

Before you break the rules and develop your own style in any pursuit, I think it's best to know the basics like the back of your hand. And the best way to do that here is to read the stories in this book and get to know the seven rules of the STORIES checklist. Next, use them to analyse your favourite and not-so-favourite experiences from the past. Then, play with them, have fun with them. Try something that resonates with you from the *Intensity* chapter this Saturday. Spice up the weekend after with something from the *Story* chapter. Inject a learning from the *Extraordinary* chapter into next Thursday evening.

Some of the rules, as you've probably noticed, are simple – get outside, for example. Some are more subtle – transformation, perhaps. Depending on your background, some may sound obvious. Others more original. No matter. Each is backed, as you'll see, by science, and has its role to play. And while there's power in each point, the seven rules are far more powerful when taken together. It's the whole, and the mix, that matters.

You don't have to tick every box every time you do something, just as not every track the DJ plays has the same dance-floor-go-wild energy as Daft Punk's 'One More Time' – oh dear, am I showing my age? But each is selected based on how it fits into a set. And just as not every drink goes with every dish – have you ever drunk dessert wine with roast beef? – each is chosen to reflect the stage of the meal and the food it's paired with. So, not every weekend has to involve the sort of sparkling story that you'd wheel out and wow people with at dinner. You don't have to crowbar a bit of exercise into a night at the opera to make it valid. (Extra points for trying though.)

If your experiences tend to include a lot of intensity, but you're lacking great stories to share, or if you're spending a lot of time with people, but you're never offline and rarely outside, the STORIES checklist will help you bring some of what's missing back into your life. This isn't just about balance, though, it's about making sure you're following all the paths most likely to lead to a resilient, meaningful life.

The checklist will have a different impact for different people – just like the last book I wrote, *Stuffocation*. For some, it was validation. For others, it was revelatory. For many, it was life-changing – in ways both large and small. One guy, named Daniele, told me that, after reading *Stuffocation*, he reduced the amount he was spending on stuff each month by so much that he was able to give up his job and do something that mattered more to him. One woman, called Michelle, told me it helped her be more present and get more enjoyment from the time she spends with her kids.

I hope this book will have a positive effect on your life. You might spend a bit more time outside and offline next weekend, for instance. Or, when you go on your much-deserved beach holiday, instead of coming home with very little in the way of story – Friend: 'How was your holiday?' You: 'We just sat by the pool' – you might design your break so that you go and do some extraordinary activities as well.

At the least, I hope that the next time you're deciding what to do, you use this simple checklist to work out if it's worth your precious time. And when you have chosen, that you use the checklist to make the experience better.

The difference may feel subtle at first, marginal even, but it will be profound in the long term. Apply the seven, science-backed rules and the STORIES checklist to your life, and you'll increase your experience intelligence. You'll waste less time on junk, and spend more on 'superfood' experiences. You'll create better individual moments, and curate a lifelong, standout collection of extraordinary memories.

How the STORIES checklist will help you choose better experiences

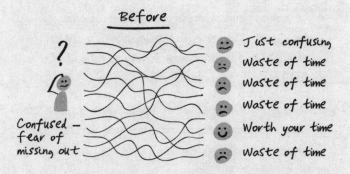

Before

? Confused — fear of missing out

Just confusing
Waste of time
Waste of time
Waste of time
Worth your time
Waste of time

So many choices - don't know what's worth your time

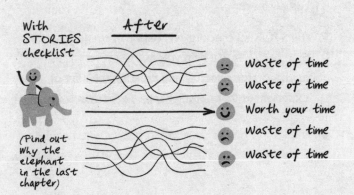

With STORIES checklist

After

(Find out why the elephant in the last chapter)

Waste of time
Waste of time
Worth your time
Waste of time
Waste of time

Why Experiences are Critical — A 7-point Summary

1. Experiences —> Happiness —> Success

2. Experiences —> Resilience —> Success

3. Experiences —> Happy, resilient success

4. As well as general intelligence and emotional intelligence, 'experience intelligence' is a critical life skill. Or, put another way, as well as IQ and EQ, ExQ is vital for success.

5. Through stories, science and practical exercises, the seven core chapters of this book will increase your experience intelligence.

6. When anything becomes complicated, checklists make people more likely to succeed. Life today is complicated.

7. The STORIES checklist will help you spend your time better. It will help you put the seven rules into operation for selecting and creating the sort of experiences that deliver happy, resilient success.

1

STORY

Kurt Vonnegut and the Shape of Stories

'You are the hero of your own story.'

JOSEPH CAMPBELL

t is 1995. The American writer Kurt Vonnegut is seventy-three. On a stage in a lecture hall packed with students, Vonnegut still fills almost all his burly six-foot-one frame. He has hangdog eyes. They're behind brown-framed glasses that he removes whenever he wants to connect with the audience, which he does often. His curly hair ruffles around his head and over his ears. There are a few mentions of grey above his temples. His grey-brown moustache droops around his mouth.

He wears a white shirt, grey tie, dirt-brown V-neck jumper, and tan, loose-fitting jacket. But if his look is typical teacher, his delivery isn't. His talk is halfway between lecture and stand-up comedy routine. And why not? He is about to talk about one of his favourite subjects.

If anyone ever asked Vonnegut what his 'prettiest' contribution to culture had been, he wouldn't mention his *New York Times* bestseller *Slaughterhouse-Five*, or any of his other thirteen novels, his three short-story collections, his five plays, or his five works of non-fiction.

Instead, Vonnegut would talk about the master's thesis he'd written when he was studying anthropology at the University of Chicago in the 1940s. It had been rejected, because, as he would later recall, 'It was so simple and looked like too much fun.'

'The fundamental idea,' he would later write, 'is that stories have shapes which can be drawn on graph paper.'

Onstage, he turns to the blackboard and clears his throat. He reaches up to the top left, draws a chalk line straight down.

'This is the "G.I. axis" – good fortune, ill fortune,' Vonnegut begins. He has a deadpan tone and a smoker's rasp in his voice. 'Sickness and poverty down here. Wealth and damn boisterous good health up there. Here's the very middle.'

He draws a horizontal line from left to right.

'Now – this is the "B.E. axis". "B" stands for "beginning".'

The college kids laugh and clap. Someone whoops. He pauses. Just as this man knows how to write a sentence, so he knows how to play audiences.

'"E" stands for electricity.'

The college kids really laugh this time. Vonnegut takes his glasses off, turns to them.

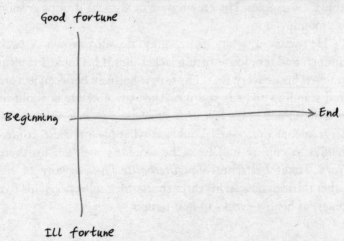

The Axes of Story, according to Vonnegut

Good fortune

Beginning → End

Ill fortune

'Now, this is an exercise in relativity really. It's the shape of the curve that matters, and not the origins. So, we'll start a little above average. Because why get a depressing person?'

Vonnegut draws a chalk curve that droops down like one side of a moustache, or water going gently over a waterfall, then dives down, far into the bottom half of the graph, the part labelled 'ill fortune'.

'We call this story "Man in Hole". But it needn't be about a man, and needn't be about somebody getting into a hole. But it's a good way to remember it. Somebody gets into trouble ...'

As he draws, the chalk line curves away from the vertical, then bottoms out and curves back up again.

'... gets out of it again.'

The line ends squarely in 'good fortune'. It looks like this:

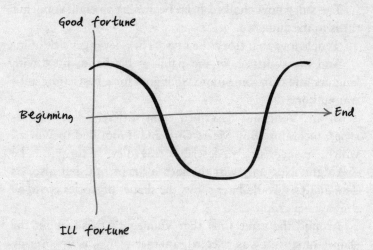

Vonnegut's Man in Hole Story

The Man in Hole Story (including the man), according to Vonnegut

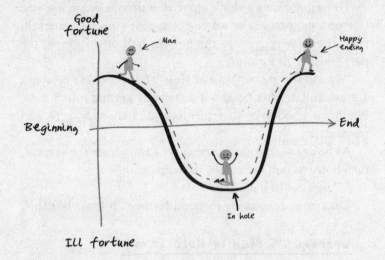

The story now chalked from beginning to end, Vonnegut turns to the audience.

'People love that story,' he says. 'They never get sick of it.'

And his audience, in the palm of his hand, hoot with laughter and clap some more. So it goes for a bestselling anti-war author.

In all, Vonnegut described eight different story archetypes, including 'Boy Meets Girl' and 'From Bad to Worse', which, unsurprisingly, describes tragedies. It turns out he was right. Not only was the idea a lot of fun, but also, as data analysis would later show, the shapes of stories could be drawn on a graph.

Around the same time that Vonnegut's thesis about the shapes of stories was rejected, another man was uncovering something startling about the mythical stories that different cultures around the world tell: they all follow the same shape.

The Hero's Journey

Joseph Campbell once spent five years living on his own, in Woodstock, upstate New York, in a rented shack with no running water. He lived there so he could spend more time reading. He read nine hours a day, every day, during those five years.

Campbell read a lot of books: modern books, medieval books, books in Old French, Provençal and Sanskrit. His friends included the author John Steinbeck, and a man named Heinrich Zimmer. Zimmer was a comparative mythologist and Indologist. He specialised in Indian literature and comparing the ancient myth stories from different cultures. When he died in 1943, Campbell edited his letters and papers.

After all those years of study, Campbell noticed something strange and wonderful. It didn't matter if you were reading the traditional stories of the Celts, Jews, Greeks, Romans or Egyptians. It made no difference if you were looking at the myths of the Minoans of Crete, the Khoikhoi of Tanganyika, or the Pawnees of Kansas and Nebraska. It was the same if you were reading the folk tales of the Eskimo of the Bering Straits, or the Yoruba of West Africa.

The details were always different, always local. But no matter whose story you come across, there was one recurring, underlying pattern. It's a pattern which many modern stories also follow. The central idea in Campbell's 1949 book *The Hero with a Thousand Faces* is now known as the 'hero's journey'. Its shape can be drawn on a blackboard. And, if drawn simply, it looks a lot like Vonnegut's 'man in hole'.

Each hero's journey begins with the ordinary world. Harry Potter is living a normal life with Uncle Vernon and Aunt Petunia. Dorothy lives on a farm in Kansas. Luke Skywalker lives with Uncle Owen and Aunt Beru on a farm on Tatooine.

Then, something happens. This can be internal or external. It can be personal or global. But it must shake the foundations of the hero's ordinary world. It must make Harry or Dorothy or whoever the hero of the story is ask, 'Is this all there is?' It shows them that there is something else – a secret garden, a better way, an answer to the problems that have been whispering to them in the night. This is their 'call to adventure'.

The hero may initially refuse this call, but once they've seen that this other choice exists, we know they have to take it. When they answer the call, they cross the threshold into the world of adventure, beginning the journey into what Campbell calls the 'zone unknown'. Dorothy is now in Oz. Luke Skywalker goes to Mos Eisley with Obi Wan Kenobi.

Now, the adventure begins. Campbell called this the 'road of trials'. A Hollywood script editor named Christopher Vogler, who simplified the hero's journey for film writers in his book *The Writer's Journey*, called this 'tests, allies, enemies'. This is our chance to see our hero face challenges they have never come across before, to learn new skills, to show their true character.

And we see that they cannot do it alone. Along this road, some of the tests, trials and obstacles are inert: mountains that must be climbed, rivers that must be crossed, buildings that must be scaled. Some of the trials are living, breathing things: aliens, monsters, people, stormtroopers, wicked witches, mean bosses. Because they want our hero to fail, and at the least because it makes them look bad, they must become enemies. And as well as creatures who don't want to help, there are those who do.

The challenges become bigger, forcing the hero to discover and reveal more of their true character, and learn greater, more powerful skills along the way. Ultimately, they will have a showdown in a mighty battle with the biggest, baddest baddy imaginable. Campbell called this the 'supreme ordeal'. This is the moment when George slays the dragon.

Now that our hero has won the ultimate battle, they get the reward. Bilbo gets the ring. Jason gets the golden fleece.

And now, they have to get home. Campbell called this the 'return'. Vogler called it 'the road back'. It's the chase scene in many Hollywood movies. Some returns are easy. Some are nasty. To buy Jason and his Argonauts some time, Medea slowed their pursuers, who included her father, by chopping her little brother into pieces and scattering his remains across the water.

When the hero gets home with the reward, everything changes. Because of their adventure, and what they've learned, the old world is, in some way, made new again. Luke Skywalker brings peace to the galaxy. Dorothy wakes up at home in Kansas, but now we know she will be OK.

There are a few ways of drawing this. There's the traditional way, where the hero goes around a circle, from ordinary world to new world. And there's a new way, which overlays Campbell's hero journey onto Vonnegut's man in hole story.

The Hero's Journey as it's usually drawn

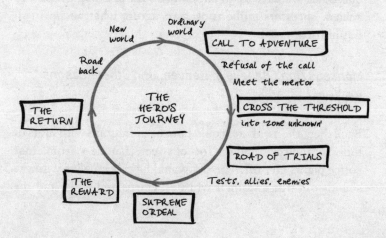

The Hero's Journey on Vonnegut's Man in Hole Shape

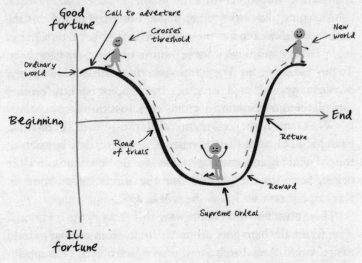

Why do so many stories in so many cultures have such a recognisable shape – this shape? And what does that mean for the shape of our experiences and our lives? To answer these questions, we have to go back, way back in time, to visit our ancient ancestors millions of years ago in what we now call East Africa.

Monkeys Don't Believe in Heaven, and Other Reasons Why We Love Stories

Back then, the air there would have been fragrant with hints of hibiscus and rose, and the sort of sweet, jasmine-y aroma that coffee plants give off. The sky would have been alive with the sounds of birds and their whistles, chirps and trills; and the sight of their feathery coats of many colours: black, white and red, with splashes of blue here, flashes of orange there.

On the ground and in the trees, four- and two-legged animals scratched, groomed, hunted, and often ate each other. Some were almost hairless. Some were furry. One two-legger had big fur around its face, like a lion's, but since it was a monkey, it looked more like it could have been an animal guitarist in a 1980s big-rock, big-hair band like Whitesnake.

Another group of two-leggers were, in hindsight, a curious bunch. There wasn't much noticeably different about them back then. They had fur like many of the others, but not all over. They weren't that big. They weren't that small. They didn't have especially big teeth, or particularly strong arms. They were around the midway point on the food chain. They hunted, and they were hunted too.

But then, something happened. Something that would propel them from the middle to the top of the food chain, and lead them to do all sorts of things, like create computers called Apple and bands named Whitesnake.

No one knew why then, and no one knows why, for sure, today. Call it luck or magic or a gift from the gods. Better yet, call it evolution. What we do know is that over the next few million years the brains of our ancestors would expand to three times the size of our nearest relatives. And while our brains got bigger, our muscles got smaller.

This trade-off, for brain over brawn, seemed to work. Slowly, imperceptibly at first, those early humans started surviving in greater numbers. Millions of years later, around two-hundred thousand years ago or so, a few made the decision to boldly go where no *Homo sapiens* had been before.

We don't know why. Perhaps there were too many for the area they'd first populated, this eastern side of Africa? Perhaps it was a group of young male upstarts who were frustrated at the lack of opportunities for food and sex and power? Perhaps some were just fed up with the old ways and wanted to strike out on their own?

And so they began a journey beyond what we might think of as the 'original lands', and went in search of something new. They didn't know it then, of course. But what began with these small steps was the beginning of a giant leap for the species. Their descendants would one day spread to every part of the planet.

On the way, there were many trials to overcome. There was food to find. There were poisonous and not poisonous berries to discover. There were cold nights, cold winters and ice ages. There were seas and hills and mountain ranges to cross. There were enemies to overcome: tigers in India, Neanderthals in northern Europe, cave hyenas from Spain to Siberia. And there were allies to make: dogs, cows, horses.

They kept going for thousands of years until they had not only spread from the 'original lands' to everywhere on the planet. They had also risen from clambering about in the middle to standing at the very top of the food chain. We now hunt, but our species are very rarely hunted.

The question – asked over and over by our enquiring minds, housed in these weighty brains of ours – is: why? What was it that helped our ancestors not only to survive, but also to climb to the top of the food chain? What makes us different from all the other animals?

The answer isn't tools. Chimps, octopuses and crows use tools. It isn't opposable thumbs. Gorillas, gibbons, pandas and koalas have them. It isn't even language. Green monkeys can tell their friends to 'Watch out! A lion's coming!' Parrots can say way more things than we can. Not only can they sound like a dead ringer for Amy Winehouse when they sing, they can also perfectly mimic your alarm clock, your car alarm and a pneumatic drill.

The simple, short answer to the question 'what makes humans different?' is this: story.

The longer answer is that it's a type of story that historians call 'collective fictions'. These aren't just lies. They're complex, made-up stories that make sense of the world around us and, as we all collectively believe in them, enable us to cooperate on all sorts of things, and in large numbers.

No other animal does this. After all, as the historian Yuval Noah Harari puts it in *Sapiens*: 'You could never convince a monkey to give you a banana by promising him limitless bananas in monkey heaven.'

Armed with great stories – stories of creation, terrible events, legendary battles, mythic heroes and shared destinies – our ancestors came together and achieved things no other species has ever achieved. They built ziggurats and pyramids and temples and empires. They invented money, conducted trade and established businesses. They created ideas of justice, and wrote down laws. They constructed societies in which we could all thrive.

No wonder evolutionary psychologists – who make sense of how we think and what we do today based on the aeons-long history of our species – call us the 'storytelling animal', and say that we're 'hard-wired for story'. If you think about stories this way, you can see they are nothing more, and nothing less, than an evolutionary adaptation.

Just as we've evolved to enjoy sweet, salty and fatty foods, and hunting and sex, because, throughout our species' long journey, they've meant surviving and thriving – so we've evolved to love stories.

No wonder, then, that we enjoy stories so much today: telling them, listening to them, reading them, watching them, creating them. No wonder there are so many people working in so many story-led industries creating books, movies and TV shows. You think sex sells? Look around. Story sells even more.

The Story of Our Lives, and the Domino Line to Happiness

To tell the 'story of story' properly – as well as listening to the lessons of history, anthropology and evolutionary psychology – we should also hear from the fields of psychology and neuroscience. A branch called 'narrative psychology' has emerged that looks at how we use stories to make sense of our lives: rather than think of the events that happen in our lives as unconnected dots, we join the dots into stories that not only reflect who we are, but also show how we'd like to think of ourselves.

As these personal narratives develop across our lives, they pass through three levels. The first stage is Actor. This is when we just act and react in the moment, the role kids typically play. I can see it in my four-year-old son. He bounces from home to park and to his grandparents' houses, just playing. He's taking part, but he's not planning. The next level up is Agent, when, as well as acting and reacting, we're more aware of where we've come from, and where we're going. This is what happens when kids turn into teenagers and start thinking about what they'll do in the near and medium-term future. The highest level is Author, when we consciously see our actions and decisions in a wider context, and start directing the story of our lives.

These personal stories are critical for happiness because, so psychologists have found, they provide unity, purpose and meaning to our lives. And while you can get away with not having these and still experience moments of joy, they're critical for achieving what the philosopher Aristotle called *eudaimonia*, and what psychologists today call a 'more enduring sort of happiness'.

Author

Seeing the whole picture; actively, consciously understanding who you were, who you are, and who you'd like to be in the future; not only writing the story, but directing the action.

Agent

Seeing the wider context, as well as the moment that came before and what comes after; acting, as well as reacting; making decisions and taking actions knowing that they'll lead to consequences.

Actor

In the moment; reacting to events as they happen.

Narrative psychology, if you think about it for a moment, is about 'inward facing' stories: the tales we tell ourselves about who we are.

What about 'outward facing' stories, the sort of tales we tell other people? They're also good for happiness, psychologists have found – thanks to a curious mechanism that neuroscientists call 'mirror neurons'.

Ever seen someone stub their toe and thought, 'Ow'? That's mirror neurons. Ever read or watched a romantic scene and found yourself feeling amorous? Mirror neurons. Ever watched a sports game and found yourself 'playing along' – a football match, say, and, as the winger puts a corner into the box, nodding as if you're the one heading the ball? Again, mirror neurons.

Whenever you read a good book or watch a great movie, your brain fires up as if you're living that experience. And it's the same when someone tells you a story, or you tell them one. Your and their neurons mirror the story's real-life action.

The upshot of all this mirroring is a whole domino line of positivity that begins with your friend telling you a story, and ends with increased happiness for both of you. As your neurons reflect each other's and your brains operate in sync, you have increased understanding and empathy for each other. Empathy brings you closer, and creates a connection. This leads to a feeling of kinship, and that leads to relationship. And relationships, as we'll see in the chapter of that name, lead directly to happiness.

The domino line to happiness

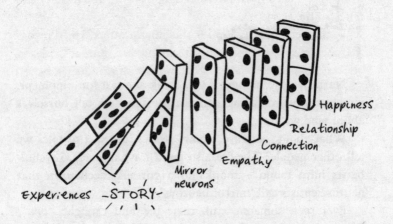

Experiences -STORY- Mirror neurons Empathy Connection Relationship Happiness

Better Shape Up ... 'Cause I Need a Man in a Hole

So now that we're clear why stories are utterly compelling for us, we can turn to the next question: why is it *this* shape that's proved so popular? Again, we can refer to the same experts for information and inspiration.

If we believe that story itself is just one of our many evolutionary adaptations, then just like any other adaptation, the shape of the most popular stories should also be the one that's most likely to help members of our species survive and thrive and pass on their genes.

If you think about what we've learned from the historians, evolutionary psychologists and neuroscientists, it seems clear that, for a story to endure the test of time, it has to contain two essential ingredients.

The ingredient at the top of the list is resonance – when one person tells a story to another, it has to resonate with them. Not only must their mirror neurons fire up, but the best stories, the ones most likely to bring storyteller and audience in sync, must be those where the neurons are already primed to fire up. That's most likely to happen when the listener can relate to the story.

In the perfect situation for this mirror effect, you'd recognise the details of the story as it's being told. But, at the least, you'll recognise the shape of the story, even if unconsciously. Think of someone telling you about a date they went on. We've all been on dates, so we get the basic structure. Or, think of someone telling you about a holiday they had in a place you haven't been – Havana in Cuba, say. They'll tell you about the old town, the crumbling walls, the nail-varnish-pink, open-top Cadillacs, the bands playing music at every corner. And while you've never been, you've been to old towns, islands, perhaps the Caribbean, you've felt the warm wind blowing down a dusty street, you've heard bands playing. So you have enough neurons ready to fire so that you can picture it.

But if the story they're telling is too far from your own experience and interest, it's less likely to resonate for you. When I tell my wife about a football match I've just watched or played in she nods, but no one's home. This is what happens on millions of dates that fail every night around our planet, as the person listening discovers that the person talking is really passionate about things they really don't have the slightest bit of interest in.

So, for the storyteller to connect with their audience, whether that's one person on a date, or a thousand people at a rally, the story must be as familiar as possible. Even if the content is new or different, then the audience should at least recognise the shape.

And I think this is why man in hole or hero's journey has entertained for at least the past few millennia. Because the hero's journey reflects the human experience at the deepest level. This shape can be summed up even more simply as problem and solution: a bump in the road and getting over the bump in the road; coming to an impassable river, sea or ocean, and then crossing that river, sea or ocean, or, at least, finding another way forward.

Isn't that the story of our lives? You wanted something. Something stood in the way. You figured out how to get over it, under it or around it, or moved forward some other way.

Isn't this the story of humanity? On the long journey from East Africa to today, your and my ancestors came up against huge boulders and vast oceans – and got over them and across them.

So, when a storyteller tells any kind of man-in-hole or hero's-journey story, they're telling a shape that resonates as deeply as any shape possibly could.

You may be reading this and thinking, 'What about other popular story shapes, like tragedies?' And it's true that tragedies – where things start either good or bad, but always go bad and then just get worse and worse, like *Oedipus the King*, *Macbeth* and *Romeo and Juliet* – are enduringly popular. And you could use this same way of thinking to suggest that telling a tragic story is just as likely to connect with people. After all, a lot of what millions of humans have endured over the years looks a lot like tragedy. And while tragedies will continue to resonate for people as fictional stories, if you're trying to connect with your audience and inspire them to be your friend, follower or mate, it's not very aspirational, is it?

So, there's another ingredient that also strikes me as essential. It's this: the story should have a positive ending. To borrow from Vonnegut, 'because why get a depressing person' at the end? If you're going to sell someone on the idea that they should follow your lead, you'd want to tell them that, yes, things are hard now, but they'll get better. If you're going to sell someone on the idea that they should become your mate, you'd want to tell them that the future will be even better than it is now. As you read this, I imagine you're thinking of politicians who try to sell us on a better tomorrow, and people you've dated who've tried to tell you that if you go with them, life will get better.

So, the classic shape of story is, like story itself, an evolutionary adaptation. The shape of man in hole and hero's journey has become the classic one because, since time immemorial, it's the story form most likely to enable a human to lead and mate.

The man in hole shape is also, so psychologists have discovered, the one most likely to lead to personal happiness. Studies in narrative psychology have found that there are two distinct types of personal narratives that people tell, and that these stories follow two very different 'emotional sequences'. In one, the story begins with an event that seems good, but ends with some sort of bad outcome. Or, in the language the psychologists use, an emotionally positive scene is 'ruined, sullied, contaminated by what follows'. This is known as the 'contamination' pattern. The other, opposite emotional sequence is called the 'redemption' pattern. These are when the story begins with a bad or difficult event, but ends with some sort of good result. Or, again, in scientific language, 'an emotionally negative life scene turns positive; the bad is salvaged or redeemed by a positive outcome'.

Contamination pattern of Storytelling

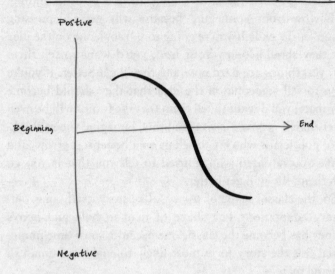

Redemption pattern of Storytelling

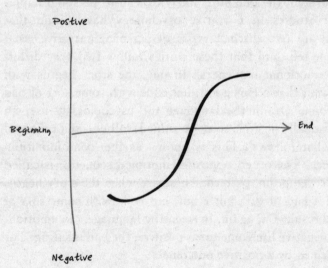

Think of your own stories for a moment, or those of people you know. Do you tend to tell stories that are contaminated or redemptive? Can you think of someone who tells them in the opposite way to you?

What's interesting here is not only that the shape of redemptive stories mirrors the man in hole and hero's journey shape. What's really interesting is that people who tend to describe their life through contaminated stories are more likely to be depressed, have lower levels of life satisfaction, and feel that they can't make a positive contribution to others. But people who tend to tell redemptive stories are more likely to be happy.

So, stories lead to happiness and success and sex. And if you want to be happier and more successful, and have more sex, then you should tell stories in the shape most likely to make you happy, resonate with your audience, and enable you to lead and mate: the classic shape of the man in hole and the hero's journey.

We Can Be Heroes

'But,' you may be thinking, 'isn't it hard to be a hero?' After all, you've seen movies, read books, and heard stories about heroes like Achilles and Batwoman and T'Challa. They all seem to say that being a hero is mighty tough. But there is an easy way. You don't have to learn to fly. You don't need to put on a mask. You don't even have to *want* to save the world.

All you have to do is follow the 'mud map' of the hero's journey. Mud map is Aussie slang, by the way. It means a rough map that someone draws in the mud. I guess the clue's in the name. I don't know how it came about, but I imagine Aussies spending a lot of time with sticks, in the outback, explaining to each other, *mate*, how to get from here to there.

The man who drew me to this mud-map idea goes by the name of Clive Williams. Now in his late fifties, Williams – who lives in Brisbane, Australia – has close-cropped, greying hair. He wears black plastic glasses, and black-and-white checked, military-fit shirts. You could say he looks like the civilian version of a superhero, right before he disappears into the phone booth to take the glasses off and put the cape on.

In real life, though, Williams is more your everyday sort of hero. He's a practising psychologist, has been for a couple of decades. He's worked in public hospitals, helping mentally ill patients and drug addicts. He's run a private practice, helping people with difficult children, parents, marriages. He's helped all sorts of people with all sorts of problems, in other words, using tried and trusted, evidence-based techniques like mindfulness and cognitive behavioural therapy.

But before he became a psychologist, Williams was an actor and playwright. To improve the structure of his stories, he learned about the hero's journey, both Campbell's original version and the simplified one Christopher Vogler wrote for screenwriters.

The more he'd read and thought about Campbell's and Vogler's work, the more Williams noticed the stages of the hero's journey happening in his own life, and he'd found it empowering. Not that he suddenly had superhuman powers. But now, he had a new way to view the challenges he faced and to help him overcome them. When obstacles or people got in his way, he'd see himself on the 'Road of Trials', facing the tests, allies and enemies that Vogler wrote about. Instead of getting annoyed by people and any other sort of thing in his way, he'd ask himself, 'What's the lesson I'm supposed to take from this test? Who's the ally I'm supposed to find? How can I learn to deal with this type of enemy better?'

Like the time a lawyer tried to rip him off. Williams was with three actor friends at a law conference and they were backstage, about to act out a scene to bring the law to life.

'This guy was a real dickhead,' Williams says now. 'We'd agreed three hundred dollars, and suddenly, standing there in his three-piece suit and Armani watch and shiny shoes, he said he wanted to pay us a hundred and fifty.'

Williams panicked.

'I was really practised at smiling,' he says now. 'I wasn't good at having a voice and saying no.'

But he breathed in, held firm. If the man wouldn't pay the $300 they'd agreed, they wouldn't do it. Furious, the lawyer looked down at his shiny shoes, checked the time, looked out at the conference, and backed down.

As Williams went onstage, he was shaking – with anxiety, nerves and elation. He'd just made an enemy. But he'd also faced a test, and come out the other side of it.

He knew there'd be more and bigger tests to come. But, with the hero's journey by his side, suddenly these tests felt like opportunities to learn and grow.

Williams didn't tell anyone for ten years. How do you tell a friend you've decided that, actually, you're a hero – like Wonder Woman or Harry Potter or Han Solo – and they're just a bit part player in your story?

Years later, Williams was part of a team of psychologists running group therapy sessions in a psychiatric hospital. He wondered, if the hero's journey was working so well for him, could it work for these people too? So he crossed the threshold. He started giving group therapy sessions called 'How Change Really Happens'. It was based on the hero's journey, but he never mentioned the hero, the dragon or the need to make enemies – instead he talked about the 'mud map' of your life.

This is a rough version of the hero's journey. Because, of course, a person's life doesn't follow its perfect step-by-step circle. That's for fictional tales told, retold and honed over months, years and millennia to be as entertaining as possible to their audience. Since we live life forwards, you can't be certain what stage you're at. But, by offering a rough version, Williams turned the steps a fictional hero takes into lessons that people with real-life problems can use to get over hurdles they might be facing, and progress to the next stage of their journey – just as he'd been using it in his own life.

If you're not happy with how things are in your ordinary world, for instance, maybe you're refusing your call to adventure? Perhaps what you need is to hear and accept your call and maybe a mentor will help. Or, if something or someone seems to be deliberately trying to stop you achieving your aims – no need to fret, this is just a test or an enemy on your road of trials. They're just an opportunity for you to discover more about yourself and learn a useful skill.

Suddenly, Williams's group sessions got a lot more popular. Before, a handful of people would show up. Now, they crammed the couches. They perched on the armrests. They sat on the floor. When he ran those 'How Change Really Happens' sessions, the other psychologists who ran group sessions at the hospital were confused and curious. Why wasn't anyone coming to their sessions any more? What, they really wanted to know, was going on in there?

When Williams told them, and about the hero's journey, their reaction was strange.

'They went quiet, just like patients do,' he says now. 'It's what always seems to happen when I tell people about it. People go quiet, they don't say much at all. What's happening is they're trying to identify where they are on the hero's journey.'

That's exactly what happened to me too. When I came across Williams's idea of the mud map and how a person could apply the hero's journey to real life, I had one of those funny moments, a *coup de foudre* – a lightning strike, the French would say – but instead of falling in love with a person, which is how the French use it, I was struck by an idea.

The more I've thought about Campbell's and Vogler's books, and the more I've understood Williams's point of view – from reading his scientific studies and talking with him – the more I've agreed with him. The hero's journey is an incredibly useful, easy to use, and inspiring metaphor for life, for every one of us.

FIVE WAYS TO BE A HERO

The hero's journey can be a metaphor for life. You can use it for longer experiences – journeys that take months or years, like becoming a writer or a good partner or parent. You can use it for medium-length experiences, like holidays or real-life long journeys – hiking the Coast to Coast Walk, for instance, or crossing the Greek islands. Or, you can use it for shorter, even individual experiences – especially micro-adventures like wild camping or visiting a new city.

Here are a handful of ways you can apply it today, tomorrow and in the coming years to all of those experiences.

1. CHOOSE YOUR ILLUSION: ALL THE WORLD'S A STAGE AND YOU'RE THE HERO

From one point of view, you and I aren't special. But, as *Dilbert* author Scott Adams once wisely pointed out, we're probably wrong about a lot of things, so why not choose an illusion that puts you in a positive light? Once you see yourself as a hero of your story, and your life as a journey, you stop judging yourself for having not reached this point or achieved that goal. You stop seeing setbacks as dead-end defeats. Instead, failures are simply tests on your road of trials. They are opportunities for you to find allies and enemies, and build skills.

2. SAY, 'YES!' MORE

Modern life is full of opportunities. Each opportunity is, in some way, a call to adventure. The more you say, 'Yes!' the more often you'll cross the threshold and start down a road of trials. Don't worry whether or not you think it's the adventure for you. You'll find out on the way, as the character Santiago did in Paulo Coelho's *The Alchemist*. So, if you've always wanted to learn the guitar, or play rugby, or kite-surf, or visit the Alps in summer, or have more picnics – say, 'Yes!' to the call to adventure, make it happen, and see where it leads.

3. HEAD FOR THE HOLES

Most of us try to avoid problems. When things go wrong, we tend to think we've gone wrong. But if you see it through the perspective of the man in hole, redemptive story, and hero's journey, you know the tough times are vital. So, instead of hoping for the best experience, revel in imperfect ones. Instead of holidays that are perfectly planned, leave some things to chance, make room for challenges. Sound awkward? Toughen up, buttercup. Head off the guidebook-recommended path. Instead of taking a taxi everywhere, take public transport, walk or ride an animal. If you go to Machu Picchu in Peru, take the traditional route. Instead of flying in by helicopter, walk the hills. When you arrive, it'll feel more authentic, and you'll have earned your sense of wonder.

4. MEET YOUR MENTOR, MAKE SOME ALLIES

Too often we struggle, and think that asking for help is a sign of weakness. But heroes get help, so why not you and me too? While mentoring has become a big thing in the world of work, who looks for a mentor for their leisure time? I think we should. If you're thinking of taking up trail running, find someone who knows more about it than you. Chances are, they'll be only too willing to talk about something they love doing. Of course, once you're on your adventure, if you find others who like it too, it'll be easier to keep going. That's one reason why people join book clubs and walking clubs. If there isn't already a group for your passion, why not set one up? You'd be surprised at how much even strangers like to talk. More on that in the *Relationships* and *Status & Significance* chapters.

5. TELL YOUR 'MAN IN HOLE' TALE

Tell your stories in the redemptive shape of the man in hole story. Don't skimp over the tests you faced, the enemies you made, and the allies who helped you. For instance, when someone asks about your weekend away, don't just tell them the highlights; tell them about the challenges on the way. Or, if you've completed a fifty-mile cycle, tell them about the hill or the moment you 'hit the wall'.

If you start to see your life as a hero's journey, you suddenly feel far more in control, as though everything has its place. Instead of feeling hard done by when things don't go your way – when you're struggling for money, or when people annoy you at work – you realise these are just necessary parts of your journey. They're just 'tests, allies and enemies' on the 'road of trials', opportunities to grow and learn.

Once you start seeing your life as a hero's journey, you realise that each experience you choose is, or at least can be, a part of that. I don't mean that every single experience has to encompass a full, transformative arc from call to adventure to slaying the dragon, reward and return. But, with a little thought, you can see that every experience forms part of your overarching adventure.

As you do that, you'll find that not only will each experience make more sense and be more satisfying, but as a whole, you'll have better stories, better connections with other people, a stronger sense, even, of your own humanity, and more happiness. Oh, and did I mention that you'll have more sex?

As you not only seek and discover who you really are, you'll also become who you have the potential to be. So, don't worry when things get tough. Answer your call to adventure. Walk your road of trials. Enjoy the obstacles: they're the way of the hero. If more of us design and plan our experiences with story in mind, we can all be heroes.

Story Summary

1. We are hard-wired to enjoy stories, because they are the critical evolutionary adaptation that has enabled humans to punch above our size and strength to become the dominant species on our planet.

2. When you tell a story, the brain of the person, or brains of the people, listening fire in synch with yours. This is called 'mirror neurons'. This creates empathy between the storyteller and her audience.

3. The storyteller with better, more inspiring stories is more likely to lead others – to war and to bed.

4. The shape of the story most likely to resonate with your audience and fire their mirror neurons is the oldest story of all: the problem and solution, man in hole, hero's journey.

5. If you tell stories in the shape of the hero's journey, you will be more likely to connect with others and inspire them to follow you.

6. People who tell stories about their own lives that follow the 'redemptive pattern' – which is the same shape as the hero's journey – are happier.

7. All experiences set off a domino line of positivity that leads directly to happiness: experiences lead to

story, story leads to connection, connection leads
to relationships, relationships lead to happiness.

8. The experiences most likely to lead to success and
happiness are those that produce stories that follow
the shape of the hero's journey.

How to Bring More STORY into Your Experiences
and Your Life

At the end of each chapter, I'll share two sets of questions to
help you apply the learnings to your life, and a list of five
things you can do to experience the rule this weekend. The questions on the next few pages will help bring more and better
stories into your life.

In *Past Times*, the questions are designed to help you think
about experiences from your past, so you can identify the sort of
things you've done before, and already do, that inspire stories –
and those that don't. That way, you'll be more likely to understand the idea, and more likely to plan experiences you should do
more of, and those you should have fewer of, so you can increase
your chances of having more and better stories. (Personally, I've
found this approach really useful to understand why some experiences I had in the past were memorable and meaningful and
made a difference to my happiness, and why others have faded
away.)

In *The Way to Happy Days*, the questions are designed to
help you design your experiences and life in general. Instead of

asking you to rate your experiences on a scale of 0 to 5, these are designed to inspire creative thinking. You can do this on your own, of course. I find them useful for a long train ride, or before I take a walk or a swim. Or, even better, use them to brainstorm and discuss with your family and friends. I find they really get conversation going.

Past Times: How Much STORY Was There in That Experience?

Think about a few of the larger experiences you had in the past, like a long-term project you took on, or a trip that covered a long distance, or perhaps just a time you had an adventure. Compare this with a simpler experience, maybe just a normal holiday. Then, ask yourself these questions about each of the experiences, giving an answer on a scale of 0 to 5, where:

> 0 = Not at all
> 1 = Very little
> 2 = A little
> 3 = Some
> 4 = A lot
> 5 = A great deal

1. To what extent did [insert experience here] give a good story – where *something happened*, where you faced a challenge and overcame it, or where you made an ally or enemy on your journey – that tells you more about who you are?

2. To what extent did it give you a good story you'd like to tell others?

3. To what extent did it give you the sort of story you'd like to hear someone else tell?

4. Even if the experience went wrong in some way, how much of a good story did it give you?

5. How much of it looked like a man in hole story – where you may well have had some tough times, but overcame them, and emerged triumphant?

6. How much of it included elements of the hero's journey? Maybe you heard some sort of 'call to adventure', then crossed a threshold, embarked on a road of trials, and encountered obstacles, enemies and allies, and learned new skills?

7. Afterwards, to what extent would you say you returned to the old world with some sort of elixir, a new learning, a new way of seeing things?

8. To what extent did you see yourself, at any point, as some kind of hero, facing down a challenge?

If your answers are mostly 4 or 5, it was a good experience. If mostly 3s or less, consider the questions below, and see if you can increase the story factor in your experiences in the future.

The Way to Happy Days: How to Get More STORY into Any Experience

Use these questions to think about how you can increase the amount and quality of story in the experiences you choose and your life in general.

1. What's your story? How is it progressing? Where are you on *your* hero's journey? Are you refusing your call to adventure? Do you have a yearning you haven't dared admit to others? Do you have a dream you've kept buried? If so, what can you do to surface that? What steps – small or big – can you take to move forward, cross the threshold and begin your journey?

2. What kind of hero would you like to be in your next experience?

3. When did you last hear a call to adventure? Did you cross the threshold? If not, what held you back? And can you find a way to say, 'Yes!' next time?

4. How can you be more aware of calls to adventure?

5. What will the road of trials look like in your next experience?

6. Who will be your allies?

7. Have you ever been around the wheel of the hero's journey before, where you faced down the supreme ordeal – an inner demon or external monster – and returned to the old world with some sort of elixir, an answer, new knowledge, new confidence and belief in yourself?

8. Are you an Actor, Agent or Author in your story?

SOMETHING FOR THE WEEKEND

To get you not only thinking about the ideas in each chapter, but also using them in your life, here's a handful of ideas you can use next weekend. Besides things you can do that cost and require commitment, there are ideas that are free.

On the page opposite, write down three ideas of your own.

1. Watch *Star Wars* with a friend

OK, it doesn't have to be *Star Wars*, you can choose your own favourite film: *Casablanca*? *The Usual Suspects*? *La La Land*? When you watch it this time around though, watch out for the telling moments that mimic the hero's journey. Keep the hero's journey on page 53 open by your side to make the task easier.

2. Get stuck into an escape room

E.g., Handmade Mysteries' rooms in London or the Escapement's Egypt Room in Margate.

3. Go to immersive theatre

E.g., Secret Cinema or Punchdrunk.

4. Take a hike

By foot, bicycle, rail. A hero's journey can be a literal journey. But there should be an element of challenge. Have a target destination that'll stretch you.

5. Get lost!

And let serendipity into your life. Go somewhere random without taking your phone with you, so you don't have a map.

2

TRANSFORMATION

How to Live the Dream We All Dream

'I guess that's the thing about a hero's journey.
You might not start out a hero, and you might not even
come back that way. But you change, which is the
same as everything changing.'

KAMI GARCIA

Some events can change a man's life, and a woman's too. Sometimes, when those things happen, in the right place at the right time for the right person, they can do a lot more than transform one or even two people's lives. They can lift a nation. An event like that happened on 30 July 1976.

On that day, a Friday, about two hundred years after the United States of America was founded, a group of men were shaking their legs, their arms, their hands. About an hour's drive north of the US border, in the newly and purpose-built stadium in Montreal, the Big O, they were limbering up for the 110-metre hurdles race.

Carefully, each man crouched and put his hands on the track. Next, he put his feet, one at a time, on the angled edges of the starting blocks. Then, primed like a wild cat, he readied himself for the race.

There were five events to go: two track, three field. Then they would know who would be called the 'World's Greatest Athlete'. The man who won gold in the decathlon had been called that ever since the decathlon had been an Olympic sport.

The starter lifted his starting pistol, fired it – and the coiled men sprang into action, accelerating like cheetahs, leaping over the hurdles. Seen from the finish line, there's a poetry in their forward motion: bursts of frenetic running, followed by half-moments of calm as they fly over the hurdles.

It's almost as if time speeds up, then slows down for a tiny split-second as athletes become airborne, floating over each hurdle, before hurtling along to the next, and the next, and the next. Until there's no more ballet, it's just that final, desperate race to the line. And then it's all over – and the Russian had won.

The decathlon had always been an American event. Hell, it had been invented there in the 1880s. A US athlete had won it nine out of the thirteen times it had been contested at the Olympics. But things hadn't gone so well in recent years. The Americans had only won once in the three most recent Olympics, losing out to a German and a Russian.

And now, the Russian who'd taken decathlon gold at the last Olympics had just won the first track event of the day. Mykola Avilov was a tall, lean, muscular man, with dark hair and a small, dark moustache. He'd whistled his way through the first day. He'd started the second leading the pack. And now an American named Fred Dixon, one of the two with hopes of a medal, had fallen over one of those hurdles and blown his chances. So American dreams all rested on the shoulders of one man, a man who, when Avilov was claiming gold four years earlier in Munich, had come in tenth.

This was, remember, during the Cold War, when trust between Russia and America was far worse than it is today, when thermonuclear war felt like a realistic option, and the only thing stopping that happening was an idea so crazy it was actually called MAD – mutually assured destruction.

In summer of 1976, mutual suspicion was high. The Americans were licking their wounds after defeat in Vietnam. The Soviets had supplied guns, bullets and surface-to-air missiles to the victorious Viet Cong. And now, the Russians were winning again, at an event the Americans considered their own.

It wasn't all over yet, though. Not by a long javelin throw. Avilov may have sailed through the 110-metre battle, but to be named 'World's Greatest Athlete' you have to do well in all ten events, and the points you get in each are more important than how high you place. The decathlon, you could say, isn't about one battle. It's more a war of attrition.

If Avilov was going to win, he'd have to beat the last American standing between him and the gold medal, a man by the name of Bruce Jenner. While Avilov was lean, Jenner was shaped like a comic-book character invented just a few years later, He-Man. On top of his thick thighs, his body was shaped like a broad V. As it went upward from his hips, it went outwards to his pecs, lats, deltoids and trapezius muscles. He even had the same ear-covering man-bob as He-Man. If the job of protecting America's honour should fall on anyone's shoulders, at least he looked the part.

There were four events left for him to beat Avilov in. Three of those were relics from the Greek forerunner to the modern decathlon: the discus, the pole vault and the javelin. And then there was the 1,500-metre run.

In official Olympic footage from the era, filmed inside the Big O, we see Jenner, his left arm outstretched, holding a discus in his hand, like a living, breathing, updated Greek god in skimpy shorts and a red vest. He spins, spins, shouts as he hurls the discus: 'Roar-aaaaaargh!'

He throws a mighty 50.04 metres, beating everyone, beating Avilov by almost 5 metres.

Now, the pole vault. Jenner runs towards the camera, the pole pointing straight at us. He picks up speed, plants the pole firmly, throws himself after it. It bends under his weight, then launches him into the air. Suddenly, Jenner is upside down, his huge He-Man thighs the wrong way up, pointing up at the sky. Then he twists in mid-air, his legs go over the bar, his stomach curls over too. He flings his arms straight up and over, and lands, flat, on the mat.

He's just jumped 2 metres. Second place, but he's beaten Avilov.

Now, the javelin, and we see Avilov. He takes his spear, reaches back, launches it. It sails through the air, but when the camera cuts to Avilov after the throw, his joy has evaporated. He isn't whistling today. There's no smile beneath the moustache. Instead, he's rubbing his elbow. He ices it.

Now it's Jenner's turn with the javelin. As he hurls his spear into the air, he wills it forward with a battle-cry: 'Aaaa-aaah!' Fourth, but he's thrown further than Avilov. The camera goes to Jenner. He's smiling, confident, comfortable with the camera.

There is still one more event to go, the 1500-metre run, but he knows he has enough points, that his time has come.

To bring the decathlon back home, all Jenner has to do is finish with a respectable time. After the starter's gun, he eases around the first bend. A Russian, Leonid Lytvynenko, who'd taken the silver medal four years before, kicks early in the race. Lytvynenko isn't in the running for a medal this time around though. He poses no threat to Jenner. There's no need to chase him. And, as every athlete knows, if you kick too soon, you blow up. What should Jenner do? Play it safe? Risk it? Jenner goes. He passes Avilov. He passes the pack. He passes everyone, except Lytvynenko, and sprints down the final straight, setting a new world record.

Someone passed Jenner a US flag and he punched the air with it. And while the other athletes were crossing the line, falling on the floor, exhausted, the all-American hero jogged a victory lap around the track. Everyone cheered, especially the thousands of Americans. And why not? Here was the 'World's Greatest Athlete', and he was one of them, wherever they were from.

Born in New York State to a mom who stayed home and a dad who was a tree surgeon, Jenner had gone to school in a place called Sleepy Hollow. He moved to Iowa in the Midwest for college. And now he was living in San Diego, California. Every night, after a day of training for six or seven hours, he'd sold insurance to make ends meet.

At last he had his reward. Thanks to four years of hard work, he'd transformed himself – from just another hard-working guy into the world's greatest athlete, an all-American hero who was about to be feted by the media and big brands, and become very rich in the process.

At the end of Jenner's lap of honour, he went up to the crowd, and to a woman overcome with emotion described by the *New York Daily News* the next day as 'a pretty blonde'. Jenner took the woman in his arms and kissed her. She was his biggest fan and his wife, Chrystie.

Keeping Up with the Jenners

Every society has its myths and, as Joseph Campbell discovered, they follow a predictable pattern. Few countries, however, have a myth as explicit as the US's American Dream. A writer and historian named James Truslow Adams built on the original idea of the right to life, liberty and the pursuit of happiness that was written in the Declaration of Independence in 1776. He spelled out the modern version of the idea in his 1931 book *The Epic of America*.

'The American dream,' Adams wrote, 'that has lured tens of millions of all nations to our shores in the past century has not been a dream of material plenty, though that has doubt-lessly counted heavily. It has been much more than that. It has been a dream of being able to grow to fullest development as man and woman.'

If you were to look at this dream through Kurt Vonnegut's glasses, you would see it's a version of one of the most popular stories: the tale of the man in hole. But, as Vonnegut said, 'It needn't be a man, and it doesn't have to be a hole. It's just a way of remembering it.'

Since the material progress of the twentieth century propelled the US to become the world's leading nation, almost all societies have copied at least a part of this model. Most people now believe in some version of this story. Even you.

You might well scoff at the idea of the American Dream, with its designer brands and McMansions and country clubs and Donald Trump. You might think I'm pushing it too far to say there's a version of it over here. If anyone is ever fool enough to mention 'the British Dream', everyone laughs – because it sounds artificial, copycat, crass.

But that's a mistake. Because the dream of a mostly free, equal, post-feudal, capitalist society where we can all achieve material plenty and pursue happiness and be able to grow to fullest development is what we all want, for ourselves, for our society, for our children. Who doesn't believe that we should all have equal opportunities, and that everyone should have the chance to better her- or himself and their family? Who doesn't believe that society should be set up so that it's perfectly possible for us to fully develop – that is, to transform our circumstances and ourselves for the better?

That's the dream, at least roughly speaking, that we all believe in. We believe that we can do better, that our families will be better educated, will eat better, and live longer lives. We hope to be richer. We want longer holidays. We believe in better. We believe in transformation.

Like a flag of many stripes, this idea of transformation – the positive, meaningful sort we believe in and strive for – includes all sorts of related ideas. It incorporates purpose, personal growth, realising our potential, and reaching our 'fullest development'. It includes becoming the person we want to be, doing what we want to do, and living the life we want to live. It means becoming a better basketball player or lover or parent, learning to sew or play backgammon or move like Jagger, saying, 'No!' to a life that feels fake to you, and moving ever closer to the person you dream of being, and have the potential to be.

Philosophers and psychologists have been waving the flag for transformation for millennia. The idea sits at the heart of two of the most influential and enduring conceptions of the good life. Aristotle thought personal development was key to achieving the sort of practical wisdom a person needed to make the smart decisions that would lead to a good life. Confucius believed learning and self-improvement were essential.

This idea is also central to many of the most influential and respected models that psychologists have formulated for happiness in recent years. Growth is named as a key ingredient, for instance, in Corey Keyes's tripartite model for flourishing rather than languishing. Doing what you want to do – also known as autonomy – is fundamental to Edward Deci and Richard Ryan's Self-Determination Theory. Meaning and accomplishments are essential for Martin Seligman's PERMA model. Personal growth and self-acceptance are core for Carol Ryff's six-factor model: these can be measured by asking people to what extent statements like these seem true for them: 'For me, life has been a continual process of learning, changing and growth', and, 'I like parts of myself'. And the highest goal in Abraham Maslow's hierarchy of needs is 'self-actualization': 'the desire for self-fulfillment ... to become more and more what one is, to become everything that one is capable of becoming'.

And, finally, according to studies in narrative psychology, people who tell stories of growth – as long as they're towards intrinsic goals like personal development rather than extrinsic goals like money and fame – achieve higher levels of happiness.

But while philosophers and psychologists have been saying and showing that transformation is essential for enduring happiness for many years, I think these ideas are more likely to resonate with us when they're expressed by artists. And so, here are three, more poetic ways of saying that autonomy, self-actualisation, growth – and all the other stripes on the flag of transformation – are vital for happiness.

The first is from a play written more than four hundred years ago. In Hamlet, as Laertes is about to escape, Shakespeare has his father Polonius give him this seminal piece of farewell advice: 'To thine own self be true.'

The second is something the singer Janis Joplin said almost fifty years ago. In an interview with a journalist at US weekly newspaper *Parade*, she said, 'You better not compromise yourself. It's all you got.'

And the third is from the actor Sir Ian McKellen, from a couple of revealing statements he made in the late 1980s and the late 2010s. Asked about his coming-out in the middle of an interview on BBC radio in 1988, McKellen said that it was 'the best thing I ever did'. He elaborated on that in a message posted on Twitter on the thirtieth anniversary of that interview: 'Life at last begins to make sense, when you are open and honest.'

So Bruce Jenner, the everyman who turned himself into the 'World's Greatest Athlete', was a hero for us all, and remains so to this day. Because just as, back then, he was following the mythic dream that we all aspire to, so Jenner continues to pursue happiness and, to borrow Truslow's words, 'to grow to fullest development as man and woman'.

In case you're one of the few who hasn't kept up with Jenner's next transformation, here's a brief update. In the first years after his triumph in Montreal, his life took off. He made millions. He became the famous face of a cereal called Wheaties. He appeared on talk shows, and he became a sportscaster for TV channels NBC and ABC. Later, after his marriage to Chrystie failed, and another marriage, to an ex-girlfriend of Elvis Presley's he'd met at the Playboy Mansion, failed too, he married a whip-smart business-woman by the name of Kris Kardashian.

Kardashian got Jenner working again, using his name and fame to make infomercials about sports equipment. In 2007, she sold the idea of a reality-TV series about herself, Bruce and their children. It was called *Keeping Up with the Kardashians*. Jenner the athlete became Jenner the reality-TV star. And then, well, there were hints and allegations and leaks.

Jenner grew his hair long, into a ponytail. He booked a 'tracheal shave', a procedure that reduces the tell-tale Adam's apple on a man's neck. He was photographed with a hot-pink manicure. It became the biggest open secret in Hollywood, though no one knew for sure – until Jenner emerged, fully developed, like a butterfly, as Caitlyn for the cover story for *Vanity Fair*. There she fluttered her eyelashes for photographer Annie Leibovitz, and she shared how being Bruce had always felt wrong, and how being Caitlyn felt so right.

'If I was lying on my deathbed and I had kept this secret and never ever did anything about it, I would be lying there saying, "You just blew your entire life,"' she said.

Not everyone can accept the change. Fred Dixon, Jenner's old decathlon colleague, for instance.

'Bruce was one of the best athletes who ever existed,' Dixon once remarked. 'Now, to see that photo ... somehow it doesn't compute.'

But Jenner expected this sort of reaction, and she's accepted it too. She has to. Besides, she is now following Polonius and Joplin and McKellen's advice. To her own self, she is being true. She's no longer compromising herself.

Jenner's story isn't over yet. But, however her story ends, in her life she epitomises the American Dream and the ideal that the rest of us believe in: that we can and should be who we want to be.

By doing that, not only is she seeking her 'fullest development' and exercising her right to the pursuit of happiness, she is also more likely to achieve it.

So, I think that Bruce *and* Caitlyn Jenner are beacons of hope for the rest of us. *He* was a beacon for what can happen if you work hard to transform yourself, from everyman to hero. *She* is not only a beacon for the trans community – sure, she has made the idea more acceptable and possible – but she is also a beacon for the idea that we should all live our lives in whatever way feels best to each of us.

There is one question left to ask. Since it's clear that transformation is critical for enduring, satisfying happiness, how big a change should you make? Do you need to be as extreme as Bruce, training 365 days a year for years to transform himself into a hero? Do you need to do something as drastic as Caitlyn – when he became she?

And anyway, what would *you* change? Where are you compromised right now? Are you on autopilot, going with the flow of what you've always done or was expected of you? Are you still playing a sport or following a hobby you've fallen out of love with? Are you hanging out with friends who, truth be told, you've had enough of? Are you trudging down a path that, if not boring you to death, is not making you feel fully alive?

If It Ain't Broke . . .?

You may be thinking, as you read this, that you can see how *other* people need to change, but you're mostly done. You can't imagine a future where you're someone completely different. And you don't want to. After all, you've worked hard to get to where you are, and, well, this is who you want to be. Answer these two questions and you'll see what I mean:

1. On a scale of 1 to 10, where 1 = no change at all and 10 = drastic and complete change, by how much have your ideas, beliefs and preferences changed in the past ten years?

2. On the same scale of 1 to 10, by how much do you expect your ideas, beliefs and preferences to change in the next ten years?

If you're like most other people, including me, you'll have a higher score for the first question than the second. Think about that for a moment. It makes no sense. What it really says is that because we find it easier to look back and see how we've changed, and harder to imagine how we'll change in the future, we end up kidding ourselves that we're the finished article. A psychologist at Harvard named Dan Gilbert, who constructed this two-question test, calls this the 'end of history' illusion.

People like you and me who know about this end-of-history illusion don't need to ask ourselves the question, 'Will we change?' We know that we are going to transform in exciting, strange ways in the future – even if we can't imagine what that looks like yet. The question we should be asking is, 'What type of change is best?' Should you opt for some sort of sudden, 'road to Damascus', disruptive, rip-it-up-and-start-again change? Or, should you aim for slower, more subtle, incremental changes?

The answer is, 'It depends' – on whether your starting point is desperation or inspiration. Let's say things aren't working out and you're desperate. You're in a hole, facing the sort of test on your road of trials that seems impossible and impassable. Maybe you're not getting any satisfaction from the things you do, or any meaningful connection with the people you're spending your time with. Perhaps, instead of feeling energised and happy after you go out with a certain set of friends, you come home feeling washed out. Or, instead of feeling relaxed and ready to sleep after a few hours on the sofa with your smartphone in one hand, your tablet in another, and one eye on the TV, you end up feeling drained and more alone than when you started.

If you recognise these feelings, I'd say you need disruptive, spin-your-life-around transformation. Or, to begin with at least, you've got to throw some disruptive, different activities into the mix of the experiences you have.

I've had these feelings a number of times in the last few years. They've led me to make changes ranging from very small and marginal, to very big and scary. Looking back at just the past decade, for instance, desperation has led me to leave a job, write a book, take up Pilates, start a university course, change who I spend my time with, delete Twitter and email from my phone, and download an app that limits how much time I spend on Facebook. (There's more on the problems with technology and the magic of reducing all sorts of distractions in the *Intensity* and *Outside & Offline* chapters.)

Or maybe desperation doesn't sound relevant for you. Maybe things are working pretty well right now, you're expressing the real you in most things you do. If so, you're in a good place for inspiration. How could you change what you do with your time to get more from it? How could you tweak what you're doing to get more outputs from the same inputs?

This is how I think about many of the new things I've taken on. I've heard about them from friends, from contacts, from the research work I do; and then I go and try them. Inspiration has led me to transformative experiences like rock-climbing, stand-up paddle-boarding, a course in stand-up comedy, Secret Cinema's *Star Wars*, and horse-riding with friends and a real cowboy in Utah.

Only you will know if desperation or inspiration is your reason for change. Only you will know if you're ready for a big, hairy, turn-your-life-around change, or a take-it-easy, learn, grow, develop type of transformation.

But whatever is right for you, one thing is clear. Whether it's major change, simple change, tweaking what's there, or the richer idea of growth and becoming, transformation is, as the science has shown, vital for your happiness. Because it's an essential human trait and exciting ingredient in life's journey. Because it reduces the compromises that stop you from being yourself, and will lead you to become the person you always wanted to be. And because it'll help you achieve your fullest development.

How to Holiday: Three Degrees of Transformation

If all this transformation and achieving fullest development sounds like a lot of *work*, and you're wondering, 'What if all I want to do, at the end of the day, is to kick back and take it easy? After all, I've deserved it. Is there room for *that* in this new world of richer, happier days?'

I think I have a solution.

Now, I should mention: I've worked in and around the travel business for more than twenty years now. I was a holiday rep for Thomson Holidays, which is now called TUI, and Crystal Holidays. I've written about travel, advised tourism firms, and given talks about travel from Amsterdam to Beijing and Cannes, and at the Association of British Travel

Agents and Tour Operators (ABTA)'s annual conference. So my solution is based on a few years of practice and thinking.

We can find the answer to the question, 'Is there a place for taking it easy?' in an idea I think of as the 'three degrees of transformation'. The three degrees are: fly and flop, find and seek, and go and become.

Don't take these names too literally, by the way. You don't have to fly to flop. You don't have to go somewhere to become something or someone. And you'll most likely seek *before* you find. Those are just useful labels to remember the difference between them.

A little more detail: fly and flop is for those holidays when the last thing on your mind is achieving your fullest development, and the only transformation you're looking for is what a friend of mine, the author and travel journalist Sophy Roberts, once called 'the fantasy of the other'. When your life is busy and pressured and mostly getting by under a grey sky, the idea of swapping all that for a few days or weeks of doing nothing under blue skies sounds appealing, no?

Find and seek, as it sounds, is when you go sightseeing with your explorer's hat on. You may be walking around the island of Delos or the Ta Prohm jungle temple in Cambodia. You could be hiking the Rob Roy Way or across Zambia's South Luangwa National Park. You could be at Big Sur, riding your Honda Gold Wing along Highway One. You could be at Benicàssim or Burning Man or Bestival. Or, you could be on a bus tour across London or on a coach trip to Skegness.

Go and become, as you'd expect, is when you travel for personal growth. You could be learning how to cook Szechuan cuisine, how to sail or pilot a boat, how to paint or appreciate the paintings of the Renaissance, or how to do a downward dog – more on that in the *Extraordinary* chapter. Or you could be seeking deeper change: attending the Hoffman course, going to Mecca for the Hajj, taking part in an ayahuasca ceremony, or walking the Camino de Santiago.

Three thoughts on the three degrees:

One – it's perfectly possible to have all three degrees in the same trip. Perhaps the best trip contains all three. Who doesn't want a break from their busy life? Variety, as psychologists Kennon Sheldon, Julia Boehm and Sonja Lyubomirsky have noted, is the 'spice of happiness'. And who doesn't want to 'find and seek' new things and come home with stories that help build and shape your identity, and that you can tell others too? And who doesn't want to grow and learn new things?

Two – you can apply these same ideas about holidays to the rest of your free time. At the end of your day or week, you can flop in front of the TV or go for a quiet drink in the pub. You've worked hard. You deserve it. Or, you can 'find and seek': go to a comedy night, have dinner with a friend, play table tennis. Or, you can 'go and become': in a yoga class, in prayer or meditation, or by contributing to the wider community. Learn more about that in the *Status & Significance* chapter.

Three – just as you can get all three of these in a single holiday, or weekend, you can find all three degrees in a book. Reading can be 'fly and flop' entertaining. It can be 'find and seek' sightseeing: the pages and your imagination can take you places. And it can be 'go and become' thought-provoking. The ideas can change what you think, how you think, and how you approach life. Like experiences, perhaps the best books contain all three.

Three Degrees of Transformation

Degree	Fly & flop	Find & seek	Go & become
Keyword	Passive	Active	Transformative
Typical holiday destination	Beach resort	City, festival	Mountains, yoga retreat
Typical activity	Lounging	Looking	Learning
Before work example	Listen to radio	Dancing and singing	Meditation, sun salutations
Lunchtime example	Read a gossip magazine	Read a book	Go to the gym
After-work example	Watch TV, go to the cinema	Go to a comedy club, dinner with friends	Course to learn Szechuan cooking
Weekend example	Have a lie-in	Hiking	Ayahuasca ceremony
Example in Ibiza	A day at the beach at Cala Gracioneta on the west coast	Party in the capital, Ibiza Town	Make a new you at Body Camp in the hills near the north coast
Opportunity for story	Low: not much to talk about	High: lots to talk about	Medium: harder to tell, easier to see

> ## Transformation Summary
>
> **1.** Becoming who you want and have the potential to be –
> which is also called personal growth, development and
> self-actualisation – is vital for happiness.
>
> **2.** Once you've got there, being who you want to be
> and doing what you want to do – which is also called
> autonomy and self-acceptance – is essential for happiness.
>
> **3.** Wherever possible, and without harming others, we
> should not compromise ourselves, but be as true to
> our dreams as possible.

How to TRANSFORM Your Experiences and Your Life

As before, the questions in *Past Times* are about specific experiences from your past. The questions in *The Way to Happy Days* will inspire you to think about your life in general. All will help you bring the benefits of transformation into your life.

Past Times: Was That Experience Transformational?

Think about an experience you had in the past, like a course you took, a time you lived somewhere, a long trip you took, or just somewhere you went. Try this using experiences that were really good, ones that were just average, and ones that were downright awful. Then, ask yourself these questions, giving an answer on a scale of 0 to 5, where:

> 0 = *Not at all*
> 1 = *Very little*
> 2 = *A little*
> 3 = *Some*
> 4 = *A lot*
> 5 = *A great deal*

1. How much did [insert experience here] help you grow?
2. To what extent did you come out of this experience with new learnings, skills or capabilities?
3. How much were you changed as a result of this experience?
4. To what extent did you have an epiphany about your relationships, or become closer to someone?
5. How much did the experience change your world view?
6. To what extent did the experience move you forwards toward a quest that matters to you?

This isn't about adding up your scores. This is more about peaks. Did you get any 4s or 5s? The more 4s and 5s your experience scored, the more it helped you grow and transform, and is therefore a more compelling experience.

If, when you think back to what you've been doing recently, you see a sea of experiences that were fun, but didn't help you grow much, consider the next questions, and see if you can't build a bit more growth and transformation, and therefore meaning and longer-term happiness, into what you do in the future.

The Way to Happy Days: How to Get More TRANSFORMATION in Your Life

Use these questions to think about how you can ride the horse of change into a brighter, better, transformed future.

1. What sort of person do you want to be? What sort of experiences will take you there? And when can you book one in?

2. When you holiday do you look to 'fly and flop', do you 'find and seek', or do you 'go and become'?
    I ask because I think those three descriptions represent the three very different levels of transformation. There's a time and a place for each, of course. But 'go and become' offers the greatest transformation.

3. What would you like to become next? Remember the end-of-history illusion.

4. Do you do what you want with your time – at work, in your free time?

5. Have you 'come out' to others, and even to yourself, about who you really are and want to be?

6. Are you, in your life, 'treading water'? That is, are you really busy, but not going anywhere that matters to you?

7. Do you have a clear image of what 'fullest development' looks like for you right now?

8. Is your reason for change desperation or inspiration, that is, the problematic place you're coming from or the exciting destination you're heading for?

9. What obstacles, enemies and, even, allies stand between you and your transformation?

10. Can you break your thousand-mile journey to transformation into smaller steps? Can you draw a series of stepping stones from here to your final destination? What do the first, second, and third steps look like? Can you take the first one this month?

SOMETHING FOR THE WEEKEND

Here's a handful of ideas you can use next weekend to get a taste of transformation. On the following pages, write down three ideas of your own.

1. Work out at your gym

They're often much quieter then.

2. Learn to cook something new

Invite four friends round this Saturday to eat something you've never cooked before. Then, read up, watch YouTube videos, get the ingredients, and get cooking. Or learn from an expert: learn how to cook all sorts of Asian foods at the School of Wok cookery school in Covent Garden.

3. Get high

Oops, I know it's not very fashionable to advocate drugs nowadays. And I'm not quite doing that. But altered states are fun, and humans have enjoyed them since anyone can remember. Your version of transformation could simply be having a gin and tonic in a bar, or a beer in a pub. It'll most likely work best if you only drink a little. Recent studies suggest people are happier at the moment of drinking, but there are only small overspills of that happiness into the rest of your life. Also note that drinking does not lead to higher life satisfaction. So, just enough to give you that sense of other that we looked at in the three degrees of getting away.

4. Be silent

Take yourself to a place far from usual distractions, probably in nature, and allocate a time to be silent. Try to quiet your inner voice too. You will emerge different.

5. Sign up for comedy improv

When I met a girl called Tizz many years ago, she thought I was pleasant, but not quite funny enough. So she sent me on a comedy improv course at a place called The Spontaneity Shop, run by Deborah Frances-White, who runs *The Guilty Feminist* podcast, and her husband Tom. Now Deborah and Tom's stars have risen, they're too busy to run it, but there are plenty of other companies running improv workshops. It's much easier than it sounds. You don't have to be an extrovert to enjoy it. And since, reader, Tizz married me, they must work *a bit*.

_____

_____

_____

_____

OUTSIDE & OFFLINE

Outside: Oh, We Do Like to Be Beside the Seaside

> *'There is no Wi-Fi in nature, but you'll get a better connection.'*
>
> ANON.

Thirty-seven miles adrift of Kyushu, the most southerly of Japan's four main islands, is a tiny island called Yakushima.

Midstream in the Kuroshio, the Pacific Ocean's version of the North Atlantic's Gulf Stream, the water around Yakushima is warm and salty and rich with sea life. Formed only 15,000 years ago by volcanic eruption, Yakushima is young, tall and green. Sometimes called the Alps in the Ocean, its highest peak is 1,936 metres. Its mountains are green with trees and bamboo grasses, from sea level to the very top. The real magic here, the reason people come, is the giants.

If you were a tree, and you could choose where to live, and you were basing your decision on rainfall, you would choose here for your home. It's the wettest place in Japan. It rains twenty-seven days a month: 4,500 millimetres of rain falls in a year, nine times more than in London.

And yet, if you were a tree, and you were basing your choice on soil, you might think twice. The granite left over from the island's formation has produced soil that is very low on nutrients.

This combination of exceptional rainfall and terrible soil has made the cedar trees here special. Elsewhere in Japan, the cedars are called Sugi and live for 500 years. Here, because the granite soil is so poor, the trees grow incredibly slowly. This, tree experts have figured out, makes them produce more resin, which makes them more resistant to disease and decay. So trees here can live much longer. Trees which have seen 1,000 years gain the title Yakusugi. Some of them live even longer.

The grandmother of the Yakusugi is Jomon Sugi. She is only 25 metres tall, just 5 metres around. But she is named for the Jomon period, Japan's prehistoric era, because she may be as old as 7,200 years, which would make her the world's oldest tree.

The Yakusugi may be the reason people come, but, as you'll see when you visit, there is much else to see and hear. There are camphors and epiphytes. There are waterfalls crashing into worn granite pools. There are streams gliding past green rocks. In many places, it's as if nature has taken a big, broad brush, and painted everything a mossy green. There's plenty of forest stillness and silence too, besides the sound of raindrops drip, drip, dripping down from the leaves they fell on during the latest downpour.

It was here that an NHK film crew came in 1990. They were following a young researcher by the name of Yoshifumi Miyazaki. He was trying to find out if there was any truth in the Japanese Forestry Agency's claims about an activity the agency was promoting called *shinrin yoku* – or, in English, 'forest bathing'.

Trees Are Good

If 'forest bathing' sounds like a made-up marketing slogan, that's because it is. It was coined by a man named Tomohide

Akiyama. He made it up back in 1982, when he was head of Japan's Forestry Agency, because he wanted to encourage more people to come to the woods.

Shinrin yoku was a neat stroke of marketing genius. People like bathing. Bathing sounds like a head-back, toe-twiddling sort of relaxing break from our ever busier lives. So why not pair it with something else people think is relaxing, like a walk in the woods? The idea of *shinrin yoku* caught on.

'But nobody had researched *shinrin yoku*, no one knew if it was just a nice idea, or if it was true,' says Miyazaki, who is now vice director at the Centre for Environment, Health and Field Sciences, at Chiba University in Japan.

So, there Miyazaki was, in 1990, in the green, green forest of Yakushima, trying to figure out if 'forest bathing' was just a good marketing slogan, or if spending time in the woods really did make a difference to people's health.

Miyazaki began his investigation by getting a group of people to walk on a treadmill in his lab for forty minutes, and then asking them to walk again for forty minutes – but this time in Yakushima's primeval forest. He asked them to record how they felt before and after. He tested their blood pressure and cortisol levels by analysing their blood and their saliva.

The results were simple and clear: forest bathing is good for you. Compared to the lab-based walk, after a stroll in the woods people's mood improved more, and any feelings of tension or anger or fatigue were lessened. Also, their blood pressure and the levels of cortisol in their system, key indicators for stress, went down further.

It's easy to read these words, think, 'Yes, that's a statement of the obvious,' and move on. But it's also important to realise that this is far from obvious. For centuries, millennia even, we humans have tried to get away from the woods. We chopped them down and made fields. We chopped them down and made houses, villages, towns, suburbs, cities. We chopped them down and made newspapers and paper for writing on. We chop them down without much thought when they're in the way of roads, driveways, extensions, housing developments. In folk tales, woods have been painted as dark and dangerous, places to stay away from, unless you're an outlaw. Our culture doesn't seem to value forests much. Sure, there's the green belt movement, our concern for the Amazon rainforest, the ramblers' associations, and the romantic writers like Henry David Thoreau and William Wordsworth. But these are relatively new complaints against the human-development machine whose dominant message has always been: forests – who cares?

And it's important to realise that, even if it sounds obvious, there's an ocean of difference between something that sounds sensible, and what science has proved to be true. Because, after all, things that sound unquestionable today weren't always so obvious. It isn't so very long ago that many in the medical profession thought smoking was a good idea, and tobacco companies used images of doctors and even sports people in their advertisements. 'More doctors smoke Camels than any other cigarette,' read one ad. 'The cigarette for me,' quipped legendary footballer Stanley Matthews in another, for a brand called Craven 'A', with a smile on his face and a cigarette in his hand.

What Miyazaki's research had done was to transform an idea from a nice romantic notion and a neat marketing slogan into real, practical, scientifically verified advice. As it happened, he did much more than that. He'd planted a seed that would blossom into a forest of research.

Since that first study, Miyazaki has continued to research the benefits of being in forests and nature, and inspired others to investigate the idea. Scientists in Japan and around the world, from Australia to Finland, the US and the UK, have been investigating forest and nature therapy from all sorts of angles. The findings always point along the same path.

Getting outside, into nature, is really good for every one of us. It turns the volume down on stuff no one wants. It reduces stress. It makes people feel less hostile. It decreases depressive symptoms. It lowers cortisol, blood pressure, pulse rate. It helps us feel less fatigue.

Getting outside and into nature turns the volume up on good things too. It helps people sleep better. It stimulates the all-important parasympathetic part of the nervous system, better known to you and me as the 'rest and digest' system. And it gives people a sense of vigour, a feeling of liveliness.

We Really Do Like to Be Beside the Seaside

Summertime in Britain is a funny business. Most of the time, it doesn't quite happen. But when the dial goes up, knowing that summer might only last a few days, out we come in our hundreds of thousands. We do our dutiful best to make the most of it before it's gone. We have the family round, dusting off the barbecue for its once-a-year outing. We fire it up, and do our level best not to burn the sausages or the chicken, while we cook them enough so that no one gets food poisoning. We pack into parks, carrying picnic blankets, bottles of rosé and beer, bags of ice. We strip off. And we pour on to beaches from Brighton and Bognor Regis, to Blackpool and Skegness.

Some of my earliest, and fondest, memories from the hot summers of the 1970s are of family barbecues, and of me and my brother, in the back of the family car, stuck in traffic jams ten miles long as everyone headed to the coast, the windows wound right down, whining and asking, 'How long till we get there?'

To keep us quiet, my dad would sing songs and try to get us to join in. One of his favourites was an old music-hall song his parents had sung with him when they'd been heading to the coast, by bus and train, back when he was a boy in the 1950s:

Oh, I do like to be beside the seaside,
Oh, I do like to be beside the sea,
I do like to stroll along the prom, prom, prom!
Where the brass bands play, tiddley-om-pom-pom!

As it happens, there's a ray of truth in that old song, as some researchers at the London School of Economics recently discovered.

A few years back, I heard about an app called Mappiness. It was created by George MacKerron and Susana Mourato in London. I liked the sound of it: to create a map of happiness. I downloaded it and signed up.

Every now and then, the Mappiness app would beep at me and ask questions: Who was I with? What was I doing? How happy was I, on a scale of 1 to 10? Like with many apps, I kept it up for a while, and then ignored it. But not before I'd unwittingly contributed to the largest data set for a study like this ever conducted. Because, as it turned out, another 21,946 people had downloaded Mappiness, and between us, we delivered 1,138,481 pieces of data.

When MacKerron and Mourato analysed the data, they not only compared what I and the other 20,000-odd participants told them, but also cross-referenced our answers with GPS data. They used that to figure out what the weather was like when we answered, and what sort of place we were at: such as urban, suburban, farmland, woodland, 'marine and coastal margins', and 'inland bare ground' – that's the sort of derelict, no-man's land that's mostly just gravel and a sense of desolation. Those million-plus pieces of data led to some obvious conclusions, and some surprising discoveries.

The obvious first. We are unhappiest of all when we're ill in bed. We're even unhappier there than when we're commuting or at work.

We're happier when it's hot and sunny. According to the analysis by the scientists, when it's 24°C or more, we're happier by 5.13 points. Or, in language you and I would use, much happier.

We're generally happier outdoors than indoors. The only time that doesn't work is when we're outdoors but at one of those 'inland bare ground' places.

We're also happier in natural environments than cities. According to the research, we're happier by between 1.8 and 2.7 points when we're in natural environments: 1.8 when we're in fresh water, wetlands and floodplains, rising to 2.7 when we're in mountains, moors and heathland.

But the least obvious, and perhaps you'd agree most surprising, discovery from the research was that when we're at 'marine and coastal margins' we are 6 points happier than in urban areas. Think of the joy you feel when you open the curtains to blue skies that tell you it's going to be a super sunny 24°C day, and compare that to how you feel on a normal, grey sort of day. That's the sort of increase in happiness we're talking about here. Or, as MacKerron and Mourato said in their scientific paper, that's the difference between attending an exhibition and cleaning the bathroom. So, yes, we really do like to be beside the seaside.

Why? Why does being beside the seaside, and outside generally – in grasslands, woods, heaths, moors and mountains – make us happier and healthier? Scientists think there are four likely reasons.

First, there's an idea called biophilia. The imprint of a million years of living among natural sounds means that our brains process natural sights and sounds in a different way to man-made. 'We may not realise this but we have been living in artificial environments since we were born,' says Miyazaki. 'So because of that our bodies are under certain stress. When you expose yourself to nature, like forest or flowers, your body will relax and the immune system which was lowered under stress would recover.'

Second is an associated idea. If we like natural sounds because we're used to them, there's the stress of city living, the 'environmental bads' that come with modern life, like the noise and air pollution in cities. Swap the blare of sirens, your neighbours playing music too loudly, and some joker revving his engine in the middle of the night for the chirp of song-birds and the whistle of the wind through leaves in trees – and you've less stress, more happiness. It's similar if you stop sucking in bus exhaust fumes, and start breathing in the clean breeze that's just crossed acres of sea, field or hillside.

Third is a fascinating theory specifically about forest bathing, put forward by a medical researcher at Nippon Medical School in Tokyo called Qing Li, that trees emit something called phytoncides. They're sort of essential oils that actively protect trees from microbes that could harm them. When people breathe in these phytoncides, they spur healthy biological changes in us too. In Li's experiments, he has found that when people walk or stay overnight in forests, they receive a free immunity boost, as their bodies produce more of the natural killer cells that form our crucial first line of defence against viruses and tumours.

And the fourth reason why being outside is good for our health? To answer that, we'll have to go back to the 1960s, to a Sunday, in fact, and to a strange man bobbing up and down in one of London's best-loved parks, Hampstead Heath.

A Very Strange Man on Hampstead Heath

In the early 1960s, a very odd thing happened in north London. As people took their usual, leisurely Sunday stroll enjoying the woodlands, the fresh air, and, as we now know, the phytoncides on the side of Hampstead Heath furthest from the city, they suddenly came across something quite silly: a man, dressed in his Sunday best suit – except for his tie and coat and jacket – and running.

The man, whose dark hair had been crew cut, was clearly not an athlete or a bank robber. For one thing, he wasn't going that fast, so he didn't look like he was trying to win a race, or escape from someone. Besides, he had two children with him, a girl with long blonde hair, and a boy also with a crew cut. He looked, so people out walking that day might have thought, a bit like a bank manager who was late for his train. But then, on second thoughts, only late by a little bit. And even then, on third thoughts, as if he was late for a train he wasn't too bothered about catching.

Rather than galloping at full-tilt, the man appeared to be taking his time. He looked a bit like a buoy bobbing up and down, along a gentle river. What he was doing – you may have guessed already – was jogging.

'I was the first person,' Jerry Morris would say later, in his thick Glaswegian accent, 'to run on Hampstead Heath. Every Sunday morning, if the weather was at all possible, I took off my coat and my little boy carried my coat, I took off my jacket and my little girl carried my jacket, and I ran for twenty minutes. People thought I was bananas.'

Morris wouldn't look out of place on the heath or anywhere else today, of course. Seeing people out jogging is as ordinary as seeing a bus, though nowadays joggers tend to dress differently: skimpy shorts, Lycra trousers, and £100 trainers that look like the owner ate a handful of highlighter pens and was then sick all over them. Back then, though, you were as likely to see a jogger as you were to see a man in Lycra. Because, though the idea that exercise might be good for you went as far back as Hippocrates, no one knew for sure.

It was Morris who changed that. He was born in Liverpool, in 1910, only weeks after the family arrived by boat from

Poland. They were escaping the Jewish pogroms back there. When they landed in their new home, they took the surname of the ship's captain as their own. Not long after arriving, they moved to Glasgow.

'We were next door to a slum street,' Morris would later say. 'I still remember the screaming women on Friday night and Saturday night, when they were beaten by their drunk husbands.'

His first memories of exercise were with his father. 'My father used to take me on a four-mile walk from Glasgow once a week, when I was a schoolboy,' he said. 'We used to aim to do the four miles in an hour. If we did that OK, I got an ice-cream. If we did it in even a minute less, I got a choc-ice.'

As Morris grew up, he became increasingly interested in improving people's lives. He studied medicine at the University of Glasgow and then University College London Medical School. He served in the Royal Army Medical Corps during the war.

Afterwards, Morris started studying public health at the London School of Hygiene and Tropical Medicine, just as a surprising new public-health problem arose. Only a few short years after the war had ended, a worrying new life-or-death issue was knocking down more men than ever before. It was rapidly getting worse and would be the leading cause of death for more than half a century.

The problem was coronary heart disease – when fatty deposits fur up your arteries and reduce the flow of blood and oxygen to your heart. Why was this suddenly affecting so many men – making them feel sick and short of breath, giving them pains in their chest and heart attacks, and killing them?

Morris searched for clues in all the data he could gather. He looked at post-mortem documents going back as far as 1907 and developed a hunch that it might be linked to how active the people were. 'There were some hints,' he would later say, 'in the national statistics of mortality that it might be connected in some way to occupation.'

To test his hunch, Morris would need thousands of volunteers to exercise regularly, and thousands who didn't. How was he going to recruit those sorts of numbers? We don't know for sure when Morris had his eureka moment. It might have been at work. It might have been in the bath. I like to think it was when he was on the way from his office in Bloomsbury to his home in Hampstead, sitting on the bus.

Back then, London's red double-deckers were operated by two people: the driver and the conductor. These men, Morris realised, were a perfect group to study, because they were very similar in every respect except one, which was the thing Morris wanted to test. They came from the same part of the country. They lived in the same sort of houses. They were served by the same health and welfare services. Their one key difference was how much they moved. The driver sat down all day long. The conductor was always on the move, going up and down the stairs all day to sell tickets. Conductors climbed between 500 and 750 steps a day. How on earth did Morris and his team know that? Simple. 'We spent many hours sitting on the buses watching the number of stairs they climbed,' Morris would say later.

With the cooperation of London Transport, Morris and his team followed 31,000 men aged thirty-five to sixty-four for two years, from 1949 to 1950. When you look at the original paper published in 1953, the first thing that strikes you is this: 40 per cent of men who had heart attacks were dead within three months, far more than today. The second thing that strikes you is how surprisingly clear the findings are. Conductors had fewer heart attacks than the drivers, and the attacks were less likely to be fatal. In fact, the drivers had twice as many heart attacks as the conductors.

The reason why seems obvious: because they moved more. But as a good scientist, Morris reasoned there could be more explanations. It could also have been, as the paper he published states, because the drivers and conductors had different constitutions, or because they were under different mental strains.

This experiment didn't prove conclusively then that the reason was exercise. So, to be sure, Morris conducted another study with another large employer of men. From 1949 to 1950, he and his team also followed the health of 110,000 men aged thirty-five to fifty-nine working for the Post Office. The men ranged from your regular postmen to higher grade postmen, postal and telegraph officers, supervisors and telephonists.

Of all the postal workers they followed, only the regular postmen's work day included plenty of physical activity, even though it was, as the paper noted, 'not particularly strenuous': walking, stair-climbing, cycling, and carrying. Again, the results were clear. 'As with the transport workers,' the 1953 paper states, 'the early mortality of the physically active group (0.6 per 1,000) is substantially less than that of the physically inactive (1.2 per 1,000).' The regular postmen, in other words, were half as likely to have a heart attack.

This meant Morris could now confidently conclude that the more your job involved exercise, the less likely you were to have coronary heart disease, and the less likely you were to die.

But while the study answered some questions, like any good study it created more questions. What about how much a person exercised out of work? And what sort of exercise was best?

Morris tried to answer those questions too. He made a study of another group of British men who were similar to each other, like the bus drivers and conductors. He found them in civil servants. But rather than being working class, these chaps were middle class and, as it happened, almost all gardeners in their spare time. 'It's what keeps us sane,' they used to tell Morris and his team.

Morris thought gardening was the sort of exercise that would protect them. But it turned out, it didn't. What protected your heart, and your life, Morris found, was more vigorous exercise, like swimming, cycling and jogging. Regular aerobic exercise like that reduces your risk of heart attack by half.

And so there Morris was, with his children David and Julia, that Sunday morning on Hampstead Heath. You could say that he was taking the science to heart and standing by his research. Or, better, that he was not only talking the talk about the importance of exercise, but walking the walk. Or, perhaps even better, jogging the jog. No matter what you call it, it worked.

Through his pioneering work on exercise, Morris fired the gun for the rise of an industry that would give us Nike, Adidas and Lululemon. And he gave tens of millions of people much longer lives, including himself. He swam, pedalled an exercise bike, or walked outside for half an hour almost every day. He only stopped swimming aged ninety-seven, because he could no longer get himself in and out of the pool. After he finally expired, in 2009, at ninety-nine-and-a-half years old, his neighbours in north London would say, 'It's just not the same without Jerry, walking up and down the road every day.'

Can You Run to Success and Happiness?

Morris's research fired the gun on the exercise revolution. It's the trigger behind the government campaigns to try to get us to be more active, and initiatives to get children exercising more, like the Daily Mile. It's the inspiration for the hundreds of marathons and half-marathons now taking place around the world, from Cornwall to the Orkney Islands, from Walt Disney World to Nashville, from Kangaroo Island in Australia to Gothenburg in Sweden. It's the motivation that inspires millions to get off the couch, put on their trainers and join a 'park run' each weekend. Organised by volunteers in parks around the world on Saturday and Sunday mornings, park runs are for people who want to join others on a shorter, more leisurely run – something similar to the sort of jog Morris first took back in the 1960s. At the time of writing, more than 3 million runners have now completed these free 5K runs. They've racked up more than 184 million miles between them.

The starting point for all these is the irrefutable evidence that exercise helps us live longer. There's plenty of evidence that exercise makes us happier too. It boosts our mood in the short term. How? For one thing, exercise is good for our general health, and, as the Mappiness team found, people are unhappiest when they're sick in bed. For another, exercise is good for our brains. When you give your body a workout, your brain releases a protein called BDNF, brain-derived neurotrophic factor. This repairs your memory neurons and acts as a reset switch. That's the most likely reason why, after exercising, we often feel so at ease.

But while you have to really rev your heart rate to get the best health and happiness benefits from exercise, you don't have to try too hard, it turns out, to get a simple mood boost. When researchers at the University of Cambridge used smartphones to measure happiness and activity levels in 10,000 people, they found that any sort of physical activity, like getting up every now and then to walk the dog or get a cup of tea, can have a positive effect on how happy people feel.

I don't know about you, but thinking about that makes me smile. Just knowing that all I need to do to lift my mood is to step away from my computer every now and then, to go for a walk or make a coffee – it feels like I've discovered a zero effort, secret shortcut to happiness. And since smiling can trick your mind into feeling happier, that's another shot of free joy right there. How nice is that?

So, we know exercise improves mood in the short term. How about the long run? Oddly, the relationship is a bit murky here.

It's clear that happiness and exercise come as a pair in the long term, but no one knows how the relationship works: whether it's happiness that causes people to exercise more, or exercise that makes people happier. At the end of an eleven-year study at Harvard University, the researchers decided that the two just go hand in hand or, as they wrote in more scientific language, that there is a 'bidirectional feedback loop and upward spiral' between happiness and exercise.

Based on all of this, the conclusion seems clear to me. OK, so we're not exactly sure if exercise causes happiness over the long term. It may just be that happy people exercise more. But I'm not taking any chances. And I don't think you should either.

To paraphrase the conclusion of Jerry Morris's years of work, when it comes to exercise there's a clear message that you might recognise from a company which has done very nicely, thank you very much, from the boom in exercise and our increasingly sedentary, indoor lifestyles: just do it. And now that we have the benefit of the findings from people like Morris and Miyazaki, and the insights from the Mappiness app, we can create our own, updated haiku-style poem from Nike's strapline:

Just do it,

Now and outside,

In a wood, in a park, or near the seaside.

Outside Summary

1. We are happier in nature. Because our species has spent 99 per cent of its existence in nature, we are hardwired to find the sights, sounds and smells of nature relaxing and pleasant. This is called biophilia.

2. We are happier outside because we are more likely to be exercising there.

3. Exercise improves our mood in the short term.

4. No one knows if it's exercise that causes happiness in the long run, or happiness that causes people to exercise more. But it's clear that the two go hand in hand. Why risk it? Exercise more.

5. We really do like to be beside the seaside. Of all places, we are happiest when we are near water, according to the largest in-the-moment study ever conducted.

6. The difference between how happy we are at the sea, compared to the city, is the same as the difference between visiting an exhibition and cleaning the bathroom.

OUTSIDE! How to Make Your Experiences and Your Life Wild, Free and Happy

As before, the questions in *Past Times* are about specific experiences from your past. The questions in *The Way to Happy Days* will help you think about your life in general. Both will help you bring the benefits of the outside into your life.

Past Times: Are You Getting Outside Enough?

Think about how you spend your free time. When you get a chance to choose, what's your automatic habit? Do you tend to stay in, or head outdoors? Try these questions a few ways. Think of your three favourite hobbies. Think of the activities you spend most time on. Then, think about last weekend. If you're really keen, fill out a time form of what you actually do, like you'd do at work. Hey, this may sound geeky, but we are talking about *playtime* management here. It's also fine to skip that part and get a general sense, though the truth may surprise you.

And now answer the questions, giving an answer on a scale of 0 to 5, where:

> 0 = *Not at all*
> 1 = *Very little*
> 2 = *A little*
> 3 = *Some*
> 4 = *A lot*
> 5 = *A great deal*

1. How much were you outside?
2. To what extent were you in nature?
3. Were you in a forest?
4. To what extent was there a chance to spend time in nature?
5. Were you by the sea?

The answers will tend towards the extremes. Hey, you're either outside or you're not. (Except for parties where there's a roof terrace.) If you haven't been down to the sea or the woods, or spent time in some other nature recently, there's a simple question: When can you go next?

The Way to Happy Days: Wood You Take More of Your Experiences OUTSIDE?

Use these questions to think about how you can increase the amount and quality of nature time in your life.

1. When you get the chance to get outside, do you take it?
2. How could you design your life so you spend more time outside?
3. If you have a garden, do you spend much time in it?
4. When did you last consciously spend time outside? By consciously, I mean listening to the wind, the water, the birds, and really looking at the colours, the shapes, the leaves. Watch out for sitting in the park, but spending all the time on your smartphone.

5. What's your favourite tree in your local park? What are your three favourite trees?

   What's the colour and texture of their bark? What colour leaves do they have at this time of year? How does that colour change? What shape are the leaves? How do they sound in the wind? When did you last stop and listen to them?

6. When you're feeling stressed, angry, tired or just a bit down, do you make yourself a G and T, reach for the crisps and the TV remote, or go out for a walk instead?

7. Do you have pictures of nature in your home and at work?

8. How could you design some nature time into your daily activity?

9. How could you change the design of an experience so that it includes more time outside, preferably in a green or forest setting?

   Instead of having your next business meeting in a coffee shop or conference room, for instance, why not meet in a park, or have a walking meeting? This will increase your creativity. If the person you invite to a walking meeting laughs at you, mention the phrase '*solvitur ambulando*', which is the Latin for 'it will be solved by walking', and point out that it's an ancient *and* modern idea. It's been used by philosophers and thinkers from Diogenes to Thoreau. Jeff Bezos recently installed a mini-forest at Amazon's HQ in Seattle. The Spheres contains 40,000 plants, and is, according to Amazon, 'a place where employees can think and work differently surrounded by plants'.

10. Can you move your next experience and increase its 'g' force – as in 'green' force – its 'forest factor' or its sea breeze?

- A city break will bring you plenty of excitement – and you'll achieve many of the key elements of the STORIES checklist – but where you can, take time out in nature instead. Or, while on a city break, include some forest time. Or, choose a city that's by the sea.

Offline: To Tune In, You Need to Turn Off

'We limit how much technology our kids use at home.'

STEVE JOBS

One evening in September 2015, at the back of a stage that's hosted legends like David Bowie, the Beatles, Bruce Springsteen, Public Enemy, Prince and Queen, machines puff dry ice so that anyone who steps through it will emerge to the cheering audience of three and a half thousand people like some kind of god: a comedy god, as it happens, on this particular night.

A vast, red electric billboard, as big as a double-decker bus, slowly descends to earth. Round the curved edges is a join-the-dots line of star-bright, Hollywood mirror lights. In the middle, in huge letters, more showbiz bulbs announce the immortal words: 'LIVE AT THE APOLLO'.

Then, walking through the cloud and on to the stage, wearing grey trainers, grey trousers, a dark sports jacket, black-framed glasses, a bushy beard and a big toothy grin, is the comedian Romesh Ranganathan.

'Good evening, Hammersmith Apollo!' he says, and the volume on the cheering goes even louder. 'How we doing? We good?'

Ranganathan is what you might call one of the Bright Young Things of British comedy. He's in his forties now, so by 'young' I mean he's fairly new to the scene. He was a maths teacher till 2012. He was nominated for the Best Newcomer at the Edinburgh Comedy Awards in 2013. Since then his star has risen fast. He's been on TV a lot. He's a regular on panel shows like *Mock the Week* and *Have I Got News For You*. He's had his own show. And he deserves it all. He's very funny. He takes smart, sideways glances at ordinary life, and serves up politically incorrect jokes with deadpan delivery.

On this night, he's talking about one of the defining features of the modern world: mobile phones.

'The shit battery life on smartphones is the best thing about them,' he says. 'Because when the battery runs out I'll interact with my kids.'

He looks up at the audience, checking we're with him.

'Because I've got no willpower. I'll be down the park ...'

He holds out a hand, looks at the imaginary phone he's holding.

'Oh, that's run out, better find out where they're going with those old men.

'The phone companies,' he continues, 'have got to admit that they've made the phones too good. They're too good for humans. Because I'll be out with my wife, and she'll say to me, "Why are you constantly on the phone?"'

He holds his imaginary phone up again, moves his thumb like he's scrolling down the screen. He turns his head, changes his tone, as if he's replying to her.

'Why not, madam? I've got a little box here that can access any website. I can play games. I can play films. Why the fuck would I want to hear about your rash? There is nothing you can say to me that can compete with this ... I'm watching *Game of Thrones*. Say something better than that.'

And there, with a simple swipe of comedy genius, he's summed up something that's now bothering a lot of people.

The Girl Who Selfie-Harmed

Once upon the Internet, a few years back, there was a girl called Essena. She lived, in real life, on the Sunshine Coast in northern Australia. Sunny more than 260 days of the year, it's a photographer's paradise.

The people are beautiful. Essena was especially beautiful. She was five foot eight inches tall, with big green eyes and beach-blonde hair. She was teenage-girl slim but grown-woman curvy.

'I had the perfect body,' she would say later. 'I had the perfect hair. I did my makeup perfectly well. I was always tanned.'

By nineteen, Essena was famous on the Internet. She would post pictures online every day. Some shots were of the healthy Sunshine Coast food she ate, like a banana, papaya and pomegranate smoothie she'd made; or a breakfast bowl with, as she captioned the picture, 'Pawpaw, lychee, passion-fruit, organic oats and lemon dressing. YUMM.'

Most of the posts, though, were pictures of her. In one, for instance, she's on a veranda, palm trees in the background, wearing a figure-hugging mini-dress and holding a breakfast smoothie. In another, she is on the rocks facing out to sea, wearing a black-and-white bikini top and mint mini-bikini bottoms. Her curly blonde hair is blowin' in the breeze and catchin' the sun.

So many shots, so many friends. Essena built up a huge following. She had 60,000 friends on Snapchat, 250,000 subscribers to her YouTube video channel, and 600,000 followers on Instagram.

But then, suddenly, a glitch appeared in Essena's social matrix.

Her pictures had often been posted with no comments. Sometimes, she'd added simple captions, like, 'Uhhhhh sunshine Happy Sunday loves x,' and, 'Wearing the Strawberry Delight plunge bandeau top by La Biquini!' and, for a shot featuring her in a white cotton bikini top and matching skirt, framed by palms and holding a crate of fruit, 'A box of bananas and pineapple ready for a huge beach day.'

But now, suddenly, someone – a hacker perhaps? – was going through her pictures, deleting thousands, leaving only ninety-one images, and changing the captions on those left behind. It was like the person was trying to let us know how Essena really felt in the photo. It was like someone had pulled the curtain back, and was showing us a whole new side to her, a side that wasn't so postcard perfect.

The new captions claimed that, actually, Essena was unhappy and the images were fake. Now, instead of saying things like 'Bikini: Elle Aqua Ice neoprene bikini. Shot on Bondi Beach' the captions said, 'Anxious,' 'Hungry,' 'Sad,' and, 'Emotionally drained.'

Before, one photo had been captioned, 'Things are getting pretty wild at my house. Maths B and English in the sun.' Now it read, 'See how relatable my captions were – stomach sucked in, strategic pose, pushed-up boobs. I just want younger girls to know this isn't candid life, or cool or inspirational. It's contrived perfection made to get attention.'

Another new caption said, 'Please like this photo, I put on makeup, curled my hair, tight dress, big uncomfortable jewelry ... Took over 50 shots until I got one I thought you might like, then I edited this one selfie for ages on several apps – just so I could feel some social approval from you.'

And it wasn't a hacker. It was Essena.

Next, she made a video in which she appeared with no make-up, and was clearly upset. 'I'm leaving my Instagram up as a symbol, hoping my re-edit captions serve as a wake-up call,' she said. 'People should know my life was edited and contrived.'

Less than twelve hours later, the video had been viewed more than a million times. Essena's follower count had shot up – to more than 800,000 on Instagram alone. But that wasn't the point! Essena created a new website called *Let's Be Game Changers*, calling on her followers to put down their phones and join her. Soon, she deleted it. She deleted all her Instagram pictures. And she disappeared for a few months.

She reappeared briefly, to send a long, personal newsletter to her 'friends' and followers.

'Online it looked like I had the perfect life,' she wrote in the letter, 'yet I was so completely lonely and miserable inside. I hid it from everyone. I smiled and laughed in pictures and vlogs ... I felt exhausted trying to keep up this bubbly, funny, happy façade.'

She talked about the time she 'stopped wearing makeup and using my phone for about 3 days straight' and how that 'changed my life'.

'I realised how I am never present, I don't really talk to people,' she wrote. 'How my days had morphed into constant shoots, constant planning to do things to make my life look good on a screen.'

And then, as if she'd almost never been a part of the social-media whirl, almost as if she'd only ever been a hoax, Essena was gone. She said she was seeing a therapist, and planned to get a job in her local bar, far from the glare of the Internet, back home on the subtropical Sunshine Coast.

Mirror, Mirror, On the Internet ...

Northumberland, in the north-east of England, is about as far away from Australia's Sunshine Coast as you can get. There, a few years back on the edge of a tiny village called Guyzance, an hour north of Newcastle, a fourteen-year-old boy called Danny took one last look in the mirror in his bedroom.

He pushed his blond hair across his forehead, and checked out his reflection: Nike trainers, blue jeans and his black-and-white Newcastle Falcons rugby shirt. And he looked good in it. He was one of the forwards, an open-side flanker, in the rugby team at his new school, Newcastle School for Boys. When brute strength and raw aggression were needed to push or pull the opposition off the ball in the scrums, rucks and mauls, he was always in the thick of things.

'Looking good!' Danny thought to himself. And he was gone – on his way to the Falcons' stadium. Not for a rugby match, though. This was for the birthday party of some girl called Olivia. She was old friends with some of the boys in the rugby team.

And now an invite meant Danny had arrived. Finally! This was the first party he'd been invited to at his new school. That meant he wasn't only a player in the team any more. He was now one of the guys.

At least, that's how Danny felt – right up to the moment he walked into the party. Because, so he found out that night, the best thing to wear to a party at a rugby club isn't necessarily a rugby top. Everyone else was in what Danny calls 'fancy clothes'. The girls were wearing 'frocks'. The boys wore red or blue or yellow chinos, polo shirts with the collars turned up, and cable-knit jumpers.

Danny's family weren't rich, but they weren't poor either. His parents were both managers in the mental-health service. He'd led a simple life till then. His two older sisters had liked going into town, but he'd spent lots of time near home, with his mum and dad, in the outdoors and playing rugby. On Saturdays, his dad would come and cheer him on as he played for the local side, Morpeth Rugby Football Club. On Sundays, the three of them would go mountain biking in the local Cheviot Hills.

A birthday party, to him, had always meant Grandma making a chocolate cake, and a few friends from the village school coming round. They'd drink squash, eat sandwiches and play on his PlayStation.

There was no squash at Olivia's birthday party. It was all fizzy drinks like Coke, and served in cans. And the sandwiches, as Danny says now, 'weren't just sandwiches: all the crusts had been taken off!' And there's no way Olivia's gran had made that cake, unless she was a confectioner. 'It was a great big pink thing,' says Danny, 'with white icing on the top.'

'I looked around, and I just felt really alone, really detached,' Danny says now. How on earth was he going to become part of this crowd? Simple: he went shopping and bought bright-coloured chinos, chunky-knit jumpers and polo shirts. He turned the collars up too. But he still didn't feel like he fitted in.

Then, the iPhone came out, and Danny knew he'd found the answer. It would be his passport to social acceptance. 'Everyone's got one,' he told his parents.

Now that was strange. Danny had never badgered Penny and Robert about anything before, except for that Sony PlayStation, new boots to train in and the new season's rugby top. Still, he'd passed his exams to get into this fancy private school so they should help him fit in. They got him one. As soon as he unboxed it, charged it up, and turned it on, he installed Facebook, took a pic, checked it was OK, posted it.

'I felt a sense of achievement,' Danny says now. 'I'd managed to get to the point where I was able to start acting on what I wanted to do – to take pictures and put them online. And I had this feeling of excitement too. Like I was moving forward. Like I was going to get "liked".'

At first, nothing happened. No likes, no comments. 'But it was the weekend,' says Danny. Perhaps people were out and weren't checking Facebook. The next day, comments started flooding in.

'HAHAHAHAHAHAHAHAHAHA you look rediculous!' wrote one girl called Charlotte. Others kept theirs simpler, with better spelling: 'Spotty Danny needs spot cream,' 'Disgusting,' and, 'Hello fatty.'

What? That wasn't what Danny had expected. Still, he was sure this was the best route to fitting in. So, he started taking more pictures, perfecting them, posting them online, then waiting to see the comments. He'd take ten pictures a day, consider them, post the three or four he thought were the best, and look for the comments. They were overwhelmingly negative, nasty even.

As a rugby player, he knew what it was like to cop a bit of stick. Though he got more than his fair share, at least that was in training or in the changing room or on the coach on the way to a game, when it was just him and the other guys. Online, it was public.

'I felt ripped apart,' says Danny. 'It was very public. Other people could see it. The girls at the school Olivia went to. The people from my old school. It was embarrassing. I felt like a failure.'

At this point, Danny might have thought, 'Hey, this isn't working, maybe I'll try something else.' But he didn't. He just took and uploaded more pictures. Because Danny wasn't a quitter, you see. His life in sport had trained him to think that if you wanted to succeed, you had to give it your all.

That's what his dad said: 'As long as you've given one hundred and ten per cent, you can't give any more.'

That's what his coach at Morpeth RFC, a man named Mike Elliott, had said too. Once, when Morpeth's Sevens team had made it to the semi-finals of a tournament for the first time ever, Elliott had gathered the lads, covered in sweat and mud, in a huddle at half-time. 'You can do this,' he'd barked at them. 'You need to forget the other team. If you play well, you'll win.' He'd been right. They'd won the game, they won the next game, and they won the tournament.

Danny had learned the same lesson from his middle-school running coach Mrs Blizy. 'She used to run us hard, up hills and down hills,' Danny recalls now. 'I really enjoyed pushing myself to the absolute limit. It was fulfilling to know at the end I'd given everything.'

So, you see, though it might seem obvious that Danny should simply have stopped taking those pictures and posting them, he couldn't. It wasn't his way. He just took another picture, and another, and another, and kept posting them to Facebook.

He had a routine. He'd brush his teeth, see how he looked in the mirror. He'd wash his face, check for spots. He got through two tubes of anti-spot cream a week. He'd brush his hair forward and to the side, like Justin Bieber's. He'd put on his red polo shirt, and turn the collar up. He'd put on a chunky-knit jumper.

He worried about his nose. 'I thought it was a bit "hooky",' he says. He worried about his tummy. 'I'd do some exercise, some sit-ups, then check in the mirror. Did it look any better?'

His teachers worried about his grades. They plummeted, from As to Cs and Ds.

He avoided eating. 'I started restricting my food to no more than an apple and maybe a bowl of couscous a day,' he says, 'and went down to about seven stone.'

His parents worried about his weight, and his face was getting dried out and reddened from all that washing. 'What's going on?' Penny asked.

Danny hid behind platitudes. He just said he was feeling stressed, that he felt like he had a lot on his plate.

'Come on, Danny,' Robert asked. 'What is it?'

How could he tell his dad, a typical Northerner and proud Geordie who never complained about anything, what was going on?

'I shut down, I wasn't going to tell them anything,' Danny says now. 'I thought they'd be saboteurs, that they'd stop me from doing what I wanted to do, they'd stop me from achieving my goal. That they'd take my iPhone away. That they'd take my mirror away. That they'd make me delete my Facebook account.'

But Penny and Robert could see the distress he was going through. As well as the weight loss and his flushed face, he'd act like a zombie at mealtimes, uninterested in anything, and then suddenly burst into tears. They took him out of school to take the pressure off, to help him relax. At first it was for a week, then a week became two, then two weeks became a month, then a month became two.

But while they were trying to do their best by their son, they were helping to make it worse.

Because Danny was a boy on a mission. Now he didn't have school and homework and rugby and real life to worry about, he could focus on what really mattered. He couldn't face leaving the house and seeing people. But he wasn't being lazy. And he wasn't giving up.

'I was never going to quit, I was going to keep going even if it hurt my health,' says Danny. 'I knew it would be worth it in the end.'

To fulfil his mission, Danny would be up by 6.30 a.m. and stay up till midnight: brushing his teeth, washing his face, looking in the mirror, taking and checking and posting photos. The longer he stayed off school, the worse it got. Six months after leaving school, he was taking 200 pictures a day – in the hope of getting a better reaction when he posted on Facebook. But all he got were more negative, nasty comments. It was, as you can imagine, an incredibly lonely existence, and exhausting.

'I couldn't take it any more,' says Danny. 'But even though I couldn't quit, I couldn't admit defeat.'

So one day, when everyone was out, Danny thought of a way out. Looking in the bathroom mirror, he remembered there were other things in that room besides spot cream. He took out a pack of aspirin, went to the kitchen, got a can of Diet Coke, and downed as many as he could.

The next thing he remembers, he was throwing it all back up in hospital. His mum was there. She'd found him. He was given some 'horrible black charcoal' stuff to eat. He stayed in hospital a few days, to recover physically. Then he went down to London, to the Maudsley Hospital, for mental-health support. They diagnosed Danny with 'body dysmorphia', and helped him slowly get better.

Danny went back to school, but a different one. He studied hard, got his grades back to where they should have been. He's still on Facebook, but he doesn't post selfies that he's spent all day perfecting any more. He's too busy living his life to do that: completing his degree at the University of York, and being an activist. He's now the mental-health spokesman for a think tank called Parliament Street, and an ambassador for a charity called Men Get Eating Disorders Too.

And that means the stuff he posts on Facebook is, paradoxically, far more impressive. He still posts pictures, and they're often pictures of him. But his face isn't dried out and red any more. His smile looks a lot more genuine. And he's often wearing a smart shirt, or even a suit and tie.

Because that's what he tends to wear when he's making an appearance on Sky News or *Good Morning Britain* or chairing a meeting at parliament about mental health. Because Danny doesn't give up. He isn't a man who admits defeat. He always gives 110 per cent. So now, he isn't posting to show off who he is. Instead, he posts pictures to promote the message that matters so much to him: beware of social media, it's very addictive and can be toxic for your mental health.

Do You Text During Sex?

You might be thinking, 'I can see that Facebook and Snapchat and things like that can be a problem for teenagers. In an age where there's the Internet and mobile phones, that's where their problems play out. But I'm OK. I'm not addicted to my phone. Tech hasn't got a hold on me.'

Or, if you're a teenager reading this, 'I can see that Facebook and Snapchat and things like that can be a problem for *other* teenagers. But I'm OK. I'm not addicted to my phone either.'

But are you sure? Do you reach for your phone first thing in the morning? Do you check your email before talking to your parents, your partner or your children? If you do, you're not the only one. Eight out of ten people check their phones within fifteen minutes of getting up. The average person picks up their phone 150 times a day. Extreme users check their phones 300 times a day. That's about once every three minutes they're awake.

And at work – how often do you check email? How quickly do you respond? Most office emails, so research suggests, are answered within six seconds. Six seconds! What are people doing: sitting at their desks waiting for an email to come in so that they can be first to respond? When did replying to an email become like one of those fast-draw gun fights in a Western movie?

How about when you go to the loo? Do you take your phone with you then? Here's a good reason not to do that: one out of six phones actually have faecal matter on them. Eurgh! OK, so maybe that isn't you. But are you so confident that you'd lick your phone?

How about during sex? And yes, you read that right. I am asking that question – because there really are people who check their phones during sex. One in ten people do it. One in ten! Really, I didn't just make that up. This hair-raising, libido-lowering fact was discovered by social scientists at a respected university, the University of Virginia in the US, and it's been reported by that bastion of journalism the *Economist*.

One in ten ... That's one of those statistics that really sets me thinking – because it raises essential questions about the sort of society we live in today. What, for instance, does it say about modern people that one in ten of us can't leave their phone alone during the most intimate act of all? What's so damn important these people can't wait three and a half minutes to find out? And, perhaps, just as importantly, since so many of us are addicted to our phones, how does it work, and how do you get away with it?

There are three key approaches to figure all this out. First, answer the questions in the *Are You a Mobile Addict?* quiz, all inspired by the official Internet Addiction Questionnaire, to find out if you're hooked or not. Next, discover the damning evidence that makes it clear: too much time online is bad for your health. And then, finally, come with me and we'll boldly go where no one has ever gone before.

ARE YOU A MOBILE ADDICT?

Answer these questions on a scale of 0 to 5, where:

0 = Does not apply

1 = Rarely

2 = Occasionally

3 = Frequently

4 = Often

5 = Always

1. Do you check your phone first thing in the morning?
2. Do the people you live with – your parents, partner, friends, or children – complain about the amount of time you spend online?
3. How often do you stay online longer than you're meant to?
4. Just before you start something, do you check your email, social media, messages or the news?

---

5. Do you find yourself at spare moments, or even when you're in the middle of something, checking your phone 'just in case'?

6. How often do you try to cut down the amount of time you spend online and fail?

7. Do you ever try to hide how much time you've been online?

8. If you find yourself somewhere with no connection, do you feel anxious or worry that you might be missing out on something?

9. Do you ever catch yourself choosing to spend time online instead of spending time with your family, your friends or your partner?

10. Do you check your phone last thing at night?

Now add up your scores.

If your score is 10–24 points, you're in the safe zone. Sure, you like to surf the web a bit too long at times, but you're no addict.

If your score is 25–39 points, you've got mild issues.

If your score is 40–50 points, you seriously need to skip to the end of this chapter and try at least one of the ways to escape the tech trap you've got caught up in.

In case you'd like to know, I got 31 points. I'm getting better at switching off: I often leave my phone at home, or on airplane mode, and we charge ours far from the bedroom, in the kitchen. I've taken the email app off my phone, and Twitter and Facebook. But I still almost always check email before settling down to work, and I often check it when I should be focused.

Now you know how addicted you are, here's the bad news: spending too much time online is bad for your health and your happiness. Scientists in Sweden, the US, Denmark and the UK have studied thousands of people over thousands of hours, and the conclusion is simple. If you spend more time online, you're more likely to feel isolated, stressed and depressed. You won't sleep as well. Even checking in every now and then is bad for your ability to get things done. Clicking on to Facebook may only take a few seconds, but research shows that when interrupted, people take an average of twenty-three minutes to return to their original task.

But there's good news. If you reduce the time you spend online, so a study by the Happiness Research Institute found, you'll feel better quite quickly. Wean yourself off Facebook for a week, and you may miss out on the latest cat video and update from that person you met once, but you'll soon feel much better.

And now I hope you've put your phone down, stopped messaging and Facebooking, and you're ready for the third and, for me at least, the most personally revealing part of this section.

There are some writers who run from the great baffling issues of our age, questions like: how on earth do people text during sex? There are those who, at the mention of questions like this, would cough politely, make their excuses and turn away. My writing heroes are the great gonzo journalists Tom Wolfe and Hunter S. Thompson. So, rather than leave these questions hanging, I decided to bring you the inside scoop, and investigate personally.

A gentleman, of course, doesn't like to talk too much about what happens in the bedroom. But what I can reveal to you, in my experiment intended to contribute to the scientific litera-ture about this delicate, and socially important, issue, are the two things I learned that night: that Donald Trump had just fired someone from his team, and that I wasn't having sex for a month afterwards.

Will that add to future historians' and anthropologists' understanding of life in the early twenty-first century? I like to think I've done my bit. One thing's for sure. As Romesh Ranganathan said, and as I tried to explain to my irate wife that night, and as I suspect you'll agree, phones today are just too good. How do they make them so good? How do they make products and services so good that you, me and millions like us can't help but check them morning, noon, night, in the middle of the night, on the loo, during dinner, and, even, during sex?

The Wizards and the WMDs in Silicon Valley

It's funny to think that, till recently, one of the world's richest, most powerful and profitable companies, a company whose products 2 billion people use each day and which knows intimate details about their lives – like where they went on holiday last year, where they're going this year, and who they fancy at work – had its home in a nondescript, low-rise headquarters that you could almost mistake for any old out-of-town office.

Almost, because although the glass-fronted buildings, connected by roads and bikeways and parking lots, only rise a little higher than the trees, many of them have the company's name written on them, in the brand's signature primary red, blue, yellow and green: Google.

It was here that Tristan Harris worked. Harris looks a bit like a computer geek, the sort you'd meet for a beer. He has short gingery-brown hair and a close-cropped beard. He wears tight-fitting shirts with the top button undone, the sleeves rolled up.

Each day, he used to take the company bus down from his home in San Francisco to Google's headquarters, better known as the Googleplex. Harris was a product manager. It was his job to make sure people spent as much time as possible using the company's web browser, Chrome. He was one of many product managers, but he was no ordinary employee.

Harris was a local. He grew up in the Bay Area, in a single-parent family. Besides raising him, his mother helped people who'd been injured at work fight their cases. Like many children all around the world, Harris studied magic tricks and made his mom proud by performing them at her birthday party. Like not so many kids around the world, but perhaps quite a few in Silicon Valley, he made software for Apple computers in his spare time. He wrote fan mail to Steve Jobs's co-founder, Steve Wozniak. And he hoped that one day, like Jobs, he'd do something that would make a difference to people's lives.

And his dream was well on the way to coming true. At eighteen, he interned at Apple. He got accepted to study computer science at the prestigious Stanford University. There, he learned from the one of the most influential researchers in Silicon Valley, BJ Fogg.

Fogg is a behavioural scientist. He followed in the footsteps of people like Ivan Pavlov and B. F. Skinner. Back in the nineteenth century, Pavlov had figured out something called 'classical conditioning': if you ring a bell every time you bring a dog food, and then just ring a bell, the dogs salivate as if you're bringing food. In the twentieth century, Skinner worked out a similar idea called 'operant conditioning': if you reward a pigeon or a rat when they do something, you make them more likely to do it next time. Also, if you punish them when they do something, you make them less likely to do it next time. Skinner's work focused on animals. He made his discoveries by putting animals into experimental chambers that would become known as 'Skinner boxes'. But he believed his findings weren't limited to animals.

'This is actually something you can apply across species,' Skinner said. 'It applies just as well to the human as to the pigeon.'

This is one of those scientific ideas that sounds remarkably simple when you spell it out like that. After all, it's an idea we all instinctively believe in. It's the 'carrot and stick' idea we all use to manage our pets. If Fido comes when you call, you encourage him with a doggie treat. If Fido eats the birthday cake, you say, 'No, Fido!' and maybe smack his nose.

But, as Skinner suggests, we can also apply this idea to the relationships we have with other humans. If your child tidies up all her Lego toys for a whole week, you might reward her with a trip to the cinema. If she pulls her brother's hair or walks through the house wearing muddy wellies even though you've told her a thousand times not to, she has to say sorry, clear it up, take time out and generally feel bad. And if your partner is late, again, or gets out of line at a party, you call him up on it. But if he arrives with tickets to Paris, you reward him with a big grin and a, 'Mais oui, monsieur!'

If Skinner's idea of operant conditioning helps human-to-human relationships along, it works wonders in the gambling industry. It's the key concept behind the industry's most addictive and lucrative invention: the whirring, beeping, light-flashing machines in the corner of the pub, the bar, the betting shop, and in row upon endless row in places like Las Vegas and the arcade on your local high street.

Those innocent beeping fruit machines, as a researcher then at the Massachusetts Institute of Technology named Natasha Dow Schüll has documented, in her 2012 book *Addiction by Design*, are far from innocent. In fact, they're almost indistinguishable from the experiments Skinner is most famous for, especially in their use of what's known in the business as 'intermittent variable rewards'. It turns out that rewards are a great way to motivate people. But they're even better and even more addictive if people don't know what they're going to get, or when they're going to get it.

Built on complex algorithms that read the person who's playing and by delivering intermittent, variable rewards – the wins the gamblers are playing for – fruit machines are, as Dow Schüll notes, 'the most virulent form of gambling in the history of man' because 'no other form of gambling manipulates the human mind as beautifully as these machines'. They are so addictive, it's not unreasonable to describe them as 'electronic morphine' and the 'crack cocaine of gambling'.

Fogg was one of the first people to not only worry about how machines can be designed to manipulate people, but to do something about it. He set up the Persuasive Technology Lab at Stanford back in 1998, after realising something new and important: that computers were now being used to change people's behaviours and create new habits – and that they'd get even better at it in the future.

Fogg has become famous in technology circles because many of his students have gone on to high powered jobs at firms like LinkedIn, Apple, Uber, Facebook and Google, and because the most successful products and services that come out of Silicon Valley are the habit-forming ones. So what begins as an innocent 'just checking' every now and then – because you are rewarded with something each time, but you never quite know what you are going to get – can end up with you guiltily checking far more often. Thanks to simple operant conditioning that works on pigeons as well as people, the habit becomes stronger and stronger until it's almost instinctive. And then you, like billions of others, are addicted.

Google's search product, for instance, rewards you with results that save you time, and you never quite know what you're going to get. But it's the communication and social tools like email, Facebook, Twitter and Instagram that truly hook people. You never know quite what you'll find when you open the app or the website, because rewards, in the form of messages, photos and 'likes', appear on no set schedule.

Fogg's intention has always been to analyse, and teach the ethics of, computer-led persuasion. He even testified to the US government's consumer protection arm, the Federal Trade Commission, about the problems with habit-forming technologies back in 2006.

But some of his students have clearly taken what they've learned in his class to create exactly the sort of services he worries about. One, a man named Nir Eyal who attended one of Fogg's Boot Camps, wrote a book called *Hooked: How to Build Habit-Forming Products*, and ran an annual conference for firms who want to hook people called the Habit Summit.

Another former student, Mike Krieger, founded Instagram. When Krieger attended Fogg's course, he was Tristan Harris's project buddy.

After graduating, Harris also founded a start-up. His was called Apture. It made it very easy for users to search for information without leaving the website they were reading. This meant, for clients like the *Financial Times* and the *Economist*, Apture stopped the user opening up another browser window to look for more information. It prevented what Harris and his co-founder called 'search leak'.

When a publisher used Apture, their readers would spend two to three times longer on the page they were reading. A product that holds users' attention? In 2011, Google bought the firm for $18 million, along with its all-important technology and staff too. The deal was, as industry news site TechCrunch described it, 'a bit of a talent acquisition as well'.

So now, like so many of his former classmates, Harris was using tools and tricks from the persuasive technology playbook to keep people engaged and clicking. As Harris would later write, 'Once you know how to push people's buttons, you can play them like a piano.'

This reminded Harris of what he'd learned about magic as a boy. 'Magicians do the same thing,' he wrote. 'You make it easier for a spectator to pick the thing you want them to pick, and harder to pick the thing you don't.'

When you put it like that, it sounds so easy, and innocent too. But Harris didn't feel comfortable. Truth be told, he hadn't felt comfortable for a while, even when he'd been running his own firm.

'I would keep telling myself that we're helping people learn about things,' he said later. 'But then to sell the product successfully, I had to just increase time on their website or make them more money. I kept pretending that this was the same thing, and I started basically really questioning my own beliefs.'

Harris kept wondering if all this persuasion was ethical. There'd been lots of discussions about ethics in Fogg's classes, and they shared their concerns in papers and at conferences. But was anybody listening?

'Product design used to be about building a product that functions well, that helps people,' Harris would later say. But now he believes it's changed. 'Design became subsumed into, "How do I get people to use it? How do I get people's attention? How do I hold them here?" Almost all designers are now in this totally different role of just getting people's attention.'

A year or so after he joined Google, Harris was working on the firm's email product.

'I was part of conversations about how do we make it easier or delightful to use your email client, how we build a better email client,' Harris would later say. 'And I felt like we were missing this deeper question, which is: how much time do we all spend on email?'

Frustrated, Harris wrote a 144-page memo, entitled 'A Call to Minimise Distraction & Respect Users' Attention'. It was a pretty antsy memo. It pointed out that:

'Never before in history have the decisions of a handful of designers (mostly men, white, living in SF, aged 25–35) working at three companies' – he means Google, Apple and Facebook – 'had so much impact on how millions of people around the world spend their attention.'

In case you're wondering, it didn't say that was a good thing either. Harris sent the memo to ten close colleagues, and went home for the day.

If this sounds a bit like a McDonald's employee writing a memo with a title like 'A Call to Sell Fewer Burgers & Respect Customers' Health', or a Cadbury's executive writing one called 'How About They Put Fruit Next to the Till Instead?' – that's because it is.

Imagine if the person who'd written that memo was you. How would you have felt, going into work the next day?

Stepping off the Google bus the next morning, going into his office, sitting down at his computer, Harris checked in. On the software he'd made the memo on, Google Slides, there's an indicator in the top right corner that shows you how many people are looking at a document you've made. 'There was,' he recalled later, 'something like 100 people looking at it right then. I looked at it later that day, there was like 300, the next day there was 400.'

Eventually, the memo reached more than 5,000 employees, and management. You'd have thought a memo like that would get Harris fired. But it didn't. Instead, it took him to a meeting with the CEO, who gave him another role. He was named the company's first Design Ethicist. And he spent the next three years asking questions and thinking about 'how to design things in a way that defends a billion people's minds from getting hijacked'.

It sounded like a great role. But it was hard to make real changes. By late 2015, Harris wasn't convinced he was having an impact. 'It was one of those things where there's a lot of head nods,' recalled a designer at Google at the time named Chris Messina. 'And then people go back to work.'

So, in late 2015, Harris left, and really blew the whistle on the tech industry, far more widely and publicly this time. By then he had gathered a number of supporters from the tech community, like a professor at the Massachusetts Institute of Technology called Sherry Turkle; the CEO of real-world social network Meetup, Scott Heiferman; and Justin Rosenstein, who, as one of the inventors of the 'like' button, had helped shape the intermittent variable rewards mechanism on Facebook.

With their support, Harris set up the Center for Humane Technology, a not-for-profit organisation to lobby governments and businesses and people to treat tech using the sort of care with which they'd previously handled hot potatoes like gambling, sugar and tobacco. Harris wants us all to know that the WMDs we should be worrying about aren't the weapons of mass destruction that may or may not exist somewhere far away, but the weapons of mass distraction which we all carry around in our pockets.

Steve Jobs and the Low-Tech Lifestyle

I love Harris's message. I think he's right. Tech firms don't really care too much about their users' well-being. They're just businesses, after all. Their primary interest, like that of most other companies that have come before them, is to maximise profits. And it just so happens that the way they do that, like the gambling companies, is by getting people to spend more time on their devices. But today's tech firms are different from businesses of the past in a couple of crucial ways. First, they have more magicians trained in the art and science of behavioural psychology. And second, since we carry our 'Skinner boxes' everywhere, they have more opportunities to experiment with, refine and deploy their weapons of mass distraction than ever before.

At the time of writing, Harris's work seems to be paying off. There's no legislation yet that curbs the power of the lab technicians and tech magicians, and gives us a fighting chance to pick something other than the thing they want us to pick. But it looks like the tech firms are listening. Apple, Google, Facebook and its subsidiary Instagram, for instance, have introduced tools to help people monitor and limit how much time they're spending on their devices.

This is a big step in the right direction. But, no matter what the tech firms do, until their business models change and they really, really want to release their billions of addicted users, I think the smartest thing every one of us can do is make a few simple but powerful steps of our own.

Perhaps Harris could borrow some of these ideas too. At the end of one evening with a journalist by the name of Bianca Bosker from a magazine called the *Atlantic*, right in the middle of the conversation Harris received a text message. He looked down at his phone screen.

'Oh!' Harris said, and then he mumbled something about what a coincidence it was that the person texting him knew someone else he knew. He looked back up at Bosker sheepishly.

'That's a great example,' he said, waving his phone. 'I had no control over the process.'

But Harris did have some control, didn't he? If he'd had his phone on airplane mode or on silent, he could have avoided this particular distraction.

It makes you wonder, doesn't it: if today's tech is so powerful that it can even catch out a person as aware of the dangers as Harris, what hope do the rest of us have?

Perhaps we can find inspiration in one of the least likely of all places: Steve Jobs.

A tech reporter named Nick Bilton was talking to Jobs in 2010, not long after the iPad first became available.

'So, your kids must love the iPad?' Bilton asked.

'They haven't used it,' Jobs replied. 'We limit how much technology our kids use at home.'

Surprised and intrigued by Jobs's answer, Bilton talked to many other tech insiders – like Chris Anderson, the former editor of *Wired* magazine, and Evan Williams, who founded Twitter. He found that they too, because they'd seen the dangers at first hand, limited how much their children used technology. Now that really makes you think, doesn't it?

How to Steer Clear of Today's Tech Trap

So, for everyone who's worried about the dangers of technology – that is, for you, me, Tristan Harris, Romesh Ranganathan, parents, all those crazies who check their phones during sex, and, actually, just about anyone who uses modern technology – here's a starter list of seven things you can do to avoid getting caught in the tech trap.

1. Go Cold Turkey
   If you've recognised real signs of addiction, maybe it's best to go cold turkey and see how you get on. You'll most likely feel weird at first. You'll find yourself phantom-checking email. But you'll actually sleep better.

2. Let it Sleep
   Go cold turkey every night and let your phone sleep so that you can sleep too. Make your bedroom a no-phone zone. At least, move your charger to another room. If your excuse is that your alarm is on your phone, get a new alarm.

3. Fly More

   Remember the feeling of bliss, when you'd sit down in your seat, the seat-belt sign would go on, you'd hear the engines roar, and you switched your devices on to airplane mode? No interruptions for the rest of your flight. Of course, the silly idea of inflight Wi-Fi is threatening this in-the-air nirvana. But you can get this sense of you-can't-reach-me freedom by turning your phone on to airplane mode. My suggestion is that you follow the French and switch your phone off at a designated time after work.

4. Just Say No ... to Notifications!

   Turn all your notifications off. Avoid the distraction trap, and free yourself from the intermittent variable rewards by creating designated device-checking periods. During those times, go mad. Check the football, the news, email, Facebook, WhatsApp. Enjoy it. These devices are magical. And then turn it off.

5. Try the 5/2 Detox Diet

   Why not try a 'five days on, two days off' diet? Yes, that can be annoying when you're trying to meet friends. But remember how people used to do it: they'd agree where they were going to meet and meet there, about that time. Instead of phoning your friend as you arrive and saying, 'I'm here, where are you sitting?' be an adventurer and look for them instead.

6. Leave it Out!

   Sometimes, when you go out, do so without your phone at all. Yes, your partner might remember something they wanted you to get from the shops. Yes, your kids might do something so wonderfully hilarious or amazing that you feel like you're letting them down by not recording it for posterity on your phone. But the shopping can wait, and they probably won't. And even if they do, you'll enjoy it more if you're in the moment and really present to see it happen live.

7. **Lock it In!**

   If you have a place for your phone you won't lose it, for one thing. More importantly, you'll be able to leave it somewhere not near you, so that instead of texting, tweeting, checking social media, you can be truly present with the people in your home. If possible, have a cupboard to lock it into.

Offline Summary

1. Millions of us have become addicted to our devices because they've made them too good.

2. The reason they're too good is because of the wizards trained in behavioural psychology who use 'operant conditioning' to hook and hold us.

3. Operant conditioning works through a process called 'intermittent variable rewards'. When we check our phones, we don't know what sort of reward we're going to get or if there'll be one there. This is the same trick used on rats and pigeons in laboratories. It's incredibly addictive.

4. If you switch off, as with any addiction it can be hard to adjust at first, but there is plenty of evidence to suggest you will become happier.

5. We should find our inspiration in the leader of the low-tech lifestyle, Steve Jobs. When asked what his children thought of the iPad, Jobs replied, 'They haven't used it. We limit how much technology our kids use at home.'

How to TURN OFF and TUNE IN to
What Really Matters

As before, the questions in *Past Times* are about specific experiences from your past. The questions in *The Way to Happy Days* will help you think about experiences in the future, and your life in general. Both will help you bring the benefits of the 'more often offline life'.

To be clear, I'm not anti-phone or anti-pictures. Phones are great for all sorts of reasons. Pictures are great for remembering. Think of them both like alcohol: a little versus a lot, use versus abuse. *Use responsibly.*

Past Times: Did That Experience Take
You OFFLINE?

Think about an experience you've had in the past, like what you did last night or last weekend. Try this using experiences that were really good – like the best night out you've had in the past month – ones that were just average, and ones that were downright awful. Then, ask yourself these questions, giving an answer on a scale of 0 to 5, where:

0 = *Not at all*
1 = *Very little*
2 = *A little*
3 = *Some*
4 = *A lot*
5 = *A great deal*

1. While you were [insert experience here], how often did you check your phone?

2. How often did you take pics or selfies with your phone?

3. Did you post those pics on social-media sites?

4. How much did you edit those pics to make them, and you, look better?

5. To what extent were you thinking about the audience 'out there', rather than focusing on the time and the place and the people you were with?

6. To what extent were you more focused on taking pics so you could show people what you were doing, on Facebook or some other social media?

    Once at the Science Museum with my kids, we went to see the bubble show. My kids, then two and four, got a chance to be inside a huge bubble. I was so focused on trying to take pics to show my wife later, I completely missed it.

7. While you were [insert experience here], how often were you checking emails, messages, news, the football score?

8. How much, if you're honest, would you say you were physically there, but mentally somewhere else?

9. To what extent did you, truth be told, do [insert experience here], only to post a picture or an update, or, at least, think about the picture you're going to post?

If your answers are mostly 2 or below, this suggests you're in the experience and giving yourself the best chance to enjoy it. If mostly 3s or above, consider the following questions, and see if you can reduce your constant connection, and enjoy where you are and what you're doing in the future.

The Way to Happy Days: How to Disconnect from the Matrix, and Connect to the Present Instead

Use these questions to think about how you can spend more time outside, offline and in the moment.

1. How would your experience of [insert experience here] be different if you weren't taking pictures to share and post on social media?

   If you're not sure how that would feel, try an experiment. Do the same activity – like a day out with your kids, or a night out with friends – twice. Once with your phone. The next time, leave your phone at home. Each time, make a note of how you feel. Sure, it'll be harder to find your friend when you meet. But you'll really be present.

2. How often do you turn your phone off, or on to airplane mode? Do you exercise your right to disconnect from emails, news and other messages, and connect to where you are and what you're doing instead?

3. Before posting pictures, do you edit them so you'll look better and people will think more of you?

4. Do you present a more 'perfect life' on social media?

5. Do you find yourself checking your phone 'just in case'?

6. What steps will you take to manage your tech addiction?

7. How do you show respect to the most valuable resources you have: your time and attention?

SOMETHING FOR THE WEEKEND

Here's a handful of ideas to help you get outside and offline this weekend. On the following pages, write down three ideas of your own.

1. Turn off, tune in, drop out

Turn your phone, Facebook, Wi-Fi and everything off for forty-eight hours, from Friday at 7 p.m. till Sunday at 7 p.m. Try it this weekend, and see how you feel. Like giving up any addiction, such as coffee or alcohol, it may feel strange at first: liberating but also weird and even painful, like you're missing something. The key is to get organised before 7 p.m. on Friday, and then treat your weekend as special. Then do the same thing again the following weekend. Once you're in the hang of it, see if you can make every weekend a weekend off. Or at least one a month.

2. Be a wild woman

Or a wild man. Go wild swimming, or wild camping, or do some sort of outdoor adventure activity: jogging in the woods, punting, stand-up paddle-boarding, cycling, canoeing. If you're feeling brave and really want to make the most of your time, have the sort of overnight escape that Alastair Humphreys recommends in his brilliant book *Microadventures*.

3. Have a perfect picnic

Get up early, pack a picnic, and take whatever transport you need to get to a hill, river or park that at least feels miles from home by lunchtime. For me, that's most likely Richmond Park or Kew Gardens. For you it could be a glade in a forest, a beach no one goes to, a rooftop terrace but actually I'll leave that to you.

4. Get thee to the sea!

No doubt you have your own, but some of my favourites for a weekend getaway, whatever the weather, are: West Wittering, the Gower Peninsula, Skegness.

5. Book a walking date

With friends or an actual date. Instead of meeting somewhere and staying there, meet and then go for a walk, or some other sort of outside activity. If you haven't done this recently, you'll notice how nice it is not to have to look directly at the person. Plus, it's good for the brain. As they used to say, in Latin, *Solvitur ambulando*: 'It'll be solved by walking.'

_____

_____

_____

_____

OO! INTRODUCING YOUR NEW OUTSIDE AND OFFLINE JOURNAL

Use the 'OO! Outside & Offline Journal' to record how you spend your free time. 'Morning', on weekdays, refers to anytime between getting up and starting work. 'Evening' is everything after you leave the office and before bed. If, between those markers, you spend time outside, perhaps walking through a park, or playing sport, put a smiley face in the first 'O'. If you don't, put a sad face. Similarly, if you spend most of that time offline, put a smiley face. But if you act like an addict, checking your messages first thing, glued to social media, put a sad face. At the end of the week, you'll have a sense of whether you're getting outside and offline enough, and giving yourself a better shot at happiness. If you decide to compare weeks, add up the smiley and sad faces. Then, think of ways to make it easy for you to increase how many of those sections of the day – before work, lunchtime and after work – you can spend *Outside & Offline*.

OO! Your Outside and Offline Journal

	MORNING		LUNCH		EVENING	
MON	🙂	☹️			🙂	☹️
TUES			🙂	🙂		
WED			🙂	☹️		
THURS			☹️	🙂		
FRI						🙂
SAT					🙂	🙂
SUN					🙂	☹️
THIS WEEK						

4

RELATIONSHIPS

The Girl with the Opposite of Loneliness

*'It is only a slight exaggeration to say that happiness is
the experience of spending time with people you
love and who love you.'*

DANIEL KAHNEMAN

I t was spring, a few years back, when Yale University's
student paper, the *Yale Daily News*, published a farewell
essay that, within a few weeks, would be viewed more than
a million times. The essay, by one of the hundreds of students
about to graduate, captured the feeling many of us have at
pivotal moments in our lives: butterflies-in-the-stomach excitement about what's to come, coupled with a bittersweet sense
of what might have been and what we are about to lose. Here's
how the essay begins:

'We don't have a word for the opposite of loneliness, but if
we did, I could say that's what I want in life. What I'm grate-
ful and thankful to have found at Yale, and what I'm scared
of losing when we wake up tomorrow and leave this place.

'It's not quite love and it's not quite community; it's just
this feeling that there are people, an abundance of people,
who are in this together. Who are on your team. When the
check is paid and you stay at the table. When it's 4 a.m. and

no one goes to bed. That night with the guitar. That night we can't remember. That time we did, we went, we saw, we laughed, we felt. The hats.'

The writer was a young woman with a fierce talent. She was thin and beautiful. She had long, straight, reddish-brown hair. She had long legs which she barely covered with what her tutor, Anne Fadiman, would call 'flagrantly short' skirts. Sometimes, she wore a feather in her hair.

She was scatty. She often lost her keys and her phone. Usually she'd find them in her big, ink-stained tote bag. She was loud. She would talk loudly with people she knew and people she didn't. But even if she tried to keep quiet and tiptoed into a room, you'd still hear her coming. Her clanking, jangling bracelets would announce her.

She was a dreamer and a poet. She was idealistic and full of hope.

'We're so young,' she wrote in that essay. 'We're so young. We're twenty-two years old. We have so much time. There's this sentiment I sometimes sense, creeping in our collective conscious as we lay alone after a party, or pack up our books when we give in and go out – that it is somehow too late … What we have to remember is that we can still do anything. We can change our minds. We can start over. Get a post-bac or try writing for the first time. The notion that it's too late to do anything is comical. It's hilarious. We're graduating college. We're so young. We can't, we MUST not lose this sense of possibility because in the end, it's all we have.'

She interned at the *Paris Review*. She wrote for the *New York Times*. She co-wrote a play that was performed at the New York Fringe Festival. She interned at the *New Yorker* magazine. She lined up a job there.

Caught up in the whirlwind of her young life, she didn't call her mother often enough. In a poem she wrote called 'Rolling Stones', she lets us listen in on a phone call home:

Hello, Mom,
I say, hello Mom,
I'm walking to class.
I'm walking to class.
I won this prize.
I got this job.
I've gotta go.
I forget to ask about her ...

At the end of the poem, she tells us:

I need to call my mother more.
I'll call her tomorrow.
I'll make time tomorrow.

She was fascinated with life, and how short it was. She was fascinated with death, and how it was coming to all of us sooner than we'd like. She wondered what sort of legacy she'd leave behind.

The girl's name, by the way, was Marina Keegan. Marina's parents, Tracy Shoolman and Kevin Keegan, came to her graduation weekend. They clapped and cheered and took photos. Tracy stayed a bit longer to help her daughter pack her belongings up, so Kevin said goodbye to Marina on a street corner.

'I told her I was so proud of her and loved her and I had a tear in my eye,' he would remember later. 'I told her how much it all meant to me and got in the car, like I always do, and started beeping the horn and yelling. She was smiling.'

Five days later, Marina was on her way to Cape Cod to celebrate her father's fifty-fifth birthday party. Her parents were waiting with a cake her mother had made, a gluten-free strawberry shortcake. Her boyfriend, Michael, was driving. He hadn't been drinking, but he fell asleep at the wheel. The car clipped the crash barrier and rolled over twice. Both were wearing seat belts, but Marina had reclined her seat all the way back to take a nap. He survived, she died.

Marina's mother, Tracy, went through the wreckage of the car, looking for shards of her daughter's life she could hold on to. Her laptop was smashed, but the hard drive was saved. Tracy took the words and the essays and the poems, to bring a little of her daughter back to life. With help from Marina's tutor at Yale, Anne Fadiman, she would later publish a collection of her works in a book titled *The Opposite of Loneliness*.

As news of Marina's death spread, through phone calls, text messages and the news, something happened. There was an outpouring of collective grief, and her essay on the *Yale Daily News* was viewed 1.4 million times by people in ninety-eight countries.

People die every day. What was it about Marina's passing that touched so many, so deeply? Perhaps the reason is simple. A young girl, her life full of promise, had died. Perhaps it was also her enthusiasm for life, the firecracker talent in the writing, and the irony of what she'd written. Or, maybe, it was the way she captured something that philosophers and poets and psychologists have been trying to say for many, many years.

Only Marina found a way to say it better. She's right, you see. We don't have a word for the opposite of loneliness, but if we did, it's what we all want in life.

And it may be more critical than that. According to the latest research, the opposite of lonelines is not only what we all want, it's what we all need.

Help! We All Need Somebody

How many phone numbers do you know? Probably your own, the landline of the house you grew up in, the main number for your office, and that's about it. You probably don't know your partner's or your friends' numbers. Your mobile keeps track of those nowadays. But there's one number everyone knows. It's a number that says the same as the Beatles song 'Help!' – because you only use it when you really need somebody. It's the emergency number, 999.

If you work in the emergency services and you answer one of those calls, you don't know what's up, but you know someone's in trouble. On 10 November 2015, a woman in Middleton, near Manchester, called that number.

'We got a call, it was a 999 call,' Stuart Ockwell, a police constable at Greater Manchester Police, would recall later. 'The lady of this house, she was having difficulty with her husband.'

As Ockwell begins to tell the story, you can hear the years of experience in his voice, a reassuring mix of Mancunian accent and police manner. You can imagine him receiving the call that day, his brain firing into gear, listening for signs of trouble and clues as to what's going on.

'We knew from the history at the address,' he continued, 'that they were an elderly couple. My thoughts were originally that the husband's probably had a fall, the ambulance would be coming, we'd go and help them gain entry. The ambulance would deal with whatever they saw fit.'

But they arrived to find something completely different.

'There was no need for medical attention,' said Ockwell. 'There was no need for police. What we found was a lovely elderly couple who were caring for each other, probably finding it a bit difficult to care for each other with their ailments and their age. And that were in need of a bit of company, if anything.'

Fred Thomson was ninety-five years old, and the years were beginning to tell. He had a full head of hair still, though it had all turned silver. He used a walking stick, a white one with a crook in it like a shepherd's stick, to get about. And he was going blind. His wife, who, in the old-fashioned way, preferred to be referred to as Mrs Thomson, was also ninety-five.

If you were a policeman that day what would you have done? Report back to base that all was OK, fill out a form, be relieved that nothing serious had happened, and be on your way? Ockwell did something like that.

'Meself and me colleague, we spent half-hour with them,' he'll tell you now. 'Put on the kettle, while Fred told us stories of when he was in the war. He's an amazing character. He had us in fits of laughter. And to me, it made my day, that.'

It probably made Fred's day too.

'Made a nice change – to have somebody to talk to – to have somebody different to talk to,' Fred Thomson would say, haltingly, later. He talks very slowly, deliberately, as if his jaw's a bit stuck. 'The police are very civil sort of people – as you would expect. I was very pleased to know there was help about. Pleased to talk to them. Sometimes – you can be a bit isolated as you get older. But they made me feel at home.'

What Ockwell doesn't realise, as he nonchalantly tells the tale of how he spent some time with Fred and Mrs Thomson, is that, actually, he might just have saved their lives that day. Because, as scientists have now proved, loneliness is a killer.

Loneliness strangles you slowly, by putting your system into a permanent state of fight or flight. That puts more of the stress hormone cortisol into your system. It raises the amount of something called protein fibrinogens too, increasing your blood pressure, building up fatty deposits, furring up your arteries, so you're more likely to have a heart attack and develop diabetes.

Loneliness leaves you stressed, depressed, more prone to having a stroke, dementia or depression, and more likely to be suicidal. It disrupts your sleep. It weakens your immune system. The one thing loneliness does support is cancer: tumours spread faster in lonelier people.

Loneliness makes healthy people ill. It makes ill people worse. And it kills, not suddenly, of course, like a whack with a blunt instrument or a knife in your heart. Along with its close cousins – social isolation and living on your own – it kills the same way cigarettes kill you. It creeps up on you, like a shadow from storm clouds as they cross the countryside, putting villages and valleys and hillsides in the shade.

The most comprehensive investigation into this area was a meta-analysis conducted by a researcher named Julianne Holt-Lunstad. When Holt-Lunstad gathered the work of seventy studies that, together, had followed 3,407,134 people around the world for an average of seven years, she found conclusive evidence that what you might call the three amigos of isolation – social isolation, loneliness and living alone – increase your chance of death, respectively, by 26 per cent, 29 per cent and 32 per cent.

Another report, covering 300,000 people, looked at this the other way round. How, the researchers wanted to know, would better social connections make it more likely that you'd be alive when the researchers next came knocking? They found that having better social connections, that is, relationships with people who you feel are in this together with you and on your team, makes you 50 per cent more likely to be alive.

That makes loneliness worse than smoking fifteen cigarettes a day, worse than obesity, worse than type 2 diabetes. And it's getting worse. Three out of four doctors in the UK say they see at least one, and as many as five, lonely people each day. That's why health officials talk not only about obesity, but also about the loneliness epidemic.

Governments banned smoking in public places. They've put taxes on sugary drinks. They're encouraging us to get more exercise. How about loneliness and social isolation?

We've seen the first attempts to address this new problem. In the UK, there's now a 'minister for loneliness' and a 'loneliness strategy'. It encourages doctors to send lonely people to cooking classes and walking groups.

It's only a start, but at least it's something. Because we had to do something. We can't cope on our own, you see. We just weren't designed that way. What we want, and what we need, are the exact opposite of loneliness. Because, as the science has shown, we all need somebody.

There's No Shame Being Hungry

You probably think the three diseases of loneliness – loneliness plus living alone and social isolation – are an old person's problem. And you'd be right. But they're a young person's problem too. Actually, they can affect anybody. One in five adults in Britain say they're always or often lonely today. One in four Australians admits to being lonely. And a third of Americans over forty-five say they are 'chronically lonely', meaning they've been lonely for a long time. Maybe, it's even your problem. 'Ha!' you're probably thinking. 'Not me! I know people who have issues like this, but not me.'

Because you probably think loneliness is for losers, that admitting you're lonely is shameful. But a man named John Cacioppo, who was one of the world's leading experts in the field before he died in March 2018, saw loneliness in another, much healthier way. Loneliness, he said, is just like hunger and thirst and pain. It's a signal, from ourselves to ourselves, that we're missing something. But where thirst says have a drink, hunger says eat some food, and pain says get away from that thing, loneliness means go find company and connection with others.

So, a question for you: ever been hungry or thirsty? Ever felt lonely? Do you live alone? And if so, do you live the 'always on' social version, or a sometimes isolated one? Take the *Are You Lonesome Today?* questionnaire to find out how lonely you really are.

ARE YOU LONESOME TODAY?

Answer the questions in this test to get a sense of how lonely you feel.

Give each a score, where:

1 = Never

2 = Rarely

3 = Sometimes

4 = Often

1. I feel in tune with the people around me.
2. I lack companionship.
3. There is no one I can turn to.
4. My social relationships are superficial.
5. I feel part of a group of friends.
6. I have a lot in common with the people around me.
7. I am no longer close to anyone.
8. My interests and ideas are not shared by those around me.
9. I am an outgoing person.
10. There are people I feel close to.

Add up your scores, but note that 1, 5, 6, 9 and 10 are 'reverse scored', so you get 4 points for 1, 3 points for 2 and so on.

QUESTION	SCORE	POINTS
1		
2		
3		
4		
5		
6		
7		
8		
9		
10		
	Loneliness score:	

If you score around 20, you're average. If you score 25 or higher you have a recognisably high level of loneliness. If you score 30 or more, you have a very high level of loneliness.

In case you're wondering, when I took this test in summer 2018, I scored 29. I think this may be because of my life stage. I used to be quite social, but I've got young kids and don't get much time to see friends. But now that I realise this, I'm going to make an extra effort to get back in touch with some people.

This is adapted from the standard test for loneliness, the 20-question UCLA Loneliness Scale.

If we're going to fix the loneliness epidemic, and develop tools to use when every one of us feels alone, it's important to distinguish between loneliness, living alone, and social isolation.

Loneliness is trickiest to see and fix, because it's subjective. It's a feeling that exists in a person's mind. It isn't about quantity, it's about quality. You can be lonely in a city, a crowd, at a party, in a marriage. Oddly, one study found that most people who say they're lonely are married or live with others.

Social isolation is fairly simple to measure. You can ask and describe objective measures like how many friends a person has. This is a useful starting point, because, as researchers at Harvard University have found, people who have five friends have 20 per cent higher fibrinogen compared to people with twenty-five friends. Having around ten fewer friends, according to one study, can have the same impact as taking up smoking.

Living alone is, of course, easiest to observe. But even this isn't that simple. Living alone doesn't necessarily lead to social isolation, as a sociologist in New York called Eric Klinenberg has argued. 'People who live alone tend to spend more time socializing with friends and neighbours than people who are married,' Klinenberg once said. 'Living alone is not an entirely solitary experience. It's generally a quite social one.'

I think this may be a generational issue. Older people living alone don't tend to have the same busy social circle as young people living alone.

The simplest way to approach this issue, as a whole, is this: if social isolation is about the quantity of people you have in your life, loneliness is about the quality of the connection you make with those people. Ideally, you'll have a bit of both: quite a few people, and real, meaningful connections with some of them. How to make those happen? How to bring the opposite of loneliness into your life?

How to Achieve the Opposite of Loneliness – According to Science

In case you're worrying that we're about to head into some sort of la-la land, where you're supposed to spend every waking moment in the presence of people and become the life and soul of any occasion, worry no more. You don't have to adopt an extrovert's smile so wide it puts the Joker's to shame. You don't have to surround yourself with people at all times, even if they're people you love and people who love you.

Though it'll do you good if you spend at least *some* time with people like that. The longest study on happiness ever conducted, the Harvard Study of Adult Development, which began in 1939 and continues to this day, could not be more clear about this.

'Good relationships keep us happier and healthier. Period,' the Harvard Medical School's Robert Waldinger once said in a TED talk based on the study. 'People who are more socially connected to family, to friends, to community, are happier. They're physically healthier, and they live longer than people who are less well connected.'

So, the starting point to living this way and achieving the opposite of loneliness is the simplest advice in this book.

It's this: do something, anything. Do things you like a lot and things you like a little. Just engage, in some way, like you mean it, with life. Take an interest. Get out there. Even if your *doing* involves a lot of *not-doing*. While you should be active – as we'll see in the *Intensity* chapter – that doesn't mean you have to be busy. There's a place for reading and silence, for instance, and activities like yoga nidra, the yogic practice that's in between sleeping and being awake.

If this advice sounds too simplistic to be useful, it's important to highlight the science behind it. One of the key reasons why experiences are good for our happiness is because, as we saw in the *Story* chapter, they set off a domino line that almost inevitably takes us away from social isolation and feelings of loneliness, and towards the opposite: to meaningful connections and relationships that will help us live longer and happier.

How?

Three ways. First, when you do something, you often do it with someone else. Think of netball, board games and climbing – where someone has to hold the rope that stops you falling.

Second, doing something gives you an identity and a sense of belonging. People who go camping have a connection with other people who go camping.

This doesn't mean every experience has to involve other people. There's still a lot to be said for spending time on your own. Solitude is quite distinct from loneliness. Marina Keegan, for instance, would have spent a lot of time on her own, writing. And, like you and me, she would have spent a fair bit of time reading on her own too.

Even if you do something alone, like paint, or read, or go running, you'll still feel more connected to others – because you'll get a sense of what psychologists call 'belonging', which sounds almost exactly like the opposite of loneliness to me.

The third reason why experiences are so good for happiness is that if you do something, you'll have something interesting to talk about. And stories, as psychologists have shown, make us happy when we tell them, and they make people want to talk with us. And, as we saw earlier in the *Story* chapter, they set off mirror neurons, which create stronger empathy and connections between us.

So, just like the domino line we saw in the *Story* chapter, here's yet another, similar line of positivity that begins with experiences, and leads directly to another of the key ingredients for happiness.

However, since we know that one way that experiences bring us happiness is by creating and supporting relationships, there's no harm trying to support that process. If you run, join a running club, or do a park run this weekend. If you practise yoga, join a class. If you read, join a book club or start your own. Or, if you're faced with two similar choices for this evening or this weekend, choose the one that's more likely to increase or enhance your relationships. And if someone you like wants to do something you don't particularly like, maybe, this time, just go along with it.

The domino line to happiness

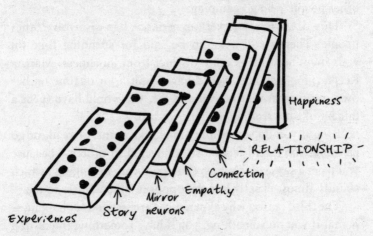

Happiness

- RELATIONSHIP -

Connection

Empathy

Mirror neurons

Story

Experiences

Once you've started bringing more of the opposite of loneliness into your own life, perhaps you'll think about how you can do your bit to alleviate the loneliness epidemic, and bring it into the lives of strangers too?

Hello, Stranger! The Surprising Joy of Talking to People You Don't Know

What would you do if, one morning, as you were about to board the 7.32 train to work, someone with a clipboard came over and asked you to take part in an experiment: would you talk to a stranger on the way to work, and then report back?

Me too. Not that early in the morning, thanks very much.

But, when a couple of psychologists at the University of Chicago named Nicholas Epley and Juliana Schroeder had research assistants ask that very question of commuters at Homewood in Illinois, an hour's train ride from central Chicago, they managed to recruit more than a hundred people to play their game. To make the experiment valid, they asked a third of the people to talk to a stranger, a third to not talk to anyone, and a third to just do what they usually did.

Then, once the people had got to the other end, they had to fill out a form, and send it in the post to them. Next, Epley and Schroeder conducted similar experiments on buses and in taxis.

The results were jaw-dropping and, in their counterintuitive way, wonderful. When Epley and Schroeder asked people if they thought they'd be happier if they talked to someone or not, they mostly said no. And when they asked if people thought the other person would want to talk with them, they mostly said no too.

What would you have said? The same, I'm guessing. That's what I thought. But you and I would both be flat wrong each time. Because while people think a bit of time to themselves is the best way to handle the daily commute, it turns out you'll enjoy the journey more if you connect with someone, even a stranger. And the reason for the mistake is that people tend to underestimate how much other people want to connect. The man staring at his iPhone? The woman flicking through emails? Those people reading the latest celebrity gossip in the free newspaper? Research clearly indicates that they're far more willing to talk than you'd have thought. And, according to Epley and Schroeder's research, the pleasure of connection is contagious: because we're social animals, people who are talked to enjoy the experience just as much as the person who opens up the conversation in the first place.

So, don't make the age-old mistake of sitting in silence and solitude. Next time you're on a train or a bus or in a cab, go ahead, passenger. Make your own, and someone else's, day by seeking connection instead of solitude.

If you're not sure what to say, consider the advice of Malavika Varadan, a radio presenter in Dubai whose TEDx talk, 'Seven Ways to Make a Conversation with Anyone', has been viewed more than 11 million times.

'Every stranger,' she says with a contagious smile, in an elegant, Bollywood accent, 'comes with an opportunity, an opportunity to learn something new, an opportunity to have an experience you've never had, an opportunity to hear a story you've never heard before.'

Her first tip?

'The first word acts as a floodgate,' she says. 'Once you've said the first word, everything else just flows. Keep it simple. A hi, a hey, a hello.'

Her best suggestion, in my view, as it's a tip gleaned from spending more than a decade talking with strangers, is:

'We have ninety seconds every day on radio and we have to make that conversation memorable,' she says. 'Here's my advice – skip the small talk and ask a really personal question.'

How personal? Ask about their name, how their parents chose it, how long they've lived in this city, if they remember the first day they landed here.

Personally, I find that small talk can be a great opener. I'm that guy who talks to people on the Tube, at the bus stop, in the sauna – really. Maybe because I'm British, and we have bad weather and bad sports teams and ridiculous celebrities and comedy politicians, one of those is usually a great way in. Because I live in London, there's always something funny going on – someone asleep and snoring on the Tube, a driver singing to the passengers – and saying something about that is an easy starting point too. If all those fail, you can always try politics or religion.

So now, you have every reason to share your experiences and achieve the opposite of loneliness – and no excuse for mistakenly seeking solitude.

Relationships Summary

1. Humans are social animals.

2. We all not only want but also *need* the opposite of loneliness.

3. Loneliness is fatal. The three amigos of isolation – social isolation, loneliness and living alone – increase your chances of dying by 26 per cent, 29 per cent and 32 per cent respectively.

4. All experiences help with this. They bring us closer to others because we tend to have experiences with others, because they give us a sense of belonging, and because they give us stories.

5. We should choose and design experiences that are more likely to bring us closer to others, even if that does sometimes mean compromising on other aspects.

PEOPLE! How to Have Better Relationships and Achieve the Opposite of Loneliness

As before, the questions in *Past Times* are about specific experiences from your past. The questions in *The Way to Happy*

Days will help you think about your life in general. Both will help you bring the opposite of loneliness into your life.

Past Times: How Important Were People in That Experience?

Think about an experience you had in the past, something you did last weekend, say, or last week. Take the quiz a few times, using experiences that were really good, ones that were just average, and ones that were downright awful. Once you have an experience in mind, ask yourself these questions, giving an answer on a scale of 0 to 5, where:

> 0 = *Not at all*
> 1 = *Very little*
> 2 = *A little*
> 3 = *Some*
> 4 = *A lot*
> 5 = *A great deal*

1. To what extent did you do [insert experience here] with other people?

2. How much would you say it brought you closer to other people?

3. During the experience, to what extent did you feel like you were in a team with others? Or, to what extent did it make you feel like there were people 'on your team'?

4. How much did the experience enhance or deepen your existing relationships? Or, did it create new ones?

5. During or through this experience, to what extent were you doing something *for* other people?

6. How much did it make you feel connected to others?

7. Through this experience, to what extent did you create or strengthen a feeling of community?

If your answers are mostly 5s, this was a good experience. If mostly 3s or less, see if you can adapt your experiences in the future so that they include people and create and support positive relationships.

———

The Way to Happy Days: How to Achieve the Opposite of Loneliness

Use these questions to think about how you can increase the amount and quality of relationships in your experiences and your life.

1. How much of your happiness is shared? Do you keep happiness close to your chest, or do you share it with others?

2. Do you tend towards team or individual sports/activities?

3. Do most of your passions involve others?

4. How can you build community and connection around your interests and passions?
   Perhaps there are local clubs or associations or groups or classes. If not, there may well be groups online.

5. How can you change your experiences so that they bring you closer to others?

SOMETHING FOR THE WEEKEND

Here's a handful of ideas you can use to improve your relationships at the weekend. On the following page, write down three ideas of your own.

1. Have lunch with an old friend.

2. Have dinner with new friends.

3. Go say a hi, a hey, or hello to a neighbour who lives on their own.
   Take a cake, invite yourself in for tea, and be honest: set a time limit for twenty minutes. That's not perfect, but that way you both know you'll be leaving soon. And you'll both be a little warmer inside.

4. Go to a festival
   Or, at least book one in. It doesn't matter whether the festival is near or far, whether it's about bands, beer, cheese or classic cars – as long as you're going.

5. Play a game with someone
   Cards? Board game? Tennis?

5

INTENSITY

Mr Mouse, the Scaredy Cat, and the Rise of the Sufferfests

'Veni, vidi, vici.' ('I came, I saw, I conquered.')

JULIUS CAESAR, 47 BCE

'Veni, vidi, vixi.' ('I came, I saw, I lived.')

MY UPDATE ON CAESAR, 2019 CE

In January 2015, I received an email out of the blue asking if I'd like to be in a documentary film. It was going to be about those muddy obstacle-course races, like Tough Mudder and Tough Guy. The email was from some American guy named Scott Keneally. When we talked on the phone, he said he wanted to shoot me in a place that would reflect the movie's theme.

'Can you come to Tough Guy?' he asked. 'It's in Wolverhampton.'

What would you have said? No one had ever asked me to be in a film before. I said yes.

'The shot would probably look best with you doing the race,' he said, warming me up. 'Why don't you do it?'

'Don't I need time to train?' I replied. This was about two weeks before the race.

'Nah,' he shot back. 'They're easy as pie, you'll be fine.'

'I'll think about it,' I replied.

Two days later, I toughened up and told him straight.

'I'll do the interview but I'm not going to do the run/course,' I wrote in an email, in what I hoped he'd read as a no-nonsense tone. 'Not enough time to do any training & actually I'm not a tough guy!'

I went up the day before the race. It was a typical January day in Wolverhampton. Which is to say, it was cold as an icy pond and there were more than fifty shades of grey in the clouds, with rain and freezing fog. To keep warm I wore a big puffer jacket that made me look like the Michelin Man.

Keneally picked me up at the train station. He was easy to spot: he's six foot five, with an unkempt beard and long shaggy hair. He was wearing a trucker cap and a big grin. I got into a van with him and his obstacle-course friends – a British guy and an American girl. The Brit was called James Appleton. He was slim, wiry, posh, like a young army officer. He seemed like a nice guy as well as a tough guy. I liked him.

But who was this American girl? What was she doing here? Wearing a fleece and leggings, she looked like a sporty version of Gwyneth Paltrow. Long, straight, blonde hair. Slim and pretty as a bird. And she was running the course. Even she was going to be a tough guy the next day.

If she had what it took, what did that make me? I can't remember a time in my life when I've felt the wind abandon my sails so quickly. What kind of man did it make me if I was wearing extra layers and a huge puffer jacket, and these people, even this slip of a girl, were about to take off almost all their clothes and muck about in the mud?

I felt completely unmanned. Like the world's biggest scaredy cat, like the wimpiest link. Suddenly, I knew why Americans think that when Hugh Grant says, 'Whoops-a-daisy,' in movies, he's speaking for all Englishmen. Had I done the wrong thing? Was I letting the side down? Because if they could take this thing on, surely I could too? After all, I was a healthy forty-year-old. I'd always played sports. I played five-a-side football once a week. I'd run a marathon a few years back. Maybe I could sign up when we got there. But I didn't say anything. Not just yet. I'd surprise them.

But when we arrived and I saw the windswept, wet farm that Tough Guy was going to be held in, and the obstacles around the course, I felt my inner wind blow once more. I wasn't unmanned. I wasn't being a wimp. I was sane.

You could see most of the route from one central spot. Some of it ran up and down the hillsides of a field horses usually grazed in. Some of the track there was steep, and some was muddy, but it looked doable.

It was the other stuff, though. For one part of the course, they'd taken one of those big yellow digger things made by JCB or Caterpillar and dug a huge pit into the wet mud. Getting through that would be like wading through cold treacle. Then, there was the part of the course where you had to dip down, like a scuba diver, but without any of the kit to keep you warm, into a freezing pond.

And even if you don't mind the idea of soggy socks and an ice-cream-cold head, how about the Cu Chi Tunnels? They're 25 metres of muddy, icy puddles, and live wires hanging down to give anyone crazy enough to go through them electric shocks. If you were to take on the Tough Guy course, as you crouched down in the mud, ready to crawl through, all you'd hear, in the blackness in front of you, would be grunting and screams of pain.

Most people, I think, would react to something like this the same way I did. After all, human societies have been trying to make things easier, better, more pleasant and more comfortable since the dawn of time. That's why we've invented things that protect us from the wet and the cold and discomfort – like central heating, goose-down pillows, memory-foam mattresses, puffer jackets, and breathable and waterproof outer layers. So why would anyone want to leave all that progress behind and spend their hard-earned money and precious time getting cold and dirty instead?

But, strange as it sounds to me, this crazy, counterintuitive idea is now attracting a lot of people – millions, in fact. Obstacle-course racing has been one of the world's fastest-growing sports in recent years. From only 50,000 people doing it in 2009, in the US, where there are good figures available, there are now more than 5 million taking part.

Meeting Mr Mouse

One of those millions is Scott Keneally. When he first came across obstacle-course racing, his reaction was the polar opposite to mine. At the time, his life was going nowhere. His fiancée was having second thoughts. His writing career was stuck in the proverbial mud. This Tough Mudder course seemed to offer something, even if he wasn't sure what that something was exactly. It was, at the least, an occasion to prepare for, a challenge to overcome, and a chance to move forward in some way. Whatever the exact reason, he heard the call to adventure, ran a race, and fell in love – with the sport, the community around it, and, in time, the opportunities it brought.

Before, he'd been a couch potato, a scaredy cat who didn't try new things, and a struggling writer. After, he got fit, discovered that he could be brave, and his journalism career took off. He wrote a report about his first Tough Mudder for a local magazine. Next, he wrote another article that ended up on the front cover of a national magazine with a circulation of 675,000 called *Outside*. And then, he got a break into TV – a job consulting for one of the US's premier TV shows,

60 Minutes, for a report on the rise of obstacle-course races like Tough Mudder. That gave him a chance to come to the UK to try the original obstacle-course race, Tough Guy, and meet its maker.

'Mr Mouse was like a superhero, like a character from a movie,' Keneally says now.

When Mr Mouse, whose real name is Billy Wilson, turned up to meet them for a drink, he was dressed in his full regalia. A former member of the British Army's Grenadier Guards, Wilson looks like a cross between an ageing Boy Scout and a dictator in a Sacha Baron Cohen film. There are four stars on the epaulettes of his green military shirt. A badge on the right side of his chest reads, 'Reg. Sgt. Major Mouse'. On his left breast pocket, it says, 'Tough Guy Veteran'. He accessorises with regimental socks, a kilt and a tie, either army green or Grenadier Guards tartan. He talks with a strong Midlands accent, and a big dose of ex-army humour. He has grey hair, bright blue eyes and a luxurious grey moustache. He carries a moustache brush.

Keneally's wife Amber, who'd come on the trip to England, remembers that first time they met Mr Mouse. 'I was stricken,' she says, 'by the way he kept brushing his moustache.'

'He's very gentlemanly, and very funny,' says Keneally. 'When he introduced himself to Amber, he took his hat off, and said something about how he'd like to impregnate her because that would get more of his sperm into the world.'

'I think he called me a breeder,' recalls Amber. 'That I'd make good stock.'

Maybe it was too many pints of warm English beer, or the excitement of the race. Maybe it was Mr Mouse's hypnotic moustache-brushing. Maybe it was his complimenting of Amber in a way that sounds, frankly, really offensive, but, as both Scott and Amber assure me, was oddly charming. Whatever the reason, some time that night, Keneally made a decision: he was going to tell the story of obstacle-course racing, and the story of the wild and crazy English guy who'd started it all, Mr Mouse.

Back in the States, Keneally got $30,000 together, enough to come back to England with a cameraman and shoot some footage. Then, he'd create a promo video and raise enough to shoot the whole film.

'Summer 2013, I was living the dream,' says Keneally now. 'I was in England, with a shooter, collecting footage of Mr Mouse to make a promo video for a massively successful crowdfunding campaign.'

Ain't No Obstacle High Enough ...

The night before he pressed 'go' for his campaign on a fundraising website called Kickstarter, a few of Keneally's supporters got cold feet.

'What chance is there that this will fail?' Amber asked.

'Zero!' he shot back, trying to sound more confident than he felt.

Then, a friend called Dan Hill, who'd put $10,000 of the original $30,000 in, asked him too.

'Buddy, I gotta tell you, I think you should lower how much you're asking for,' he suggested.

Keneally knew Amber and Dan had a good point, that his target of $297,000 was on the high side. But if he only asked for part of the money, he'd have to come back a month or two later to ask for more. Surely it was better to ask for enough to make the movie, so he could get on with making it?

Hesitant but hopeful, Keneally took a breath, pressed the button on his computer to launch the campaign, and crossed his fingers. He'd know soon enough. Sooner than he'd thought, as it turned out. They raised $7,500 that first day.

'But we needed that every single day to have a chance of hitting the target,' Keneally says. 'That campaign turned into the longest forty days of my life.'

The place where Keneally lived, Healdsburg, is a small town. It's the sort of close-knit community where people know each other's business.

'Everyone had been really excited for me,' says Keneally. 'But then, suddenly, it was like I was walking around town with egg on my face. People just totally stopped talking to me about the movie.'

Keneally had timed the Kickstarter campaign to end on the same day he ran an obstacle course called Spartan Race in Malibu, southern California. He'd hoped to go down there to announce that he was now making the movie. But he'd fallen a long way short. And on Kickstarter, if you don't hit your target, you don't get any of the money – so he didn't receive a penny of the $34,000 people had pledged.

Keneally couldn't give up now, though, not after so publicly announcing the movie. So he and Amber started another fund-raiser, this time on a site called Indiegogo, where you get all the cash, however much, or little, people have pledged. So at least he was going to this Spartan Race with some kind of positive news.

To kick-start the new campaign, Amber filmed herself strumming her guitar and singing a song. It was based on Miley Cyrus's song 'We Can't Stop', but she changed the words, 'It's our party …' to, 'It's your movie…' So, as Amber sang:

> It's your movie, you can do what you want,
> It's your movie, you can see it or not,
> It's your movie, you can help us a lot,
> If you share it we got,
> Kickstarter or not …
> Barbed wire, sweaty bodies, on your knees
> Hands in the air for your burpees,

We know why you crawl through the mud now,
So much easier than trying to crowdfund now.
If you don't want us to go home,
Can we get a hell no!
Cos we wanna tell your story,
Give you all the glory ...

Amber's not a bad guitar player, and not a bad singer either. It's a really catchy tune. Quite a few people watched it. (You can too, it's at www.howtospendit.com/amber.) Funny that she should mention burpees in that song, though – because meanwhile, down in Malibu, the campaign was beginning with a splat, thanks to a Spartan Race rule that's designed to separate the true Spartans from the just-enoughers. If you fail an obstacle, you have to do thirty burpees: a mean military fitness and agility test that, as Keneally puts it, 'repackages squats, push-ups and jumping jacks into one little horror show'.

Halfway round the course, there was a challenge called, simply, the Rope Climb. To complete this obstacle, you had to climb twenty-five feet up a rope, ring a cowbell at the top, then lower yourself back down again. It's tough, a signature Spartan Race obstacle. That day, it was smack in the centre of the festival area, surrounded by spectators. As Keneally got there, people recognised him.

'Rise of the Sufferfests!' someone shouted.

Keneally was nervous but thrilled. But then he started climbing.

'It was exhausting,' he wrote later, 'and by the time I reached the top knot, I was cashed. My arms were shaking, my nerves were racing, and the goddamned cowbell was still several inches out of reach. Worse yet, I was the only competitor on the ropes.'

The crowd willed him up.

'Rise up!'

'You got this!'

'You can do it!'

But he couldn't. He lunged for the bell, missed it, and splatted down into a trench of mud. When he emerged, wiping mud from his eyes, no one said a word. And now Keneally had to do thirty soul-crushing burpees. They took him fifteen minutes. Not long after, he admitted defeat, and did the worst thing a person can do in a Spartan Race: not finish.

The crowdfunding campaign didn't go much better. It raised $27,000 – a full $270,000 short of the amount needed to make the film. At that point, Keneally almost gave up. But then, in what he calls a 'hail Mary', last-ditch try, he sent an email to a guy he used to know by the name of Hugh Arian down in Los Angeles, at a firm called Echo Entertainment. And then, suddenly, it was like the clouds had parted. Arian flew up to have lunch with Scott and Amber, and said yes – he'd fund the movie.

'It was the biggest thrill of my life,' says Keneally. 'Suddenly, me and my cameraman Keith were up and running, booking flights and arranging shoots in different parts of the country, and England too.'

Keneally put the same effort he'd put into raising funds into making the movie. He managed to get famous people like *Super Size Me*'s Morgan Spurlock and Tim Ferriss, the author of *The 4-Hour Work Week*, to appear.

When *Rise of the Sufferfests* was released, Keneally gave a talk at the Apple campus, and it was released on Apple's iTunes. It rose to number three in their documentary charts. Next, it was on airlines. If you flew with Delta or United or Virgin in 2017, it was in the new-releases section right next to the *Star Wars* movie *Rogue One*.

'That kind of distribution was awesome, people kept taking pictures of the film playing in seat backs in planes, and posting the pictures online, and sending me texts,' says Keneally. 'I felt like I'd hit a home run.'

Beep Beep! When a Radical New Approach Signals a Revolution

In the late 1970s, a little-known scientist had a radical idea that would lead to a completely new understanding of how a person can achieve better experiences, and live a better life. His name was Mihaly Csikszentmihalyi. If you want to say it out loud, it sounds like 'Mee-high Cheek-sent-mee-high-ee'. His friends call him Mike.

Csikszentmihalyi was born in 1934, in a town on the Adriatic Sea that had been part of the old Austro-Hungarian Empire. His family came to the US just after the war. Csikszentmihalyi had always been fascinated with how and why different people experienced similar situations differently. During the war, his family had been interred in a prisoner-of-war camp in Italy. Why, he'd wondered, had some people found it so upsetting, while others were able to stay calm? How come he'd been able to shut out all the unpleasantness around him, for instance, and focus on playing chess instead?

When his family moved to the US after the war, Csikszentmihalyi studied psychology, and became a professor at the University of Chicago. As his career in psychology progressed, he became frustrated at the way so many psychologists were turning to the area that B. F. Skinner was known for: behaviourism. Sure, he understood that because behaviourism was only concerned with what was external and observable and measurable, this could make his subject, psychology, appear more scientific. But, by ignoring what went on inside someone's head, this approach also missed a huge amount of what really mattered. After all, as Csikszentmihalyi once wrote, 'Life unfolds as a chain of subjective experiences ... The quality of these experiences determines whether and to what extent life was worth living.'

As we saw earlier, as people like Tristan Harris have pointed out, the application of behaviourism is great if you want to influence people to keep watching, clicking or doing whatever it is you want them to do. But it misses out on whether that watching, clicking or whatever makes their life more worth living, or not.

Perhaps, Csikszentmihalyi wondered, there could be a way to turn feelings into the sort of data that would be observable and measurable and comparable, and therefore more useful and meaningful? One of the problems with asking people how they felt had always been that by the time you came to sit down with them, with your clipboard and pen, and ask them, the time you were asking them about had passed. The Nobel-prize-winning psychologist Daniel Kahneman refers to this as the difference between the 'remembering self' and the 'experiencing self'. When you think back to Christmas Day or a holiday at Disney World, you tend to think of the turkey and the presents, and the roller coaster and meeting Mickey, not the petty arguments or the queues, the so-so food, and the kids getting crabby. The problem with asking people afterwards is that no one remembers exactly how they felt at the time.

Csikszentmihalyi solved this long-standing problem with a then-new piece of technology called a pager. In case you're not old enough to remember them, pagers were like mobile phones that only did texting, and could only handle incoming messages. They became popular with millions of people in the 1980s, but when Csikszentmihalyi thought of the idea, at the tail end of the 1970s, they were still mostly used professionally, by doctors in hospitals, for instance.

So, Csikszentmihalyi gave people pagers, and asked them to do something very simple. Whenever the pager beeped, they were to record what they were doing and how they felt. This was, as you may have realised, the origins of the method that MacKerron and Mourato would use for their Mappiness app decades later.

The direct result of this new method was that Csikszentmihalyi could not only turn subjective feelings into objective data, he could also find out whether, and to what extent, people felt their lives were worth living.

Consider the light shone on a typical week in the life of an American girl named Lorraine, for instance, one of the first people Csikszentmihalyi tried this with. At the time of the study, Lorraine was a senior in high school, so a teenager about to leave school. She was in the middle of figuring out what she was going to do in her first year of college. Her plan was to go to Spain on an exchange programme.

At the beginning of the week, Lorraine felt fairly positive. She said she was feeling happy and friendly when talking with friends, attending class, watching Miss America on television, and speaking with her aunt on the telephone.

Her mood changed dramatically on the Wednesday. Up till around midday, she was feeling good. But then she found out she couldn't go to Spain. By 1.30 p.m., she was very sad and very angry. Her mood remained much worse than usual for the rest of the day. The only time she reported feeling happy was when she was thinking about gorging on food at 4.20 p.m.

For the rest of the week, whenever Lorraine was on her own or in class, her mood remained bad. She perked up when she was with other people. On Friday and Saturday night, for instance, she went go-karting, partying and drinking with friends – and that cheered her up. Her mood even improved on Thursday, when she watched two friends, Penny and Merri, fighting. Penny, by the way, was incensed because Merri had gone and kissed Danny.

In the follow-up interview after the experiment, Lorraine explained her mood like this: 'When I was with people, it was better. When I was alone, I'd just think about [not going to Spain].'

Since then, Csikszentmihalyi and colleagues have repeated experiments like the one he conducted with Lorraine, with thousands of participants around the world: from teenagers in Tokyo to old women in Korea, farmers in the Italian Alps, and factory workers in Chicago. They gathered over a hundred thousand pieces of evidence. The results of these experiments have led to a decisive, radical new understanding about when people are happiest, what makes people happy, and, so, what we should all do to have the best experiences and live our best lives.

Radical – because, if you think about it, when most of us fantasise about the good life, we tend to think we'll be happiest when the to-do list is complete, the work is done, and we're lazing about, sitting on the sofa maybe, or a sun lounger. But, as the data from the experiment showed, the opposite is true.

If someone was paged when they were taking it easy, it turned out that they were far less likely to be happy. Think about Lorraine: when she was alone and in class, she ended up ruminating on her bad luck. If, on the other hand, someone received a beep when they were intensely focused on doing something – like when Lorraine was go-karting – directing all of their attention and what Csikszentmihalyi called their 'psychic energy' on it, they were far more likely to be happy.

When Csikszentmihalyi spoke to people and analysed their pager data, about what they were doing when they'd felt happy and how they'd been doing it, he realised something wonderful – and critically important for every one of us. In order for someone to have what he called 'optimum experiences', it's not *what* you do that matters. It's *how* you do it that really makes the difference.

It doesn't matter if you're rock-climbing, cycling, painting, partying, performing surgery, practising yoga; playing netball, football, basketball, chess or guitar in a band; just hanging out with friends or, even, watching Penny fight Merri because she kissed Danny. So long as it occupies all of your attention and 'psychic energy', it'll almost inevitably lead you into a relaxed, happy psychological state that he named 'flow'.

Now that he'd discovered flow, this magic ingredient that leads directly to optimum experiences and happiness, Csikszentmihalyi set about finding out what was needed for a person to enter the zone of flow. Based on thousands of interviews, he found there are eight elements to consider. The first five are all clear and simple. The final three are paradoxical, and maybe even a little strange.

First, the activity – because although it's *how* you do something that matters, *what* you do can help you to reach flow, and some things are far more engaging than others. You can't be in flow if you're passive, like lying on a sun lounger or slouched in front of the TV. You have to be active, and the activity should be challenging enough to test you.

'The best moments in our lives are not the passive, receptive, relaxing times,' Csikszentmihalyi wrote. 'The best moments usually occur if a person's body or mind is stretched to its limits in a voluntary effort to accomplish something difficult and worthwhile.'

Have you ever played tennis or football against someone who is not nearly as good as you? Or who's much better? It's not nearly as fun as playing someone who's about the same level, is it? Or, have you ever picked up a children's book and realised the plot's just not that interesting, or an academic treatise that's way too complicated – compared to a thriller that keeps you turning the pages? The best activities should pass the Goldilocks test: not too hard, not too easy, just right.

Second, you should be in 'full body awareness', so both your mind and body are not only entirely focused but also completely in sync with each other, with no spare psychic energy that could be caught by a passing distraction. This 'full body awareness' is the critical ingredient that athletes talk about when they say they're in the zone. Here's an example of what this looks like: when Serena Williams throws the ball up high with her left hand, reaches up and behind with her right, arches her back to extend as much as possible, then whacks the ball to serve – or when she whizzes across the court to reach a drop shot, or smashes a scything backhand down the line – you can be sure she's operating in the intense flow of full body awareness.

Third, there should be clear goals, and fourth, there should be feedback. You should know as soon as possible if you're reaching those goals. Fifth is about the activity. It should be the sort of immersive experience that leaves you so focused you can't think about anything but this moment and this place, right here, right now. Think of cycling down a hill with your feet off the pedals, or playing one of your favourite songs as loud as you want in an empty house and singing along.

Sixth, seventh and eighth are the odd, paradoxical aspects of flow. Sixth, there should be what Csikszentmihalyi called the 'paradox of control'. You should be at the absolute outside edge of your ability, so that you're only just, not quite, but yes, just about hanging on in there. As Csikszentmihalyi wrote in *Flow*, 'What people enjoy is not *being* in control, but the sense of *exercising* control in difficult situations' – his emphasis, not mine, by the way. In skiing terms, you're haring down the hill, flying along at a pace just at the edge of your ability. In performance terms, you should be playing a piece of music that challenges your entire mind and body. This is why jazz musicians, as they constantly riff this way and that, are often thought of as exemplars of flow.

Seventh, while your mind and body are entirely present, at the same time you'll lose a sense of self during a flow experience. And, even though you've given up your sense of self during the flow experience, afterwards you'll feel an expanded sense of who you are. You'll feel taller. Maybe you'll walk taller. Maybe you've expanded your capabilities. You've probably expanded your sense of possibilities: perhaps you've moved from, 'I can't,' to, 'Maybe I can,' or even, 'Yes, I can.' After a flow experience, you'll have a sense that you've moved up the ladder of personal possibility and human existence, that you've become, in some way, a *somebody*.

Eighth, during a flow experience, time has a strange, elastic quality. On the one hand, a moment can stretch into what seems like minutes. On the other, time flies by, as you're caught in a reverie of flow. Somehow tennis players will later say they saw the ball flying across the court, even though it might have been flying close to 100 mph, and virtually impossible to see. And a painter caught up in the act of painting, or a gamer playing a video game, might be so immersed that hours pass and they don't notice at all.

So now, all those years later, Csikszentmihalyi found an answer to the question he'd wondered about as a child in a prisoner-of-war camp in Italy. Why had some people been able to shut out the unpleasantness all around when they were doing something like playing chess? The answer, so his research showed, was simple. In those moments, despite their surroundings, they were having an optimum experience and were therefore 'happy', because, despite their situation, all of their psychic energy was focused, and they were in a state of flow.

How to Be Superman

By uncovering this secret to happiness, Csikszentmihalyi not only answered the question that had been bugging him for all those years, he also inspired many others. Since he discovered flow, psychologists and neuroscientists and writers have been analysing the idea, identifying when flow happens, what it looks like, and how you can bring more of it into your life.

Two psychologists named Keith Sawyer and Charles Walker, for instance, have discovered that if you're hoping to find flow, other people are especially helpful. In studies of basketball players and musicians, Sawyer found that the more social and more involved an experience, the more likely it will be to produce flow. He called this 'group flow'. Walker even created a hierarchy of flow states. 'Solitary flow', like the sort you get when you run or read a book or cycle on your own, is good. 'Coactive flow', when you run or cycle or listen to music with friends, is better. And 'interactive flow', when you play football in a team, play jazz with others, or act in a play, is best. This idea is one of the reasons why sex and conversations can be so much fun. When you're all telling stories and listening intently and responding, in the moment, everyone's in interactive flow. Funny to think that Route 1 to an optimum experience and happiness is as easy as having a brilliant conversation, isn't it?

There are two other approaches I think are particularly useful in thinking about flow, because they offer simple rules we can all follow to have more of the sort of intense experiences that make flow happen in our lives. One comes from a scientist at Harvard University. The other is from someone you might call a 'flow pro'.

The 'flow pro' is a man by the name of Steven Kotler. Based in New Mexico in the US, Kotler is a bestselling author who's become so convinced of flow's potential impact that he's written three books about the topic, and, a few years back, he founded an organisation called the Flow Genome

Project. Its aim is to map 'the deep science of ultimate human performance' that flow makes possible.

In one of his books, *The Rise of Superman*, which is about how people are using flow to push the envelope of human possibility, Kotler described the key conditions that any man or woman can use to try to trigger it. I think of this approach as the 'R&R' of flow. But instead of referring to the military term 'rest and relaxation', I mean 'rich environment' and 'risks'.

When you look for a 'rich environment', so Kotler says, you need to look for one that offers novelty, unpredictability and complexity. This explains why city breaks are so fun. Everything's new, even the signposts. What's around that corner? Figuring out where to go, how to get around, and what the hell that architecture is supposed to look like, is complex and engaging.

When it comes to risk, it doesn't matter what sort you choose. It can be creative, emotional, social, physical, or a combination of all of them. As long as you're flying by the seat of your pants, hanging on for dear life, aware that at any moment you could fall or fail, but doing your damnedest to stay upright and see it through – that's the kind of risk that'll put you in a state of flow.

In *Rise of the Superman*, Kotler gave five examples of activities that offer the sort of risks and rich environments that typically lead to this magical state. The first of these, which he called 'on ramps to flow', is action and adventures sports like surfing, skiing and kayaking. Next, creative pursuits like painting and writing. Third, suffering, as in the 'runner's high'. Fourth, doing something for others – sometimes called the 'helper's high'. Finally, playing video games, whose success is defined by how engrossed the players become.

Don't feel constrained by those five, though. If you do something that's put you in some sort of risk, if the environment is new to you, unpredictable and tricky – you could well be on your way to flow.

The other approach that I think's really useful comes from an iconoclast professor at Harvard University called Herbert Benson. Born a year after Csikszentmihalyi, in 1935, Benson also felt unsatisfied with some of the ways psychology was approached. His frustration stemmed from the rigid, Western approach. If someone were to sum up Benson's life's work, they might say he tried to bring the benefits of Eastern, esoteric and alternative practices into normal, Western approaches to health. While many East-meets-West enthusiasts sit at the fringes of debate, you couldn't say that about Benson. Among other achievements, Benson is a professor of mind/body medicine at Harvard Medical School, and he founded the Mind/Body Medical Institute at Massachusetts General Hospital, the original and largest teaching hospital at Harvard Medical School. He has written or co-authored nearly two hundred scientific publications and twelve books.

Benson's best-known book is *The Relaxation Response*. Published in 1975, it popularised the scientific reasons why people should adopt mindfulness, decades before the idea became fashionable. But the work Benson has produced that I find the most intriguing, and that's most relevant here, is his take on flow. His approach was typical: he applied rigorous, Western, scientific analysis to an esoteric concept, and then tried to work out what the discoveries mean for everyday people like you and me. He published the results in his 2003 book *The Breakout Principle*. In it, Benson mapped out the four stages of any flow experience.

Stage 1, Benson discovered, is struggle. It could be physical or mental, like running a marathon or climbing a hill, playing chess, solving a complex problem, or creating a presentation. Stage 2 is release from that struggle. This happens at the tail end of the struggle: when you've fought and fought the dragon, and you've emerged victorious. Stage 3 is what is now usually called flow, and what Benson refers to, following psychologists like William James and Abraham Maslow, as a 'peak experience'. The final Stage 4 is recovery, when a person comes down from the inspiring, energetic, and yet also physically, mentally and emotionally draining, high of flow.

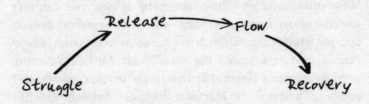

Benson's Model: The neuroscience of flow

Struggle → Release → Flow → Recovery

Think back for a moment to the arc the hero goes through in the hero's journey, and compare it with the arc a person goes through in Benson's four stages of flow – and you'll see some surprising similarities.

At the beginning of the hero's journey, right after the hero has crossed the threshold, she or he goes through difficult tests on the road of trials, having to overcome obstacles and enemies, create allies, and learn difficult skills. That sounds like a lot of hard work, struggle even. And now here's Benson saying that struggle is the essential launch pad for a peak experience.

Next, on the hero's journey, at the end of the road of trials and at the top of the arc, the hero has the supreme ordeal. She or he enters the innermost cave, slays the dragon, and gets the reward; and so, in some sense, is released from the burden of the quest – because it has been achieved. In any hero story, there's a pause here. After the storm of struggles on the road of trials building up to this final, huge, whacking great thunder crack, there's a moment of calm. Indiana Jones has the treasure. Bilbo has hold of the ring. Moana has the heart of Te Fiti. Look at this phase alongside Benson's model and it sounds, to me at least, a lot like a moment of release and its reward, flow.

Then, in the final stage of the hero's journey, the hero makes the return, coming home, re-integrating what she or he has learned, sharing this new-found reward with the world. Because of his or her heroics, everyone can rest easy, sleep well and live happily ever after. Now, if that doesn't sound like a chance for recovery, I don't know what does.

What's really interesting here isn't just the similarities between these two roadmaps for happiness – the ancient wisdom of the hero's journey and the twenty-first-century neuroscience. What's really interesting, not only for anyone aiming to be superwoman or superman, but for every one of us who likes the idea of getting more happiness and creativity into our lives, is that there's a clear process for triggering flow: road of trials/struggle, reward/release and flow, and return/recovery.

I find making these kinds of connections exciting. But there's a problem that's nagging me here too. Maybe it's occurred to you as well. If you think about flow as Csikszentmihalyi, Kotler and Benson describe it, where people get so engrossed in rock-climbing or dancing or making love or reading that they lose track of time and even themselves – it sounds a lot like the way addicts talk about playing gambling machines and how it feels when you fall into the endless scroll of social-media sites like Snapchat, Instagram and Facebook.

That strikes me as deeply worrying.

Flow: neuroscience and the hero's journey

Comparing Benson's model for flow with the hero's journey and the man in hole story shape

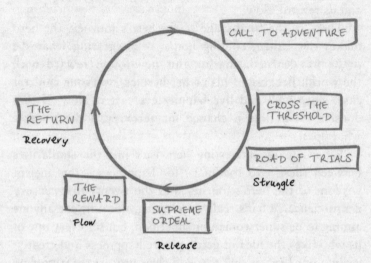

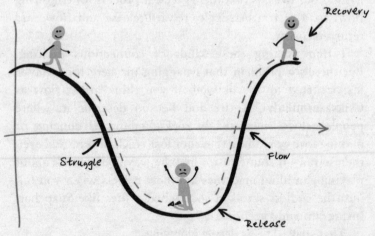

The Rat People – and the Fake Flow in Your Phone

I'd like to introduce you to Darlene.

In most ways, Darlene is normal. She's lived, as she says, 'a charmed life – never alcohol, never drugs, never running or being run on. Good and accomplished kids. Opportunities. Life has been sweet, wonderful and very blessed.'

Darlene, sixty-one, lives in Las Vegas, though not the glamorous city you know from the movies like *The Hangover*, where sharp-suited stag parties meet Mike Tyson, and the hookers look like Heather Graham.

It's late now, and Darlene is hungry, thirsty and miserable. Her hair is dishevelled. Her skin is dried out. Her clothes are wrinkled and baggy. She is hunched over a machine. She's been gambling since 5 p.m.

Here's how Darlene would later describe this night, in a post on an Internet site for machine-gambling addicts:

'3 a.m., was nearly alone, had to go to the bathroom, didn't want to leave the machine.

'5 a.m., still there, choking on smoke, starving, cramping from bladder pain, butt hurting from sitting.

'6 a.m., finally got up, put my coat on but still couldn't leave. Got attendant to watch machine while I peed. Almost cried with relief. Looked at myself in bathroom mirror, was shocked at what I saw. I do not ever want to look on the face of that woman again – the desperate one, the smoky, hungry one who doesn't have the sense to go to the bathroom or go home. Continued playing – standing up, coat on.

'8 a.m., breakfast eaters arriving and I became terrified that someone I knew would see me. Finally left ...

'How did I get to this point? 15 hours? I've never done anything in my life for 15 hours straight, except take care of my babies. I'm well past that point in my life, could be a grandmother. And what kind of Grandma would that be?

Some idiot with no self-control, who becomes paralysed, hypnotised – by what? A machine? The music? The lights? WHAT IS IT?'

Most people who read Darlene's post on the site expressed sympathy.

'I can relate to how you feel,' wrote one.

'Know the feeling,' said another.

'I was glued. I sat for 10 hours straight,' said yet another. 'I used to sit in that damn chair in the casino and COULDN'T PHYSICALLY MOVE.'

But, as Darlene wrote in comments on the site, she didn't want *understanding*. She wanted to *understand*. Eventually, someone gave her an answer. The person wrote:

'Darlene dear Darlene.

Slot machines are just "Skinner boxes" for people! Why they keep you transfixed is really not a big mystery. The machine is designed to do just that. It operates on the principles of operant conditioning. The original studies on conditioning were done by B. F. Skinner and involved rats ...

If every time the rat hit the lever he got a treat, that would be the end of it – he would just hit the lever when he was hungry. But that's not how conditioning works. Enter the concept of intermittent reinforcement. Simply put, it means that the rewards (pellets) are dispensed on a random schedule – sometimes the rat gets none, sometimes a few, sometimes a lot of pellets (sounding familiar yet?). He never knows when he's going to get a pellet so he keeps pushing that lever, over and over and over and over, even if none come out. The rat becomes obsessed – addicted, if you will. THIS, then, is the psychological principle that slot machines operate on, and how it operates on you.'

Darlene replied. 'You put into words what I knew to be the facts!' she wrote. 'Perhaps we should form a splinter group, calling ourselves "The Rat People", since we all know when the pellets drop, they could just as well be cyanide as chocolate.'

Operant conditioning? Intermittent variable rewards? As you'll remember from the *Outside & Offline* chapter, whether it's deliberate or not, and whether they'd describe it this way or not, many of today's tech firms are using these same methods to turn decent, intelligent, *accomplished* people who've never had any problems with drink and drugs – like you and me and our partners and parents and children and friends – into 'rat people'.

While I don't think Internet addiction is as negative for humans as machine gambling, there are some striking similarities. Haven't you ever found yourself checking your phone more often than is healthy? Have you ever lost yourself in the endless scroll of Facebook or Twitter or a news site?

Did you recognise the levers and pellets in your own Internet use? How many times today did you push a digital lever – look at your phone and check Facebook or Snapchat or Twitter or texts or emails or the football scores or the news or some other app? How did the pellets vary each time?

Do you ever feel like you don't have control, like you've been hypnotised, like you have no choice but to check your device? That the voice in your head, and the desire in your body, won't go away till you've just had one little look?

We all have. We've all got caught in the lure of the screen.

So this problem isn't only for machine gamblers. It's for every one of us – the good, accomplished millions of us who have addiction issues with the Skinner boxes we carry with us everywhere and check morning, noon, night and in the middle of the night.

Think I'm exaggerating? More than half of Britons – 59 per cent – say they're hooked to their devices. And many of us now spend somewhere between 40 and 60 per cent of our leisure time looking at our screens.

So, concerned with the idea that I might be promoting a practice that could turn you into a machine addict, I took another look at the ingredients and conditions for flow in Kotler's, Benson's and, most importantly, Csikszentmihalyi's work. Then, I compared them with the machine-flow that hypnotises the rat people.

I started with Kotler's way of seeing it, and couldn't see any distinction.

Real vs Fake – Flow According to Kotler

	REAL FLOW	FAKE FLOW	
Condition		Machine gambling	Phone
Risk	Yes	Yes – financial	Yes – social, reputation
Rich environment: novelty	Yes	Yes – new spins	Yes – new emails, tweets, updates, etc.
Rich environment: unpredictability	Yes	Yes	Yes
Rich environment: complexity	Yes	Yes	Yes – because the content varies so much

Then I looked at Benson and Csikszentmihalyi, and, if you'll excuse the pun, bingo! I hit the jackpot.

There are, as you'll see in the table on page 208, two key differences. One's in the input, the other's in the outcome. Let's start with the outcome. The easiest way to recognise 'fake flow' as opposed to 'real flow' is how you feel afterwards. If, at the end of your activity, you feel alive, enhanced, somehow bigger, that's real flow. But if at the end – perhaps after a late-night, longer-than-expected, zone-out on one of your devices – you feel depleted and drained, that's fake flow. Beware of it. That's the sort of flow that'll make you join the 'rat people'.

To get a good grasp of this real flow, I think you can get close by remembering what the Roman emperor Julius Caesar said after he'd invaded Britain in 47 BC: '*Veni, vidi, vici*' – 'I came, I saw, I conquered'. But you don't have to vanquish anyone. The phrase that, in my view, reflects this expanded sense you get from real flow, is an update on Caesar: '*Veni, vidi, vixi*' – 'I came, I saw, I lived'. If, as you emerge from your flow, you feel you can truly say, 'I came, I saw, I lived,' then I think you've just had real flow.

The other key difference is the input. Remember how Benson says that the four-step flow process begins with struggle, and Csikszentmihalyi's first condition is that you have to not only be active, but stretched to your limits doing something intensely difficult and worthwhile?

On some gambling machines, like the more complex poker ones, there are games that are hard – so long as the player doesn't play like a zombie or let the machine play itself by selecting 'auto hold' or 'auto play'. But that isn't true for most gambling machines, and it isn't true of almost all the mobile checking we do, is it? Of course, we need to check email every now and then, and keeping up with friends is important. But it's not worth checking as often as we all do, surely? And if it's at least a little worthwhile, no one would say it's hard to check the football scores, or see what's new on Snapchat, or check who's done what on Facebook. Checking our devices just isn't challenging. It's nowhere near the intense struggle from activities that lead to real flow, like scaling a wall, trying to beat a friend at tennis, or writing a book.

Phew. So I can recommend flow. The flow you want is the stuff you have to work at to get. The sort that's only available if you're prepared to struggle through a challenge that's worthwhile and intensely difficult. Do that, and at the end you'll be able to say, 'I came, I saw, I lived,' and know you've just had real flow.

Real vs Fake – Flow According to Benson

	REAL FLOW	FAKE FLOW	
Condition		Machine gambling	Phone
Struggle	Yes	?	No
Release	Yes	Yes	Yes – after each time you see how many emails, likes, etc. you have
Flow	Yes	Yes – during each game	Yes
Recovery	Yes	Yes – after each round	Yes – when you step away from the device

Real vs Fake – Flow According to Csikszentmihalyi

	REAL FLOW	FAKE FLOW	FAKE FLOW
Condition		Machine gambling	Phone
Active: 'stretched to limits' doing something difficult and worthwhile	Yes	?	No
Full body awareness	Yes	Yes	Yes
Clear goals	Yes	Yes	Yes – is there something there?
Feedback	Yes	Yes	Yes
Immersive	Yes	Yes	Yes
Paradox of control, at edge of ability	Yes	Yes – the magic of intermittent variable rewards	Yes
Lose a sense of self during, and expanded sense after	Yes	Yes & no – lose sense of time, but depleted sense after	Yes & no – lose sense of time, but depleted sense after
Time has an elastic quality	Yes	Yes	Yes

If you think about this distinction, and then think about Scott Keneally's journey, it becomes clear what kept him going through all those years of failure and humiliation. It wasn't the fake flow that's created by the operant conditioning in Skinner boxes. It's the sort of intensely difficult challenge that results in real flow.

HOW TO DESIGN AN INTENSE EXPERIENCE

To make it easier to find real flow, design as many of the essential ingredients that Csikszentmihalyi, Kotler and Benson identified into your experience as possible. Use this checklist to make sure that you're creating optimal conditions for a peak flow experience.

1. Delete distractions: Get offline, and perhaps outside, to give yourself a better chance of focusing

2. Active: How active will you be?
   a. Not-doing can also be active: silent meditation like vipassana requires the sort of focus that'll lead you to flow.

3. Risk: How much of a risk will you be taking?
   a. The risk can be social, emotional, financial, physical.

4. Goals: To what extent will there be goals?

5. Feedback: To what extent will there be instant feedback?

6. Unpredictable: To what extent will there be *unpredictable* elements to keep you on the edge of your seat?

7. New: To what extent will there be *new things* to hold your attention?

8. Complex: To what extent will this be *complex* enough to make you struggle?

If you read the first letters of each item, it spells 'DARG FUNC'. To me, that sounds a bit like 'Daft Punk', like 'dark', which makes me think of interesting and slightly twisted, and also like fun and funk – and all of those make it more memorable, and so more likely that I'll remember and use them. I hope DARG FUNC makes it more memorable for you too.

Use the DARG FUNC checklist overleaf to not only think about the intensity an experience is likely to give you, but also how you might redesign the experience to turn every 'a little' into 'a lot'.

DARG FUNC

How to Design an Intense Experience

And to get into a 'Good Flow' Zone

1 DELETE DISTRACTIONS
Get offline and outside

☐ A LOT
A LITTLE

2 ACTIVE
Actively choose something active

☐ A LOT
A LITTLE

3 RISK
Ensure there's social, physical, emotional or some kind of risk

☐ A LOT
A LITTLE

4 GOALS
Do you know what you're aiming for. What success looks like?

☐ A LOT
A LITTLE

5 FEEDBACK
How will you know you're getting there?

☐ A LOT
A LITTLE

6 UNPREDICTABLE
Allow space and time for random events and serendipity

☐ A LOT
A LITTLE

7 NEW
Look for things that are new for you

☐ A LOT
A LITTLE

8 COMPLEX
Will this be complicated enough to hold your attention?

☐ A LOT
A LITTLE

A Superman in the Arena

Scott Keneally's movie *Rise of the Sufferfests* is brilliant. I'm not just saying that because I'm in it, and it's the only film I've ever been in. Oh, go on then. I am. But it isn't only me who says it's good. Its rating on the online movie bible IMDB is 8.1 out of 10. On Amazon.com it's 4.4 out of 5. On Apple, 4.7.

In the movie, in which there's a lot of mud, pain and even Amber – though, sadly, not singing her version of 'We Can't Stop' – Keneally asks the same question that went careering through my mind that icy, grey day in Wolverhampton. For the love of God, why? Why are so many men and women paying for pain?

I won't spoil the movie for you by listing the reasons Keneally discovered. But, armed with insights from people like Csikszentmihalyi, Kotler and Benson, at least we can explain why, when Keneally jumped into the mud and the movie, he couldn't stop. The answer, of course, is simple: the intensity of real flow.

As Keneally went over, under and through the mud and the tunnels and the towers, the barbed wire and the electric wires, the knee-deep muddy pits and the over-head-height icy ponds, he – like anyone who takes on a physical challenge such as an obstacle race – was in flow.

And as Keneally waded through the crowdfunding, and all the other phases of turning an idea he had one night in a bar in Wolverhampton into a movie, he – like anyone who takes on the challenge of turning an idea into reality – was in flow.

First, challenge: Each experience stretched his skills. Keneally didn't know the first thing about these muddy obstacle course races – 'OCR', as they're known in the industry. He didn't know how to make a movie. Both meant he was continually facing new challenges and learning new skills, and, so, constantly in the 'flow zone'.

Second, mind-body awareness: When you're running, climbing, crawling through an OCR, it's a mental as well as physical challenge, so he would have been in full mind-body awareness. Similarly, making a movie involves all your senses, as you're always looking, thinking, wondering: Will this look good? Where will it fit? What if we shoot it from over there rather than here?

Third, goals: He had to break down these big end-goals into achievable milestones. Do thirty burpees. Get over this obstacle. Climb through this ice and mud. Get $30,000. Find a camera assistant. Shoot a promo video.

Fourth, feedback: Well, if you do or you don't get over that obstacle, or raise that amount, you'll know.

Fifth, immersion: Get so immersed in the moment that you forget all else. Go to the English Midlands in January, break a hole in the ice and jump into a pond. Do you think at that moment you're thinking about work, or something your partner asked you to do?

Sixth, paradox of control: Keneally was never in control, of who, when or how much people would fund him.

Seventh, lose a sense of self: When you're getting around an OCR course, the camaraderie, the cold and the suffering release you from that self-consciousness. And Keneally really did believe that he was making the movie for the community.

Eighth, time concertinas: Like any completely immersive experience, people remember OCR races both ways. You can tell someone what the race was like overall. And you can remember individual obstacles. You hear the screams in the tunnels, the shrieks by the electric wire, the warrior's 'Aaaaaaaargh!' at the beginning.

Now, let's look at the 'on ramps' to flow and the two Rs of risk and rich environment. To begin with, OCR is an extreme sport so there's your on-ramp right there. The risk, too, is obvious. For OCR obstacles, like hanging on to the monkey bars, it's the mental and physical, 'Can I, can't I, will I, won't I?' risk of failure. And the movie?

'Making the movie was the ultimate sufferfest,' Keneally says now. 'With a race, it's compartmentalised into a short window of time. But embarking on a film is like going on an expedition to Antarctica. I went through hell, through all that debt for this crazy dream. And I really struggled in real ways, financially and emotionally.'

As well as the on-ramps and the risk, the environment Keneally was throwing himself into, for both the mud races and the movie, was novel, unpredictable, complex. 'Every phase brought something new that we had to figure out how to do,' says Amber. When they launched the Kickstarter, who knew how many people would back the film? When he started shooting, how many people would agree to be in it? When the movie launched, how many firms would agree to distribute it, how many people would watch it?

Now, let's turn to Benson's approach. Again, each element is clear. You can see struggle, release, flow and recovery in getting through each obstacle in an OCR race. You struggle to climb up the rope, crawl through the tunnel and hang on to the monkey bars. Then, as your mind and body accept the challenge, you feel release, you find flow. And in between obstacles, you recover. It's the arc someone goes on over the entire course of an OCR, from start to finish. And it's the same arc Keneally went through with each challenge, and the overall challenge, of the movie: from fundraising to making the movie, releasing the movie, and then enjoying people's responses.

So it's clear, Keneally's ride through mud and the movie was one long, ongoing optimum experience that hauled him off the couch, and rocketed him into the intensity of flow.

In case you're wondering, Keneally wasn't aware of any of this at the time, not consciously at least. I've asked him.

He reminds me of a character which another American, a far more famous one named Theodore, once talked about. President Roosevelt was at the Sorbonne in Paris, more than a hundred years ago, when he talked about the 'man in the arena':

'It is not the critic who counts; not the man who points out how the strong man stumbles, or where the doer of deeds could have done them better. The credit belongs to the man who is actually in the arena, whose face is marred by dust and sweat and blood; who strives valiantly; who errs, who comes short again and again, because there is no effort without error and shortcoming; but who does actually strive to do the deeds; who knows great enthusiasms, the great devotions; who spends himself in a worthy cause; who at the best knows in the end the triumph of high achievement, and who at the worst, if he fails, at least fails while daring greatly, so that his place shall never be with those cold and timid souls who neither know victory nor defeat.'

Isn't that Keneally? Covered in mud, coming up short, making errors, daring greatly, failing often, striving valiantly.

Isn't that, in some way, every one of us, at least in our finer moments? Doing our best, failing, getting back up again?

The thing is – you don't have to be a six-foot-five, shaggy-haired, struggling writer in northern California to get the benefits of flow. You don't have to be a man and you don't have to be in a hole. Those are just easy ways to remember the idea. You don't have to be in an arena full of mud. You don't have to run an obstacle race. You don't have to be making a movie.

What I love about this magical idea of flow is that it's available to all of us. It's for anyone who's prepared to put down the distractions. It's for anyone who's willing to hear the call to adventure and walk down the road of trials.

You do have to come out of the shadows. You do have to accept and even embrace risk. You do have to realise that intense struggles are an energising, essential part of a life well lived. Instead of hoping for, looking for, and wishing on a star that all your struggles will soon end and you'll be able to lounge about on Easy Street, you have to deliberately choose struggle and intense experiences instead.

Intensity Summary

1. Our typical fantasy of the good life – with our feet up, lazing about, and far from busy – is a mistake.

2. We often think we'll be happier when we've got our work done and put our feet up, taking it easy. But that's wrong.

3. Humans are happier when we're fully engaged, taking on an intensely difficult challenge that focuses all of our energy.

4. This is called flow.

5. There is a difference between 'fake flow' and 'real flow'. We can be lured into fake flow by the operant conditioning in Skinner boxes like gambling machines and smartphones. But the low effort inputs are matched by the lowly outcome.

6. To get the benefits of 'real flow', you have to take on a task that's intensely challenging and causes you to struggle. Do that, and instead of emerging from the experience feeling depleted and drained, as you would

after 'fake flow', you'll get an expanded sense of who you are and be able to think, 'I came, I saw, I lived.'

7. It's possible to design experiences so that they're more likely to lead us into 'real flow'.

8. These ingredients make us more likely to find flow, but, ultimately, it isn't *what* we do, but *how* we do it that matters most. The vital ingredient is that you put all of your focus in the present moment.

How to Get More INTENSITY into Your Everydays

As before, the questions in *Past Times* are about specific experiences from your past. The questions in *The Way to Happy Days* will help you think about your life in general. Both will help you bring the benefits of intensity into your life.

Past Times: How Intense Was That Experience?

Think about a challenging experience you've had in the past three months; maybe it was a physical challenge, maybe it was something at work, maybe it was just something that went wrong and you had to figure out a way to solve it. Try this using experiences that were really good, ones that were just average, and ones that were downright awful. Then, ask yourself these questions, giving an answer on a scale of 0 to 5, where:

> 0 = *Not at all*
> 1 = *Very little*
> 2 = *A little*
> 3 = *Some*
> 4 = *A lot*
> 5 = *A great deal*

1. How much did [insert experience here] challenge you?

2. Afterwards, to what extent did you feel an expanded sense of who you are?

3. To what extent were you in 'full body awareness', completely in the zone and in the present?

4. To what extent was it the sort of immersive experience that left you so focused you couldn't think about anything but that moment and that place, right there, right then?

5. Did the experience feature the five 'on-ramps' to flow: i) action and adventure sport, ii) creative pursuits like painting and writing, iii) suffering, e.g. the 'runner's high', iv) doing something for others, i.e. the 'helper's high', v) playing video games?

6. How much of a chance was there you could fail? Was there creative, emotional, social or physical risk?

Any 4s and 5s? Run an experience you had through these questions and it's soon clear whether you were in flow at all. If your answers tended to be mostly 3s or less, consider the questions below, and see if you can increase the intensity of your experiences in the future.

The Way to Happy Days: How to Get More Intensity into Your Life

Use these questions to think about how you can increase the amount and quality of intensity and flow in your experiences and your life.

1. Ticking along in life is fine ... but are you ticking along too much?

2. Have you been craving laid-back, luxury experiences – when really you should aim for challenging ones?

3. Do you do enough things that are difficult but worthwhile?

4. How can you reduce distractions so that you're more able to immerse yourself in an experience?
   Hint: leave your phone at home, and reread the *Outside & Offline* chapter.

5. Do you play enough games? Can you 'gamify' your experiences, that is, add more of the elements that Csikszentmihalyi discovered would lead to flow? Can you create a structure of clear goals and instant feedback and stretch yourself by adding levels, points, progress, prizes and competition?

6. Do you avoid failure, or expose yourself to it? Are you a man or woman in the arena?
   Failure hurts, but it is necessary for success. Any activity that offers the reward of success also features the risk of failure – you can't achieve success without it. There's no shame in failure, as Roosevelt so rightly pointed out. But there's also power in Caesar's phrase, '*Veni vidi vici*.'

7. How can you turn a passive experience into an active one?

    This is why, on dull away days with the firm, people play 'bullshit bingo'. Next time you're stuck in the middle of a boring experience, either just let your mind wander, because down time is good for your mind, or get active and create a game that hauls you out of an unstimulating, passive experience and lands you in a fun, active one.

8. How much of your day are you in flow? How could you increase the amount of time you spend in flow?

9. How could you make your environment richer – less familiar, less predictable, more complex?

    For instance, take a different route to work or to your friend's house. Go someplace you've never been. *Work* someplace you've never been. Take on challenges that are hard enough to require as much skill as you can muster.

10. How can you make sure you're in 'full body awareness'? If your challenge is mental, making a presentation, for instance, how can you involve your body?

SOMETHING FOR THE WEEKEND

Here's a handful of ideas you can use to get more intensity into your weekend. On the following pages, write down three ideas of your own.

1. Toughen up, buttercup

Sign up for the Tough Guy, or, if, like me, you're not ready for that kind of commitment yet, the Tough Mudder Half, which is half as long and there are no electric shocks.

2. Game on

Play sport. Gamify something you're already planning on doing by adding points, challenge, levels and goals. You can play against yourself or another person, or with another person and against yourselves.

3. Play nicely

If you're already doing something, bring some coactive and interactive flow into your activity. If you run already, run with a friend or join a running club. If you play an instrument, jam with friends. And instead of just singing, sing with others: in church or in a choir, at a massaoke event – like karaoke but everyone sings together – or at Sunday Sermon – the singalong for people who aren't religious – or even just in the house. (Our family has a few choice songs we sing along to, from David Bowie and Mick Jagger's 'Dancing in the Street' to a song called *I Find My Joy* by our friend Šzárka Elias. It has a great, simple chorus that every one of us can remember.)

4. Tell a joke

Two levels to this. First, if you practise and perfect and then tell a joke, you'll help everyone else get into interactive flow. Second, sign up to a standup comedy course. You think you've done scary things before? Try telling jokes on cue in front of other people. I've honestly never been as scared as the time I told some jokes at the 'graduation show' of Logan Murray's Amused Moose comedy course.

5. Be crafty

Pick a project – paint a wall, fix the fence, sort out your wardrobe, mosaic a pot, understand what Nietzsche is on about, write a poem or a screenplay – set a deadline, and go get it done. It doesn't matter if you complete it in time, but it does matter that you finish it, that you tidy up the loose ends into some kind of end point, and that you feel good about what you achieved.

_____

_____

_____

_____

EXTRAORDINARY

The New Peak-End Rules

'The purpose of life is to live it, to taste experience to the utmost, to reach out eagerly and without fear for newer and richer experience.'

ELEANOR ROOSEVELT

I've only met God once, and that was almost twenty years ago now.

If there's anyone to thank, it was a tall, dark, brown-eyed stranger I met in New Delhi.

Her name was Victoria Grand. You should meet her. She's extraordinary. Whip smart but wears her intelligence lightly, and friendly to just about everybody. She's half-Argentinian, half-American. Her mother was a secretary, her father a playboy diplomat.

'Dad was a poor Jew from Brooklyn,' Vicky says now. 'Born in the Depression, he Don Draper-ed his way into the State Department and South America. He had a faux accent and wore safari jackets. He drove a cherry-red convertible and sailed a big sailboat. He lived in a penthouse on the most expensive corner of Buenos Aires. He met Mom at an embassy party.'

As I remember it, I met Victoria at the turn of twilight. The sunset orange that had been lighting Delhi's dust and street sellers and auto-rickshaws was just then giving way to the glow of neon signs and night markets. The last few starlings and doves were flying home, to the Red Fort and the trees near India Gate, to roost for the night.

Vicky, then twenty-six, was sitting at the back of the bus I'd just got on to, and was instantly noticeable. She would be anywhere, with her jet-black hair and Latin good looks. But here especially, because this was no luxury coach. The seats didn't recline. There were no headrests. It was like an old school bus, dusty, with tears in the plastic seats.

I'd handed over my backpack, and watched the bus-*wallahs* tie it to the roof of the bus. I was walking down the aisle and there she was: the only other non-Indian on board.

'Going to Rishikesh?' I asked, because, er, that's where the bus was going. Rishikesh is in the foothills of the Himalayas. It means 'home of the *rishis*'. The *rishis* are holy men. The town was made famous, to Westerners at least, when the Beatles went there in the 1960s.

'Sure,' she smiled. 'Wanna sit?' she added, sliding up a bit.

We both knew the driver would keep stopping till the bus was full, and that this was our only chance. If we didn't sit together now, we'd end up stuck in the middle of families on the move.

'Sure,' I said, squeezing on to the seat. There wasn't much leg room on those buses.

'I'm going there to study yoga,' she said.

'Me too,' I shot back, though I hadn't known it till that moment.

'And stay in an ashram,' she added. An ashram is like a Hindu version of a monastery.

'Yeah, me too,' I said.

It wasn't long after that, that we both confessed we were in love. The way I remember it, she went first. But she insists it was me.

'I've been travelling with my girlfriend for the past few months,' I said. 'I've left her with her family in Calcutta to write a book. But I'm missing her already.'

'Ah, me too,' she said. 'I've been travelling for a while, but I just snuck in two amazing days and nights with my guy. He's called Derek. I don't know how I'm going to make it till I see him again.'

And that was the beginning of a beautiful few weeks of friendship. Both young, in love and missing our beloveds, both on a mission to try something new in this town that was a million miles from our ordinary lives, and both of us the sort of people who like talking and meeting others – we were instant yoga mates and roomies.

We found a room to stay at an ashram called Ved Niketan. It was north of the town, a few miles up the River Ganges and over a suspension bridge called Lakshman Jhula.

The ashram was set back from the river. It was spartan, built of concrete. On some walls, the devotees had painted useful instructions in red, green and yellow, like:

'IMMODEST BATHING IN THE GANGES OR MOVING AROUND THE ASHRAM PREMISES OR YOGA HALL IN UNDERGARMENTS OR INAPPROPRIATE ATTIRE IS NOT ALLOWED.'

Ved Niketan was a few hundred yards from the place where the Beatles had stayed, and a ten-minute walk to our yoga class.

We learned our yoga from a Polish guy who'd been in Rishikesh so long he'd taken a guru name. Swami Vivekananda Saraswati was about six foot five and looked like a maths geek. He had a big, pale face, crowned with thick black hair he'd had braided. He wore loose robes in saffron orange. The word *swami*, by the way, means teacher.

His practice was in an unorthodox place: the otherwise unused basement of a very forgettable two-star hotel. Swami, as we soon learned to call him, seemed to be great at putting these Eastern ideals into words and actions that made sense to Westerners like us.

We soon fell into a routine. We were up around 5.30 a.m. so we could get to each morning's yoga class by 6 a.m. We'd do yoga till about 8.30 a.m. Pulling our bodies into *asanas* like touching our toes, standing on one foot while twisting the raised foot around the other leg, and doing headstands.

After class, we were always starving. No food for the righteous, you see. None before practice at least. So, we'd head off to a café owned by a local called Mukti to get some porridge or dhal and rice. Then, we'd have free time, hanging out with our new friends: Marcelo from the Netherlands, Simon from Ballarat, Australia, and Ellie and Geoff who'd been living in Jakarta, Indonesia.

Each day, we'd find something fun to do. We relaxed at the German bakery overlooking the river and the bridge. We played frisbee on the beach. We took photos of the sacred cows down there. We went hiking in the hills, said hello to the monkeys. We went to lectures by the Swami. We talked about what we were going to do with our real lives once we left.

I was only there for about a month, but whenever I think back to it, it feels much longer, like one of those midsummer sunsets that never seems to end. There were a few things that happened, in the midst of that rosy glow, that stand out, though.

There was the morning we got up extra early – 4.30 a.m., I think it was – to cross the Lakshman Jhula bridge and head upstream and uphill to a Shiva temple. By 6 a.m. it was like a scene from an exotic movie, at least it was exotic for a boy brought up Church of England, in middle-class Surrey, just south of London. The air was thick with the sounds, smells and sights of Shiva worship. At the front, near the statues of the gods, priests were waving incense burners back and forth. We were all chanting an ancient Sanskrit chant, '*Om namah shiva-ya, om namah shiva-ya, om namah shiva-ya,*' over and over.

There was the day Vicky took a load of us up to the roof of the ashram late one afternoon, and taught us the ashtanga yoga she'd learned in California. It might have been the wrong time of day to be giving salutations to the sun, technically at least. But there are worse places to learn the downward dog than watching the sunset from a rooftop in Rishikesh.

And then there was the evening Swami held a group meditation. The room was nothing special. It was just a big, plain room upstairs in the hotel whose basement he used for the morning sessions. About a dozen of us, maybe a few more, sat in a circle. And he guided us in meditation. He wanted us to shift our consciousness and raise it through our seven chakras, from our roots to our crowns.

Then, with our chakras and consciousness awakened, we all chanted the classic prayer, '*Om*.' Except we didn't say it like that. It was more like a collective deep breath in, and then out:

'*Ommmmmmmmmmmmmmmmmmmmmmmmmmmmmmmmmm mmmmm*.'

Then, we all took a big breath in, and again:

'*Ommmmmmmmmmmmmmmmmmmmmmmmmmmmmmmmmm mmmmm*.'

Swami directed us to not only say it out loud, but also listen to the sound as we said it. And while that was going on, to not only call out our '*Om*' so everyone in the room could hear it, but also to call it out inside ourselves, silently, to hurl it out into the universe with as much force as possible, again and again, and listen for the response. Real meditation, he explained, is this act of listening.

Sometime in that room, in that circle, in that whirl of *omming*, inside and outside, that's when it happened. I don't, to this day, know what it was or what it means, or whether it means anything at all. But it felt like a very special moment.

Do you remember the line from the Bible, 'Seek and ye shall find'? What happened felt something like that. Suddenly, where it had felt like I was seeking something, looking out, asking a question, it was as if, all of a sudden, and just for a moment, the fabric of the universe ripped apart, and instead of me asking, it was like the universe, or god or whatever it was, turned the tables on me – and asked me a question.

I don't know what the question was. It felt like I'd been looking for something, *omming* and asking, like everyone else in that circle. And that then I'd been rewarded with that singular, special moment. It's the only moment in my life when I've felt like there was something else out there.

When that thing, whatever it was, reached out and said hello to me that day, it crowned a fun, memorable, and, yes, enlightening stay in Rishikesh.

A week or so later, I packed my backpack again, crossed back over the Lakshman Jhula suspension bridge, and waved goodbye to the gang – to Marcelo, Simon, Ellie and Geoff, and Vicky. That's how I remember it all, anyway.

The Old Peak-End Rule

The way I see it, there are two types of people. There are those who, when they are at the seaside, have to go in the water, no matter what. Like my dad, for instance. And there are those who don't, like most other people. Which one are you?

Even if you're not an English Channel, Irish sea, Atlantic Ocean or other cold water swimmer, you're at least a toe dipper, aren't you? Even if you're not, play along, would you?

Because I want you to remember, for a moment, the last time you dipped your toes in cold sea water. OK, so now picture yourself in Brighton, on England's south coast. It's early summer – June or July. There's probably some blue sky, a few fluffy clouds. It's windy too, windier than you'd thought it was going to be. But you've come this far. So, dutifully, like any Brit trained in the art of enjoying the beach whatever the weather, you take off your shoes and socks, roll up your trousers or hitch up your skirt. You hobble down the stones, or wander along frigid sand. And as the wave breaks, froths and speeds towards your toes, it hits you: that cold, first bite.

A few psychologists used water around that temperature to investigate a fascinating idea: the difference between what people remember and what actually happened, or, as the psychologists say, the 'remembering self' and the 'experiencing self'.

Think of it like this. When you go through the wish-I-wasn't-here experience of a terrible date or a miserable hike – stilted conversation, pouring rain, your boots get wet, the wrong kind of moaning – but afterwards you find yourself looking back fondly at the experience. That's the difference between the experiencing and remembering self.

This groundbreaking experiment shed some surprising light on the difference between what a person remembers, and what they actually experienced. You could say it poured cold water on the idea that any of us remembers perfectly. And it led to the creation of something called the 'peak-end rule'. Simply put, this says that people are most likely to remember what happened at the highest point and at the end of an experience, and that these two elements are particularly influential in how they think about the experience overall.

Let's start with the end part of this peak-end rule, and that experiment with cold water. The psychologists had people put one of their hands, for sixty seconds, in buckets of water cooled to 14°C, about the temperature of the English Channel near Brighton in June. Next, for the second experiment, they got them to put their other hand in 14°C water for another sixty seconds, and then keep that hand submerged for a further thirty seconds, but with the water temperature raised to 15°C.

That's seawater near Brighton in July. The psychologists then asked, which experiment would you rather do again?

What would you have said? When the question is put on paper like this, the answer's obvious. The first one, right? Having your hand in cold water for the shortest time makes most sense. But, oddly, people were more willing to do the second, longer trial again. The reason, the scientists figured, was that even though their hand would spend more time at an uncomfortable temperature, the final temperature was less unpleasant. From this, the psychologists could conclude that what happens at the end of an experience is key in determining how people remember it.

This curious idea has been tested in further experiments. In one, for instance, psychologists tested it on patients undergoing an uncomfortable procedure called a colonoscopy, in which doctors push a tube up your anus and into your rectum. They split the group in two. With one, they tried to be as quick as possible, just as doctors do who don't have a mean streak. But with the others, at the end, they left the scope inside the person for an extra three minutes, but not moving it, so not causing much discomfort. When they asked people afterwards, they found that the ones who had the extra three minutes at the end were more positive about the experience. Clearly, it wasn't the total amount of discomfort that mattered to the remembering self. It was what they experienced at the end.

If the idea of a prodder up your bum sounds uncomfortable but not something you can relate to, you might find this third experiment more useful. Psychologists put people into one of the most common, and annoying, experiences a first-world human can have: lining up and waiting to be served. They used a computer programme to simulate queuing and find out how people felt. The screen showed how long the queue was, and where they were in it. People would get irritated, so the researchers found out, if the line was long, if it didn't move for a while, and when it went slowly. But they were notably happier when it moved quickly.

No matter how their queuing experience was overall, though, the researchers discovered that what happened at the end had an outsize influence on how people remembered their overall experience. If the queue moved quickly at the end, they remembered it as a far less irritating experience. If the queue moved slowly at the end, they remembered it as a far more irritating experience. Again, this supports the findings from the cold water and colonoscopy experiments, that what happens at the end is key for how people remember an experience.

While conducting these experiments, psychologists noticed something else that punched above its weight in terms of how a person remembers an experience: the extreme. During a painful experience, like the colonoscopy procedure, for instance, the biggest impact on patients' memories, besides what happened at the end, was the most uncomfortable moment. In other experiments, psychologists have shown that people are far more likely to remember events that are more intensely emotional than usual, like when they split up with someone, when they came first in a race, or when the dog died.

For some reason, presumably so they didn't alarm people by reminding them of the bad things that happen in life, instead of saying extremes, and then qualifying that by talking about peaks and troughs, psychologists only ended up talking about the high points, that is, the peaks. And this became the 'peak-end rule'.

The idea that we're more likely to remember these peak moments makes sense, when you think about it. After all, we can't remember everything. Instead, we remember life through 'snapshots'. When we try to recall something later, these moments are the ones that most easily come to mind, and we tend to think they represent the event, that they're typical. But the reason they're easy to recall is because they're extreme.

Here's a useful way of picturing it. Most of life, if you think about it, is quite forgettable, like a flat line in a grey world. You turn off the alarm clock. You brush your teeth. You commute. Maybe you drive, or you stand, waiting, on a train platform. You sit in front of a computer, pressing buttons. You talk to work colleagues. You send emails. You get a cup of tea. You watch TV. You turn over to go to sleep. Yawn.

But, sometimes, life jumps up from that flat line, turns a pirouette out of the grey, and bursts into a rainbow-maned unicorn of excitement. Sometimes, *something happens*. It can be good, and you can rise to a peak. It can be bad, and you can fall into a trough. Remember the day they said yes? The day she said no? When you got your exam results? When your team won a game that really mattered?

So this surprising discovery, of the importance of peaks, makes a lot of intuitive sense. It also creates an interesting challenge for anyone who wants to plan and design better experiences. Because it throws up a difficult question. Who are you creating the experiences for, and who matters more: the remembering self who basks in the memory, or the experiencing self who has to live through it?

Thinking about these two sides of the self can, at the least, make you think twice about some experiences, and cast quite a different light on others.

If you pause for a moment, can you think of any experiences your remembering self talks about in glowing terms but your experiencing self didn't find quite so fun? Perhaps that festival that's given your remembering self snapshots of dancing in a field at sunrise, seeing great bands, and partying with your friends – but made your experiencing self trudge through mud, get lost, shiver with cold, wish you were some-where with a decent shower, argue with your boyfriend or girlfriend or best friend at the time, and then take eighteen hours on a hangover to get home. Or, perhaps, a party, a weekend, a holiday that was mostly boring or annoying or painful for your experiencing self. It's hard to take off the rose-tinted spectacles which we use to remember. But, if you dig a little deeper in your memory, I think most of us can find, lurking behind and beside the smiling pictures, just out of shot, a lot of life that wasn't quite so amazing, captivating, or, frankly, Insta-fabulous.

When I play this game, the first experiences that come to mind are: most of my twenties; the time I took my family to Port Eliot festival in Cornwall when, even though it was sunny and there were moments of magic and we got some great snaps and we did have fun, my wife and I kept arguing; and that month I spent in Rishikesh.

Everyone Needs a Vicky from Rishikesh

You probably have a Vicky from Rishikesh, a someone who lives somewhere else, a person you connected with, hung out with for a while, lost touch with as you got on with your life, got back in touch with, keep in touch with. I think almost every one of us has a Vicky from Rishikesh. Of course, they don't have to be named Vicky, and you didn't have to have met them in Rishikesh.

Today, Vicky lives in Sonoma County, over the bridge from San Francisco. She's married with two kids. She's a hotshot legal at a big Silicon Valley firm. We keep up, mostly by Facebook and the odd email. Every now and then I make a promise about how I'm going to come to California and we'll go to Burning Man. Sometimes, when she's in London or I'm in California for work, we have dinner. And we still talk about those good ol' days in Rishikesh.

We're convinced we had a great time there. After all, it's the basis for our friendship. But did we, really?

I've given you the glossed-over, simple version, you see. You've heard the story I tell in the pub. It's a classic travel story, plus that bit about meeting God. But was it really so good when we were there, living it every day?

For starters, it was January in the foothills of the Himalayas, so it was glacially cold that time of year, and I'd just come up after months in the south of India. I wasn't prepared for that sort of temperature. It was so cold I don't think I showered for the whole month. I'm not sure anyone did. Not a chance in the bare, painted walls of that concrete ashram. And that bed. The blankets had probably been there since the Beatles had been in town. Each of us slept in every single piece of clothing we owned. I bought a cheap fur hat in the market, and wore it inside out to get all the warmth I could suck out of the fur. Once we got out of bed, we wore our blankets to keep from freezing.

Getting up early every day for yoga practice sounds great when you say it. But in January at that time, it was still night. There wasn't a day when we all just popped out of bed with big 'hello, morning' grins. And the yoga hall in the basement of a crappy hotel? It too was cold, and had less atmosphere than a municipal school hall.

Besides the early start, sometimes it felt like instead of taking it easy – '*Ommmmm*' – we were always hurrying about from this place to that, from yoga practice to lecture and to more yoga, in order to take it easy – '*Ommmmm*'. And doesn't that defeat the point of it?

And the people. Sure, there were some people I liked. But there were far more who were just annoying. There were the clichés: loud Americans, supercilious French, just-out-of-the-army arrogant Israelis, and soap-dodging, hippier-than-thou travellers who were far too enlightened to commune with an idiot abroad like me. And Swami. A nice guy, but always so willing to give any girl in the group a bit of extra help with her asanas, and he'd probably been the kid at school who'd done his maths homework early and let everyone know about it.

Mukti was a nice guy and Mukti's was a nice place. But, edible as Mukti's dhal and rice were, the Michelin Guide wouldn't have been heading up there any time soon to hand out a street-food star.

And all that hippy claptrap, especially our 4.30 a.m. trip to the Shiva temple. I had this sudden realisation there too. As I got swept along with the candles and the incense and chanting '*Om namah shiv-ya*', my inner mind suddenly shouted at me, 'You don't even worship your own God, what are you doing here worshipping this god?!'

If you read my diary, you'll see I was missing my girlfriend at the time too. And planning my next move, a trip to see some rhinos in some other place in India, and then on to Thailand. So much for loving the yoga stuff. If I'd been so into it, why spend so much time pining for a girl and planning to leave?

I'm not saying I didn't have a great time. I'm not saying it wasn't eye-opening, surreal and fun. But I am saying there was also plenty of crappy, annoying stuff going on in Rishikesh too, stuff I almost always gloss over when I think back. (It was only when I dug out my diary from the time to write this that I was able to look *behind* the pictures and remember what was *really* going on.) And I think it's essential to think about this difference between the experiencing self and the remembering self when you plan and design experiences.

One way to do that is to use this peak-end rule while recognising its limitations. So, if you were designing an experience based on what we know about this rule – a night out, or a weekend away, or a holiday, for instance – you should do three things. One, put careful thought into creating one peak moment. Two, do the same with what happens at the end. Three, make sure that, in between those memorable moments, the experiencing self won't have to endure too many joy-sapping annoyances like long queues, the everyday equivalent of not-that-cold water, and other nagging pains in the bottom.

I think an even better way to make use of this *old* peak-end rule, though, is to use it as a starting point. If we take its insights, and then consider some other research, one recent study in particular, we can devise a new set of rules – the *new* peak-end rules – that are even more likely to deliver extraordinary experiences for everyone involved, including your remembering and experiencing selves.

The New Peak-End Rules

The peak-end rule has been shown to work in some experiments. But if you consider those experiments for a moment, you'll note that they were all quite short. Does the peak-end rule also work for longer experiences? And if it doesn't, how should we think about longer experiences?

Think about the last holiday you took, for instance. Now, as we've seen, it's very hard to remember clearly, even when we're watching ourselves. But let's try. What do you remember about it? Can you remember any boring bits? Were there any peaks, troughs even? Do you remember what you did when you first arrived, or what you did on your last day?

Hold those thoughts for a moment, because your answers may hold some clues about what matters.

Some psychologists in New Zealand, led by a man named Simon Kemp, decided to find out if the peak-end rule works on longer experiences too. So, they asked a bunch of students who were going on holiday to share how they felt about their trip. They asked them during their holiday, using Csikszentmihalyi's 'pager method'. And they asked them after they'd come home too. The experiment began with forty-nine participants, but a few pulled out partway through, and a few couldn't answer all the questions because their phone batteries died, so they ended up with forty-one respondents. That summer, most of them holidayed in New Zealand, seven went to Australia, and one came to the UK.

When you compare what these people said during their summer holidays, and what they remembered afterwards, the results are enlightening, especially because of what they reveal about how long you should go on holiday for, and the update they suggest for the old peak-end rule.

The most immediately useful truths the experiment showed weren't, in fact, that new. 'Duration neglect', originally discovered back in the 1990s, says that when people recall an experience and think about how much fun it was, or not, they tend to ignore how long it lasted. This idea came through loud and clear in the experiment's data. It didn't matter how long people went away for, whether they went for four days or a fortnight, they still got the same amount of happiness from their holidays.

The experiment also backed another idea that's been explored for some years: that people, even amazing people like you and me, don't remember as accurately as we'd like to think we do. Instead, we dig out a few snapshots from our minds about the time we're trying to recall, and then use those to make up a movie about what happened.

Besides highlighting these insights, the experiment also uncovered some exciting new discoveries. The data showed, for example, that while the peak-end rule works fine for shorter experiences, it doesn't seem to work for longer experiences like holidays. The peak moment, it turns out, isn't that influential when it comes to how people rate their overall experience. The happiness people reported at the peak moment in their holiday was quite different from their overall sense of happiness from the holiday. This makes a lot of sense when you think about it. For shorter experiences, like a night out or a colonoscopy, it's easier for a peak moment to dominate the entire experience. But for a longer experience, like a holiday, while you're sure to remember peak moments like the day you hurtled down a zip-wire or took a boat out, you'll also remember if the rest of the trip didn't hit the same heights all the way through.

The experiment also stumbled upon one other curious idea worth mentioning: that when it comes to the way people look back on an experience, what happens at the beginning is just as influential as any peak moment or what happens at the end.

What to make of all these insights? My take is this: if you design your experiences with the remembering self in mind – and you should – you should probably book shorter, punchier, more exciting holidays than you do now. When four days gives as much happiness as a fortnight, why not?

So, instead of blowing all your holiday allowance on one or two big holidays, you should probably try breaking it up into smaller chunks. Valencia during the Falles festival in March, perhaps, when they make enormous effigies of famous people out of paper, wood and wax, up to five storeys high, and then set them alight? Or a 'me time' long weekend at the clifftop Scarlet Hotel in Cornwall, with nothing but a pile of your favourite books and a view of the Atlantic for company? Or three days of trail running, wild swimming, talks and live music at the Love Trails Festival?

Next, you have to accept the awkward but inescapable fact that, rather than true remembering, we tend to 'remember' by gathering a few mental snapshots and turning them into a movie memory. If you were planning an experience by the old rule, you'd have put extra energy into creating compelling snapshots in two key areas, the peak and the end. But these latest insights suggest you should also aim for great snapshots in three more areas.

First, consider not only the end but also the beginning – because, as Kemp's published paper says, 'Happiness during the first 24-hour period is recalled at least as well as the peak happiness or that from the last 24-hour period.'

Second, think carefully not only about the most obviously memorable experience, but the most unusual one too – because, again, according to Kemp's research, the happiness that people feel on the day they flag as most memorable, and the happiness on the most unusual day, are both useful indicators for the overall happiness they get from the holiday. If those days are full of joy, chances are, the holiday will be too.

And, finally, don't aim only for the one peak experience, but for many peak experiences – because, even if the one peak experience doesn't define your overall happiness that comes from the trip, peak experiences are, by definition, the most memorable and when you're happiest. Why shoot for one, when you could have far more, and raise your general level of joy?

So, while the old peak-end rule has been seen to be useful for shorter experiences, I think it's time for a new rule that incorporates these insights but also reflects the latest science. If you don't like the idea of a rule, think of this as a simple recipe for designing extraordinary experiences. And if you're worried that these ingredients seem too focused on producing great memories for the remembering self, there's no need. They'll create extraordinary experiences for the experiencing self too.

The Essential Ingredients of the New Peak-End Rules 1: The 'Awe New' Curious Peaks

The recipe has, as you'd suspect, three main ingredients: the beginning, the peak and the end. Let's start with the main ingredient. How can you put yourself into more situations where you're likely to have a peak experience? Science has plenty to say on this, but the answer can be summed up in three main ideas: flow, which we looked at in the last chapter, plus awe and new.

Trying out new things, for starters, is key for happiness for all sorts of reasons. Variety, as we noted before, is the 'spice of happiness'. Doing new things helps us get as close as possible to the upper range of happiness available for each of us. New things help people feel more positive, minimise any negative feelings they might have, and the memories they create act like protective assets. Just as homes and bank balances are assets that can protect us in times of need, so memories can too.

Trying out new activities helps us avoid the problem that comes from sticking with the same old things. Because of what psychologists call the 'hedonic treadmill', if you do the same thing over and over you'll stop noticing what's so special about it. Familiarity may lead to boredom. But more than just avoiding the negative, scientists have now identified all sorts of positive magic in the new.

Trying out new things enables us to build 'experiential CVs'. They expand our sense of self, of who we are and what we can do. They release dopamine, which makes us feel good. They stimulate our minds, make us more creative, and strengthen connections in our brains. They give us a chance to exercise one of the defining features of being human too, our innate curiosity.

So we're hard-wired to try out new things. They help with our mental wiring, they give us a thrill in the present, and they set us up for a better, more creative future.

Besides new activities, the other things likely to lead to peak experiences are those that are, literally, awesome. Typical awe-inducing activities range from the spiritual to the simple, from prayer to gazing at the stars to just appreciating nature – especially 'big nature', such as enjoying the view of, or from the top of, a hill, a cliff or the sea. All these give us a sense of the vastness of the universe, and how small our place is within it. Studies show that this does wonders for diminishing the ego and the narrow, small-minded focus that comes with it, and that it opens us up to the zen-like, transcendental experience of realising there's far more here than just ourselves.

The Essential Ingredients of the New Peak-End Rules 2: Befores and Beginnings

What to do with the beginning and the end? For clues, think of the observations about newness and curiosity, and the idea of the experiencing and remembering selves, a few paragraphs back. Remember the shape of flow and the hero's journey a handful of chapters back. And think of our ancient ancestors long ago.

Let's start with the importance of curiosity and newness. The stage of an experience most likely to offer these is the beginning. That's usually your best chance to be open and curious, and feel a sense of wonder and awe. Think of the first time you cycled with the stabilisers off, or the first day of your most recent holiday in a place you'd never been, whether it was Rome, Ronda or Rhossili Bay in Wales. But there's much more than this to the beginning.

The beginning is critical because of the pivotal stage it occupies in any experience. It's useful to think of an experience in three stages, even if so far we've only talked about two of them.

Because as well as the 'during' and the 'after', and the experiencing self and the remembering self, there's also the 'before' and the anticipating self. This 'before' is often overlooked, but it shouldn't be. It gives us anticipation, which is one of the key reasons why experiences are better than material goods at making us happy: because anticipation is free happiness. And this moment, the beginning, is critical, because it's when the fantasy of anticipation is converted into the opportunity of reality. That means that the beginning of an experience is particularly special, not only because your brain is sparked into life as it takes in all the new sights, sounds and sensations, but also because there's an extra spark as your brain compares what you'd hoped and expected and imagined, with what really is.

What does all this tell us about how to plan and design the beginning? In my view, it simply means honour it. Give yourself the time and mental space to enjoy it for the magical time it is. It's the bridge from fantasy to reality, from before to during. Don't build a bridge that's purely functional. Don't rush over it and fall headlong into the experience. As you cross, shift gears a little. Open your eyes and your ears a bit more. As we'll soon see in the next section, there's evidence that if people treat something quite ordinary as special, they get much more from it.

What's also especially interesting about this advice, I think, is that the idea is echoed in the hero's journey. Consider the shape of the hero's journey for a moment – turn to page 53 if you need a reminder – and you'll see that the beginning is also the pivotal moment from fantasy to reality. Look at the top of the diagram, from where it says 'Call to Adventure' to 'Cross the Threshold', and you should be able to see that this is when the hero stops thinking about the adventure, stops refusing the call to adventure, says, 'Yes!' instead, and then crosses the threshold. This is when the adventure shifts from an idea in the hero's mind, to reality on the road of trials.

Again, you might wonder, what does this mean? It means that when you plan and design your own beginnings, you should give yourself a chance to note the importance of this pivotal moment. You're here. Look around. The adventure has started. Breathe it in. This thing you've looked forward to all this time is now. Do this, and you'll appreciate the moment, be more present, and get more out of it.

The Essential Ingredients of the New Peak-End Rules 3: Savouring the End

Now for the final piece in this puzzle: how to plan the end. To approach this, let's turn, once more, to the hero's journey, and go even further back to our distant ancestors. When our hunter-gatherer ancestors were hungry, they would explore. They would go out looking, over the hill, curious to find out what was in the next valley. If they found an area where the trees were heavy with fruit, the bushes ripe with berries, or the game was plentiful, they'd make the most of it. They'd hunt and gather and exploit the riches they'd found. This process has been called, unsurprisingly, 'explore and exploit'.

Fast-forward a few millennia, and we still do it, all of us. We start by exploring a new city, cuisine or group of people. Then, once we've figured out the places, items and people on the menu of life that we like, we order them again. Not always. You never quite stop exploring. But as you learn more about the world out there, and yourself, so you spend less time exploring, and more time exploiting. Both the beginning and the ending should reflect this ancient and sensible idea. To begin, explore. At the end, exploit.

Think of what this idea might mean on a holiday. On the first night, not long after arriving, when the signposts and the weather and the accents are new and exciting, you'll explore, and go for dinner someplace new, order something you've never had before. But by the last night, it's fine to go somewhere you know, eat something you had earlier in the week. This is the time to exploit. Your hero's journey has come full circle, and you've now come back to the old world but with new eyes.

Let's not be too literal about this. I'm not saying the end is necessarily about doing the same things as before. The idea isn't as reductive as that. To see why I'm saying this, think of the hero's journey alongside the shape of flow again – turn to page 202 if you need a reminder. Look closely at these two, and it's clear that the end is a crucial opportunity for reflection, reintegration and recovery. The coming back should be as important as the going in the first place. This is the return, when you, the hero, have been on a road of trials and are now bringing the reward back into the old world, so that it can become new. In terms of a holiday, once again, this is the time to reflect on what you've seen and learned, who you've met, how they've made you think, or not, and how you might bring some of these new learnings and thoughts into your old world – so that when you come home, you don't just fall back into the ruts of your old life, but make your old life new thanks to your new learnings. So, instead of simply saying, 'Explore to begin and exploit at the end,' perhaps a better saying would be, 'Search at the beginning and savour at the end.'

A TRIP TO PARIS, MADE WITH THE KEY INGREDIENTS OF THE NEW PEAK-END RULES

To give you an idea of how these new peak-end rules work in practice, let me give you an example of how I used these insights to plan a trip I went on with my family to Paris – which turned out to be one of our best holidays ever, even though it was only three days long.

I should mention that my kids were four and seven, and we hadn't been on many foreign holidays with them, because of the hassle and stress involved. And my wife and I had been to Paris quite a few times, both for work and for holidays, in the past.

To make the beginning good, we did three things. Got up super early, and arrived early for the Eurostar. Avoiding stress sounds obvious, but it just saves a lot of bother. Next, the kids and I went to the café on the train for some breakfast. They loved walking down the train, bobbing about, bumping into people. They'd never bought snacks at a café on a moving train before, and loved the whole experience. When we arrived at the Gare du Nord, we put our bags in left luggage, and took a cab up to Montmartre, so we'd get a view of the city and have crepes for lunch. Suddenly, my wife and I were both transported to when we'd been there, years before, without children.

I used the other rules too. We had a constant stream of unusual, new and, ultimately, peak experiences. We stayed at a resort called Villages Nature where we got to drive a golf buggy around – parents in front, kids playing at the back. We floated around their great big water park. We slid down huge slides in their forest. We went to Disneyland on our last day. Then, to round it off, after all that searching, we had a picnic on the Eurostar home, talking about all the things we'd done, till the kids fell asleep on our laps. Designing our trip around the new peak-end rules led to much better memories. The kids still talk about it now. And we had a much better time, at the time.

So, to sum up this new recipe for extraordinary experiences, begin with the beginning. Don't rush. Instead, explore and search for flow, newness and awe. Instead of a sole peak, aim for more than one. Look for activities that sound unusual and are likely to be memorable. Finally, plan the end so that it gives you a chance to exploit, savour, recover and return, like a homecoming hero, gracefully.

Follow these 'new peak-end rules' and you'll have a thrilling journey of extraordinary experiences for the anticipating self to look forward to, and the experiencing self to enjoy, and you'll create a stunning set of extraordinary memory snapshots for the remembering self.

But, while it's easy to get excited by the bright lights of the extraordinary, we shouldn't forget the simple magic of the ordinary everyday.

The Extraordinary Magic in the Ordinary Everyday

If you're anything like me, you probably think all these tricks and triggers and on-ramps sound great for launching us, like rockets, out of our ordinary, everyday, distracted lives – and firing us into the heady, intense, focused states of flow. But you're also at least a bit concerned. It all sounds a bit busy and, frankly, tiring, doesn't it?

When I first came across all the evidence about extraordinary experiences, I felt all fizzy and excited. Here was an idea I'd somehow always believed was true, and now, armed with science, I could go out and share it. But I also felt a second, much odder sensation, like I needed to lie down – because of the intense pressure that came with this revelation.

If all this was true, what was I doing just sitting still? If the science said extraordinary experiences are *the* route to happiness, shouldn't I be out there, right now, chasing down wild, extraordinary, experiential-CV-building experiences? No more meeting a friend for a quiet drink. No more lazy nights in, curled up by the fire, reading a book. There was no longer any excuse to spend a weekend pottering about, taking the kids to the pool or the park, or doing a bit of DIY. Stumbling upon this startling truth surely meant I should be living life like my hair was on fire.

And yet, just hanging out, doing nothing in particular, can be fun too, can't it? Nice, normal, non-incredible experiences – like a walk with a friend, a cup of tea with your mum, or going to bed early – feel really worthwhile too. The good news is that, perhaps oddly, as well as pointing to extraordinary experiences as being essential for happiness, the science says ordinary experiences are too.

To have any chance of being happy, so one study found, you have to enjoy ordinary experiences. The best place to find happiness, so another study found, is in little everyday pleasures: a smile from a stranger, a tune you like, a message from a friend, the sunlight through the trees, the feeling of rain on your face, your dog's wagging tail. And rather than spend all your hard-earned cash on one blow-out, extraordinary experience, so some other research says, you'd be better off spending little and often: instead of dinner at a Michelin-starred restaurant once a quarter, choose lunch out with a friend once a fortnight. Or, instead of one big holiday a year, spread the spend over a series of short breaks. Instead of putting all your experience eggs in one big basket, as it were, you're better off spread-betting your time-spend into lots of little-and-often experiences. And then there's another piece of research that suggests that if you think of an ordinary experience – in this case, an average weekend – as if it's something special, you get much more out of it.

So there's a very strong case for ordinary experiences.

Yet, perhaps more important still is the fact that even the most ordinary of experiences can also, as it turns out, lead to the magical, happiness-inducing state of flow.

So, yes, those tricks and triggers and on-ramps *are* great for hauling people like you and me out from our ordinary, distracted lives, and launching us into intense, focused states of flow. But that's all they are. The activities themselves aren't flow. They're just tricks to get you into it.

Remember, it's not *what* you do. It's *how* you do it that really matters.

All you really need, as Csikszentmihalyi's research showed, is to manage your psychic energy and direct your full attention. The flow novice might start by racing up on-ramps, using all the tricks and triggers she can, but the true 'flow pro' is able to find the magic of flow, and the beauty of things, in what Csikszentmihalyi called 'the most humdrum experiences'.

Or, as another psychologist who was interested in peak experiences, Abraham Maslow, put it, 'The sacred is in the ordinary ... it is to be found in one's daily life, in one's neighbors, friends, and family, in one's backyard.'

How to Make Your Life a Masterpiece

So if, as the science clearly shows, ordinary and extraordinary experiences both lead to happiness, what does that mean for people, like you and me, who want to make use of the science to plan, design and have better experiences? How should we decide between ordinary and extraordinary experiences?

I spent a lot of time thinking about this. Then, suddenly, somehow, during an ordinary walk in my local park, an extraordinary idea came to me: chiaroscuro. It would be ideal if, at this point, I could tell you that an elaborate painting by Velázquez or Rubens or Caravaggio had suddenly appeared in my mind. But that didn't happen, because I don't know that much about art, and I only heard the term on a weekend break to Rome a few years back.

My wife and I had taken my mum for her sixtieth birthday. After a long lunch and a hit of espresso, we'd wandered into a gallery.

'Look at this,' I marvelled. 'It's like you can see the candlelight.'

'It's chiaroscuro!' they said at the same time, amazed at my ignorance. To say it out loud, by the way, in case your art education is as backward as mine, you say 'kee-arr-o skoo-roh'.

'It's what?'

'Chiaroscuro!' they repeated, laughing at me.

Chiaroscuro is made out of two Italian words: '*chiaro*', meaning bright or light, and '*oscuro*', meaning obscure or dark. It was a device used by trailblazing artists like Rembrandt and Velázquez to create more realistic, 3D-style paintings. It's a particularly good way to show the light and dark cast by candlelight. Paintings that show the style well are *An Old Man in Red* by Rembrandt, *The Taking of*

Christ by Caravaggio, and *The Matchmaker* by Gerrit van Honthorst. I know that because I looked it up. If you've ever looked at an arty picture of a male or female nude, where they've accentuated their curves through light and shadow, that's chiaroscuro too.

Chiaroscuro, I realised, was the answer to the problem of fitting extraordinary and ordinary experiences into the same life. Trying to have nothing but extraordinary experiences is like slapping nothing but bright colours on a canvas. Contrast is key. What if every day was Christmas Day? If every day was full to the brim with excitement, when would there be time to rest? As we saw in the last chapter, *Intensity*, the intense high of flow requires recovery. Alongside the *chiaro*, we all need some *oscuro*. If you want to see the stars, you need the night sky too.

If you think back to the extraordinary, peak moments of your life, they were probably surrounded by ordinary experiences. Picturing that time I spent in Rishikesh, it's like a handful of shooting stars across a big night sky of ordinary experiences: hunkering down in all my clothes to sleep; wandering the dark, pre-dawn alleyways of Rishikesh on the way to yoga; changing pounds sterling into rupees. But that's OK. Those moments have their place.

So, phew, there's really no need to feel oppressed by the science that says extraordinary experiences are key for happiness. There's no need to feel confused by the science that also says ordinary experiences are essential for a life well lived too.

Because we're now in an even better place to tackle the question: Should you choose ordinary or extraordinary experiences? The answer is you should have both. The right mix, of course, is different for different people. And it changes as you get older. Younger people, according to new research from two psychologists named Amit Bhattacharjee and Cassie Mogilner, prefer the 'excited happiness' that comes from extraordinary experiences that help them define who they are, and build their 'experiential CV', like jumping out of a plane. As people age, they enjoy 'calm happiness' more, the sort that comes from ordinary experiences, like dinner with a friend.

Whatever the mix that's right for you, this insight, that both ordinary and extraordinary experiences lead to happiness, is really useful, because, if you can see that your next month is full of everyday experiences, then you can throw some extraordinary ones into the mix. And if it's chock-full with wild experiences, sprinkle in a few lower-key ones. You'll soon discover the mix that works for you.

As well as using the new peak-end rules to plan extraordinary experiences, remember to include ordinary experiences too. And make a conscious note to treat them as special. You'll get more out of them, and then even everyday experiences will feel extraordinary.

How to use the new peak-end rules

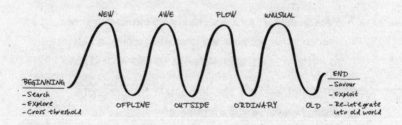

Extraordinary Summary

1. We do not have perfect memories.

2. Instead, we remember through 'snapshots'.

3. Rather than reflecting typical moments, those snapshots tend to be what happens at the beginning, the end and the extreme moments: the peaks and the troughs.

4. This means that an experience can look and feel very different to us as we live through it, and when we remember it. This is called the difference between the 'experiencing self' and the 'remembering self'.

5. We can use these insights to improve the design of our experiences.

6. We can consider the impact of the beginning and the end. The beginning is a time to search. The end is a time to savour.

7. We can design more peak moments by planning more elements that are new and unusual, that give us a chance to feel awe, and that challenge us so that we find flow.

8. For happiness, it is also important to appreciate ordinary, everyday experiences.

9. It's possible to design experiences that take both the experiencing and remembering selves into account, and that create the right chiaroscuro balance of extraordinary and ordinary moments. The 'new peak-end rules' make it easier to achieve this.

_____

How to Make Your Experiences and Your Life
EXTRAORDINARY

As before, the questions in *Past Times* are about specific experiences from your past. The questions in *The Way to Happy Days* will help you think about your life in general. Both will help you live a more extraordinary life.

_____

Past Times: How Extraordinary Was That
Experience?

Think about an experience you had in the past, like what you did last weekend or last holiday. Try this using experiences that were really good, ones that were just average, and ones that were downright awful. Then, ask yourself these questions, giving an answer on a scale of 0 to 5, where:

>   0 = *Not at all*
>   1 = *Very little*
>   2 = *A little*
>   3 = *Some*
>   4 = *A lot*
>   5 = *A great deal*

For this chapter, we'll consider two types of experiences: extraordinary, and then ordinary.

First, thinking about *extraordinary* experiences …

1. How much would you say [insert experience here] was new or unusual?

2. To what extent was it memorable? Did you think at the time, 'Well, we're never going to forget this'?

3. To what extent was there an 'Aha!' moment of realisation or a 'Wow!' moment of surprise?

4. Did you feel awe at any point – a sense of something else, something more than you, something that wasn't you – the vastness of a mountain, the sea, the universe, of a timescale that wasn't yours, or a space that wasn't you? And, if you did, how much awe did you feel?

5. To what extent did you explore or search at the beginning?

6. How much did you exploit or savour at the end?

7. At the beginning, how much of an added sense of freshness did you notice?

   This makes me think of the thrill of seeing the sunset and moonrise, staying up till after the sun's up, seeing dewdrops on a spider's web, the feeling of a different air temperature when the plane doors open, noticing how the fonts and signs are different in a new city, my kids revelling in climbing or reading or ball skills they've just learned. But, for you, fresh beginnings might mean something entirely different.

8. To what extent, during the experience, were you curious? Did the experience pique your curiosity?

Now, thinking about *ordinary* experiences …

1. To what extent was it perfectly ordinary, but still in some way meaningful? To what extent was it everyday but worthwhile?

2. To what extent did it give you 'calm happiness' rather than 'excited happiness'?

3. During the experience, how much of the 'the sacred' did you see in 'the ordinary'?

4. How much would you say this plays an important part in creating your 'stars against the night sky', chiaroscuro life?

Whether this is for extraordinary or ordinary experiences, if your answers are mostly 4s and 5s, this was a great, worthwhile experience. If mostly 3s or less, consider the questions below, and see if you can increase the extraordinary factor, and the meaning, in your experiences.

———————

The Way to Happy Days: How to Have More Worthwhile Experiences, and Live a Life That's Extraordinary

Use these questions to think about how you can increase the number and quality of extraordinary moments in your life.

1. How can you design a beginning so that it's a brilliant bridge, enchanting tunnel or elevating lift – that takes you from *here* and puts you *there*?

   The journey can be as simple as a plane or a boat ride, or it can be a literal tunnel or lift. Think of the lift ride for the restaurant Duck and Waffle in London, for instance. And the creative geniuses at Bompas & Parr and Secret Cinema do a great job of this.

2. How can you make it more likely that something extraordinary will happen?

3. How can you design your experience so that it excites your anticipating, experiencing and remembering selves?

4. Are you doing enough new things? Do you often encounter people you don't know, places you don't usually go, and things you don't do at times you're not used to? If not, how could you get a little more of those in your life?

   When, for instance, people go on a Cities at Dawn class with photographer Anthony Epes, besides the lesson in photography, it gives them a chance to see something they usually see but at a completely different time, so in an utterly different way.

5. How can you plan more peaks into your experiences?

6. Do you notice enough of the sacred in the ordinary? How much magic do you see in your daily life, your neighbours, your friends and family, and in your back yard?

SOMETHING FOR THE WEEKEND

Here's a handful of ideas you can use to deliberately bring some extraordinary and ordinary moments into your weekend. On the following page, write down three ideas of your own.

1. Go wing-walking

It's the most extraordinary thing I've ever done. Or, if standing on the wing of a biplane as it soars and falls through the air doesn't appeal to you, how about being in the cockpit and flying a small plane? Lessons aren't much more than £100.

2. Do something that's really nothing fancy

Do one of the things you do most often and enjoy the most. And notice how much you enjoy it.

3. Have a cup of tea

Cups of tea count twice: they're both ordinary and, if you give them the right ritual, they can be extraordinary too.

4. Be bigger than yourself

Look, listen, touch, and wonder at nature: hug a tree, look at a landscape, admire the moon and the clouds and the stars, and see if you don't get a sense of awe at how big and really beautiful it all is.

5. Have Saturday lunch with family and friends

7

STATUS & SIGNIFICANCE

I'd Like to Thank the Academy ... Wouldn't I?

*'The only reasonable goal in life is maximizing your
total lifetime experience of something called happiness.
That might sound selfish, but it's not. Only a sociopath or a
hermit can find happiness through extreme selfishness.
A normal person needs to treat others well in order to
enjoy life. For the sake of argument, let's assume
you're normal (ish).'*

SCOTT ADAMS

On 7 March 2010, at 6801 Hollywood Boulevard, in Hollywood, California, the Kodak Theater felt, for many of the 3,000 or so people in the audience that night, like the centre of the universe. The auditorium was packed with glittering stars and bright TV lights. The men were dressed in black tuxedos, black bow-ties and white shirts, the women in designer jewellery and red-carpet dresses. Around the planet, more than 60 million people in 225 countries were watching too, all eager to see who'd won at the 82nd Academy Awards.

On stage, Robin Williams opened an envelope, and read out the name of the winner of Best Supporting Actress. The room burst into applause. An actress and comedienne by the name of Monique Hicks, known professionally as Mo'Nique, closed her big brown eyes. She didn't look happy. She looked shocked, like someone who's just found out her car has been towed and is wondering how the hell she's going to pay for it. Then, she slowly opened her eyes, stood up, turned to her husband, Sidney, kissed him momentarily on the lips, stepped into the aisle and, in a blue velvet wraparound dress, and with white gardenias in her hair, made her way to the stage.

There, clutching the golden statue Robin Williams had just given her, she still looked like she couldn't believe this was happening.

'First,' she said, her voice breaking with emotion, 'I would like to thank the Academy ...'

As Mo'Nique said those words, she upheld one of the dearest traditions in Oscar acceptance speeches. When it comes to being thanked, the Academy wins hands down, beating God and even Meryl Streep, who's thanked twice as often as God, by some distance.

When Penélope Cruz won an Oscar in 2009, she wanted to thank the Academy. So too, that year, did Sean Penn, as did Anne Hathaway, Jeff Bridges, Colin Firth, Renée Zellweger, Jim Broadbent, Denzel Washington, Daniel Day-Lewis, Natalie Portman, Jennifer Hudson and Jennifer Lawrence when they won theirs.

They're professional actors, and I'm a mighty cynic. But, hand on heart, I suspect every single one of them meant it, too. Because, forget the news coverage and the uptick in their commercial value that comes from winning, this really is their dream come true. Why not thank the people who voted for them?

The funny thing is, if they really knew what the Academy had just done for them, I think they'd well up even more. There'd be even more 'I'd like to thank the Academy's, and it would beat God for gratitude by an even wider margin.

In a curious way, you see, the Academy is playing God. Whether its members realise it or not, when they give an actor or actress an Oscar, they also give them the sort of thing that only deities usually have the power to bestow – according to a fascinating and controversial piece of research.

This was led by a physician and researcher trained at the universities of Stanford and Toronto named Donald Redelmeier. Redelmeier was once described by the *New York Times* as someone who has 'applied scientific rigor to topics that in lesser hands might have been dismissed as quirky and iconoclastic' and 'perhaps the leading debunker of preconceived notions in the medical world'. He was one of the psychologists responsible for the colonoscopy study that we thought about (but not for too long) in the last chapter, *Extraordinary*. The idea for this piece of research came to him when he was watching an Oscar ceremony one night on television.

'I was amazed how those on stage seemed so vivacious, energetic and exuberant,' he says now. 'Each person didn't look anything like the patients I see in clinic, and the differences appeared more than skin deep.'

'The most iconic example is maybe Jack Palance when he won an Oscar for Best Supporting Actor in 1992,' he adds. 'He was aged seventy-three years then. And he celebrated by doing one-handed push-ups.'

So an idea for a piece of research was born: did the boost to self-esteem from winning an Oscar have a profound effect on people's well-being?

To find out, Redelmeier and a colleague called Sheldon Singh looked at every year the Oscars had been handed out, and compared the longevity of three groups: Oscar winners, Oscar nominees and groups of similar actors.

To do this, they began by identifying all actors and actresses ever nominated for an Academy Award in a leading or supporting role. There were 762 at the time they conducted the research. Then, they identified another cast member of the same sex who was in the same film and was born in the same era.

For example, Jack Nicholson was classified as a winner because he had three wins. Richard Burton was a nominee because he was nominated seven times but never won. And Lorne Greene, who older readers may remember as a star of the 1970s sci-fi TV show *Battlestar Galactica*, was a control because he was never nominated.

The results were startling. When you first hear them, your reaction is likely to be similar to someone who's just won an Oscar. Maybe your mouth will fall open in amazement, maybe you'll just close your eyes and let it sink in for moment, as Mo'Nique did when Robin Williams read her name out.

Without further ado, then, I'll open the envelope and read out the result: if you win an Oscar, whether it's for Best Actor or Actress or Best Supporting Actor or Actress, you'll live four years longer.

So if you ever win an Oscar, be sure to give thanks to the Academy. And if you're reading this, Denzel, Renée, Anne and Mo'Nique, next time you win, do think about how best to say your thanks to the Academy. Because people who've won more than one Oscar live even longer, an extra six years compared to normal actors.

Or, then again, maybe you don't need to. A few years after Redelmeier and Singh had published their paper, some other scientists analysed the data they'd collected, and decided they'd read it wrong. They said they'd made a mistake called 'selection bias' and that they'd considered the Oscar winners' whole lives, when they should really have only considered the years *after* the actors and actresses had won their Oscars. That's when the Oscar would have an impact, they argued. And when they ran the numbers based on the year the Oscar was won, the Oscar winners only lived about a year longer, which is insignificant in scientific terms.

Still, I've been in touch with Redelmeier, and he stands by the research. He agrees that the Oscar would only have an effect after a person wins, but points out that it's simply an unarguable and observed fact that Oscar winners live four years longer than normal actors.

To me, it isn't all that important whether winning an Oscar gives people one or four or six or any number of years' extra life – since the chances of you and me winning an Oscar this year, next year, or any year aren't that high. What is interesting, and important for you and me, is how this story illustrates a scientific discovery that no one likes to talk about but everybody should – because it impacts the health and happiness of every single one of us.

The Curious Case of the Status Syndrome

To find the origins of this discovery, we need to go back in time, way back, so long ago that Daniel Day-Lewis hadn't even won the first of his three Oscars, for *My Left Foot* in 1989. We need to go back further, to a time before mobile phones and personal computers, to the 1970s, when men wore jackets with wide ties, wide lapels and wide-collared shirts, when women worked in typing pools, and when everybody smoked in the office.

Because it was back then that a researcher by the name of Michael Marmot – now *Sir* Michael Marmot, though this was decades before he would be knighted for his services to public health – first published data from a study on the British civil service that would take almost thirty years of his life, and lead to a startling new understanding of the importance of status on stress, health, happiness and longevity.

There is a far greater chance that you are a civil servant than an actor. There's about a one in two hundred chance if you're British. But that still means you're probably, like me, not a civil servant, so you may still be wondering what all this has to do with us.

It's this: whether we like it or not, all human societies are organised into hierarchies. Even societies that say they don't want hierarchy and try to remove all trace of it fail. This idea was best expressed by some writing on the farmyard wall in George Orwell's *Animal Farm*: 'All animals are equal but some animals are more equal than others.'

The society we live in today is far more fluid than it has been for centuries, but we all sit on some rung or other of the status ladder: from shop assistant to shop manager, from teacher to headmistress, from cabin crew to captain. And the British civil service has a fixed, stratified hierarchy. People join at a certain grade and rise through the ranks. Each step up the ladder has more responsibility and higher pay. This makes the British civil service the perfect place to study the effects of hierarchy and status on people's health.

You might hear, at this point, an echo of Jerry Morris's pioneering work on bus drivers and bus conductors and postal workers. That makes sense, since Marmot was a close friend of Morris's, and he used similar methods.

I said that the results of the Whitehall study were startling, but perhaps that was a stretch. Because nowadays we all know that stress kills. We know that the fight-or-flight mode that kept our ancestors alive on the plains of Africa is useful in short bursts. It helped them escape lions. It helps us escape muggers and catch the bus and get our kids to school on time. But we also know that if we remain in fight-or-flight mode for extended periods, like a torch left on too long, we'll burn out. Our immunity will fall. We'll be more likely to catch diseases. We'll be more likely, even, to die at an earlier age.

And we also all know that those higher up the food chain carry more on their shoulders, and pay the price for their superior position and money by suffering the effects of more stress.

But this is where Marmot's research was startling. Because, as he and his team discovered, this part of the folk-wisdom simply isn't true. In fact, it's the exact opposite. The truth is that – as Marmot has written about in scientific papers and his book *Status Syndrome*, and as he has explained in person to the Director-General of the World Health Organization, who convened a meeting of his highest advisors to hear Marmot speak on this – there is what Marmot calls a 'social gradient to health'. The lower down the ladder you are, the more likely you are to catch diseases and die earlier. The higher up the ladder you are, the longer you live. And if that wasn't unfair enough, status also has a substantial impact on happiness. The higher up you sit on the social ladder, the happier you are.

When I think about that, there's a question that automatically springs to my mind: how can I learn from this in order to be happier, live longer, and pass on that information to my family, friends and you? Or, to put it more bluntly, how can you and I get more status?

Did you squirm when you read that? If you did, you're not alone.

What's Wrong with Status?

A funny thing happens when I'm giving a talk to a group of people and I ask them about the status-oriented game of 'keeping up with the Joneses'.

'Who here,' I say, 'knows someone who keeps up with the Joneses?'

Hands shoot up. Almost everyone raises a hand. They smile too, picturing their more annoying neighbours, work colleagues, old friends.

'Great, so who here plays the game too?' I ask. 'Who here keeps up with the Joneses?'

Then there's always a pause, some puzzled looks. Some close their eyes the way Mo'Nique did. I know what they're thinking. It's what's running through your mind right now. Either you're thinking, 'No way, not me!' because, of course, *you* don't. Or, you're secretly admitting it, maybe you're even smiling, but there's still no way you'd admit it out loud, not even to your partner.

A few hands tentatively go up. Then someone, usually a person who's sitting at the edge of the room and has been looking thoughtful for a while, gets it, puts their hand up too, and says, 'We all do, we just do it in different ways.'

'Exactly,' I say, happy someone's got the point.

This puzzles me. If status is such an obvious good, why are so many of us so awkward about it?

We know eating vegetables is good for us, and so there are government campaigns to encourage us to eat more vegetables, and we encourage our kids to eat more too. People proudly say, 'I've been eating more vegetables recently.'

We know getting exercise is good for us, so we go to gyms, and run, and cycle, and buy Lululemon leggings and Rapha cycling tops and super-expensive trainers in luminous day-glo colours, so no one can possibly miss that we take exercise seriously. And we're more than happy to talk about how much exercise we're getting.

But, even though the science clearly says more status is good for us too, while we're happy to show our status, we'd never, ever talk about it.

It's high time, I think, for us to get over this awkwardness. If we care about happiness, health and longevity – our own, our children's, our families' and our friends' – we really need to have an open conversation about what it is, and how to get more of it.

In his research, Marmot identified the principal ways to achieve status. These follow the folk-wisdom, more or less. It's the usual suspects: power, money and education. The social gradient of health, in fact, follows a person's level of education more closely than all of the others. Someone with a PhD, so the research shows, is likely to live longer than someone with a Master's degree. Someone with a Master's will likely live longer than someone with an ordinary degree. Someone with a degree will live longer than someone who leaves school at eighteen. And someone who completes sixth form will live longer than someone who leaves at sixteen.

If we want to know how to get more status, and the benefits it brings, it'll be helpful to also understand why higher status leads to better health, longer lives and greater happiness.

This is best explained by an idea put forward by an economist at the University of Cambridge named Amartya Sen. Sen says that for people to flourish, they need three things: control, capabilities and social participation. It's easy to see how higher status increases all three of these. Higher status – and the higher education, more money and power that come with it – will give you more control, and a greater sense of control, over what you do. It'll give you wider choice about what you do, and more opportunities to do new things. It'll provide more chances to get involved with your peers, other people and the wider community.

So, what do these insights suggest about the sort of experiences you should have, and how you should plan your experiences? I asked Marmot for his advice, and didn't get very far. His take goes something like this: First, you get the education. Then the money and power follow. That, in turn, results in higher status and provides you with a certain set of experiences.

'I don't think people do things because it gives them status,' he explained to me once. 'It's status that gives them the opportunity to do rewarding, interesting things.'

So, in Marmot's view, status is primary. It defines the experiences you have. This makes sense. If you're well-educated, wealthy and powerful, you're more likely to have high-status experiences like attend the opera, go to Singapore to see the Formula One race, and holiday in Barbados. It's also a useful way to think about societies.

But what does this mean for the individual? Where does that leave the person who now knows that higher status means more happiness, health and a longer life? Does that mean you and I have to go back to education, or simply get a higher-paying job and earn more, in order to enable the most rewarding, meaningful experiences?

I don't think so. Sure, those things clearly make a big difference. But I think it can work the other way around too. As well as higher status leading to certain types of experiences, I think certain types of experiences can lead to higher status. With a little creative thinking, it's possible to think about what those experiences look like.

This isn't about being a snob. This isn't about looking down your nose at someone who, for a weekend away, takes the bus to Bournemouth while you're taking the train to Champagne. I'm not suggesting you start looking down on the simpler things in life and experiences that have lower status, or that you start only going to the latest, high-status, fancy restaurants. As I wrote in my last book, *Stuffocation*, one of the reasons why experiences are better than material things at making us happy, and one of the reasons why I believe experientialism will likely lead to an all-round happier society, is because experiences are harder to compare, so they bring less of the downside of social comparison. But if status matters so much, for happiness, health and longevity, I think it's at least worth trying to figure out ways to choose experiences that lead to more status.

FIVE ROUTES TO HIGHER STATUS

Here are five ways you can climb the social hierarchy. These aren't instant 'status makeovers'. Actually, even the idea of an immediate improvement in status sounds wrong, like putting a Ferrari body on a Fiesta engine, or like dressing mutton up as lamb. The effects of these won't be instant, but they'll put you on the path to higher status.

1. EDUCATION, EDUCATION, EDUCATION

Since level of education is clearly so important, you should stay in school as long as possible, and reach as high a level as you can. But this isn't only about formal education. Every skill you learn may not quite double your chances of success, as Dilbert cartoonist Scott Adams suggests in his book *How to Fail at Almost Everything and Still Win Big*. But everything you learn will expand your capabilities, put you more in control, and also increase the amount of good fortune that comes your way – because the more you know, the more likely you'll understand how to take advantage of any opportunities that come along.

2. GET INVOLVED, TAKE CONTROL

Did you notice how Amartya Sen's three keys to flourishing reflect some of the other chapters of this book? Control is the autonomy we talked about in the *Transformation* chapter. You could find the experience of control in taking on tough challenges that give you an opportunity to get hold of a difficult situation: from agreeing to a demanding task at work, to conquering a climbing wall.

Social participation is the opposite of social isolation, as seen in the *Relationships* chapter. The type of social participation that most directly leads to status, as Marmot mentions, comes from joining committees, at work, in your profession, at your child's school, in your local community. So, if you're not already part of a committee, see what's around and whether you can join. Capabilities is trying new activities and learning new skills, which we looked at in the *Extraordinary* chapter, and in education just now. So, while you aim for those, you'll be more likely to get all the benefits of status.

3. GET A STORY, GO ON A JOURNEY

The definition of status is evolving. To begin with, of course, when compared with material goods, experiences give far more status than they used to. Any experience will add to yours. But, of course, as suggested in the *Story* chapter, those that give you interesting stories to tell carry extra weight. And what's new also carries cachet. So, there's no harm knowing a little of the trends in experiences and trying out some of the more innovative ideas. Instead of just going to the theatre, try immersive theatre, like that organised by Punchdrunk. Instead of just watching a movie, have an immersive cinema experience, perhaps with Secret Cinema. Rather than just go out for dinner at a restaurant, eat at a pop-up. Instead of taking a 'fly and flop' holiday, take a 'find and seek' or 'go and become' trip instead: perhaps some sort of journey, a transformative experience like those recommended by an organisation named the Transformational Travel Council, where you change your perspective and discover something about yourself and your capabilities.

4. GET FIT

Status is also increasingly equated with physical health. If you spend more time on experiences that are physically challenging, like marathons or Tough Guy-type mud races, or anything you could reasonably call an expedition or adventure – even if they're the sort of short, sweet, fairly local 'micro-adventures' that British explorer Alastair Humphreys talks about – you'll not only have more stories, you'll also step up the status ladder.

5. TURN THE TV OFF

This is inspired by an insight Marmot shared with me. 'Looking at our data, the only thing that went up as you went down the status hierarchy,' he said, 'was the amount of TV people watched. Everything else went up as you went up the hierarchy. TV is a last resort, when you have nothing else in life, that's what you do.' So, the obvious advice from this is simple: to have more status, watch less TV and, as they used to say on the old TV show *Why Don't You?* go out and do something less boring instead.

Interestingly, Marmot's insight reflects the lack of flow that comes from watching much of today's TV. As

> Csikszentmihalyi wrote, 'The plots and characters of the popular shows are so repetitive that although watching TV requires the processing of visual images, very little in the way of memory, thinking, or volition is required. Not surprisingly, people report some of the lowest levels of concentration, use of skills, clarity of thought, and feelings of potency when watching television.'

If you're still feeling profoundly awkward about seeking experiences that deliver status, there's one more suggestion that I believe will not only convince you, it'll also inspire you.

The best way to bring this to life is through a story. It's a story that rescues the concept of status from the unmentionable cellar of shame it's hidden in today, and puts this essential ingredient for a healthy, happy, long life firmly where it should be – on a proud, public pedestal. It's the rags-to-riches tale of the world's first female self-made millionaire.

From a Wooden Shack to the White House: The World's First Female Self-Made Millionaire

When people talk about slavery, they often use phrases like 'unimaginable horror'. And that's partly true. As we sit pretty and rich and well fed and centrally heated and mostly free, how can we possibly imagine the physical brutality and mental cruelty that slaves endured?

The film *12 Years a Slave* is horrific, and also amazing – as it helps us, in a small way, for a few hours, from the comfort of our twenty-first-century lives, to imagine the twenty-four-hours-a-day, seven-days-a-week, lifelong terror of being a slave.

The thing that stays with me most from the film – beyond the whippings, the beatings and the rapes – is the idea of ownership. If you're a slave, you're not recognised as a human. You're a possession. You're owned, like a belt or a teacup or a mobile phone. If your owner wants, they can throw you on the ground, smash you to pieces. They can upgrade to a better version.

Perhaps even worse than all that is if, as a slave, you have children. Because while you are doing the most magical thing possible, creating life, you are also doing the worst possible thing imaginable. You are imprisoning your child into a short, hard life of humiliation, punishment and horror.

12 Years a Slave was based on the book of the same name published in 1853. A few years before, the US census of 1850 records a man named Robert W. Burney, whose possessions included two slaves named Oscar and Minerva.

Oscar and Minerva's first five children were born as Burney's possessions too, on his cotton plantation named Grand View. Grand View was wishful thinking. The plantation was in a floodplain, on a stubby finger of land surrounded on three sides by the muddy, meandering Mississippi River.

Some years later, in 1863, the US president Abraham Lincoln made the Emancipation Proclamation, setting millions of slaves free. But while that made Minerva and Oscar and their children free from ownership, they weren't free from hardship. There was no easy-to-follow, yellow brick road to prosperity. They continued to live on Burney's plantation, eking out an existence by growing cotton on a small patch of the plantation.

In 1867, the river kept breaking through the levees, flooding their land, washing all their cotton plants away in waves of muddy water. After the water subsided, the rains failed and a drought came. So the cotton crop was terrible and then, to add insult to dreadful harvest, the price of cotton dropped.

But at the tail end of that tough year, something shiny and wonderful and full of hope happened. Minerva gave birth to a healthy baby girl, her and Oscar's first child born into freedom. If only they'd known then that this girl of theirs, born in the mud of a cotton plantation, would become a millionaire. But that was many years later, and they would be long dead.

Sarah was an orphan by the age of seven. She was married at fourteen, and widowed at twenty. By the age of thirty-seven, she'd risen from picking cotton in the hot, muddy fields of Louisiana to washing dirt out of clothes for $1.50 a day in Missouri. Then, if things weren't tough enough already, her hair started to fall out.

Sarah saw that many other black women had similar problems. Poor diet, stress, and soaps for washing clothes containing an ingredient that burns skin called lye, were causing many African-American women at the time to suffer scalp problems and baldness. So Sarah became an agent for a company that made haircare products for African-Americans, and started selling their Wonderful Hair Grower product. Seeing the market potential, Sarah decided to create her own hair products. The recipe, she would later say, came to her in a dream.

'A big black man appeared to me,' Sarah claimed, 'and told me what to mix up for my hair.'

Whatever the true source of Sarah's recipe – though who am I to doubt her? The mind moves in mysterious ways, after all – it worked.

'In a few weeks my hair was coming in faster than it had ever fallen out,' she said.

That certainly seems to have been true. In photos, Sarah always appeared with a very full head of hair. And, by the way, she is never named as 'Sarah'. In a canny move that reflected the business acumen that lay dormant till she started selling haircare products, she was always known by the name of her third husband, Charles Joseph Walker. Because she'd noticed the success of beauty products that came from France, Sarah adopted a French affectation. And so, a businesswoman and a brand was born: Mme C. J. Walker.

The new Mme C. J. Walker sold the products herself, door to door. And with the help of her husband, Charles, she created compelling newspaper ads and placed them in new newspapers read by the black community. In time, Walker's company grew strong and healthy, like her hair. She built factories. She grew her workforce to more than 20,000. She became a successful, prominent businesswoman. In Irvington-on-Hudson, where two of America's richest men, Jay Gould and John D. Rockefeller, also lived, she built an impressive house. By the time of her death in 1919, she was important enough for the *New York Times* to report on her passing, and on her fortune of around $1 million, in an obituary titled, 'Wealthiest Negress Dead'.

Think how far Sarah had come, from the nameless shack on the banks of the muddy Mississippi, to operating the Mme C. J. Walker business, and building a three-storey home named Villa Lewaro, in a tony neighbourhood on the Hudson River near New York City. Think how proud her parents, Minerva and Oscar, would have been.

The Right and the Wrong Sort of Status: Lessons from Two Self-Made Billionaires

Minecraft, in case you've never played it or heard of it, is a video game, and a curious one. It's what's known in the business as a 'sandbox' game. The term comes from how children play in a sandbox. Instead of a traditional video game, like a shoot-'em-up or a racing game, there are no rules, and no way to win. All *Minecraft* players have the same basic playing capabilities. They can pick up stones, dirt and tree trunks, and then put them somewhere else in a 3D grid that goes on forever. But what they then do with these abilities is entirely up to them. Many explore the *Minecraft* world's different areas, its jungles, caves, deserts and forests. Some create buildings, towns, even whole civilisations. Some like to fight the *Minecraft* monsters, like zombies, spiders and skeletons. Others prefer to wander about finding other players to fight.

If that all sounds pretty geeky, you should also know that Minecraft has really simple, blocky, clunky graphics. So it looks, to people like me who don't play video games, like a game for nerds. And yet my niece Honey, who is thirteen now, and doesn't seem geeky at all, spends as many hours a day playing *Minecraft* as her parents will let her. So do quite a few other people. More than 144 million copies of the game have been sold. It's the second-best-selling video game of all time, behind only *Tetris*. There's now even a big-budget Hollywood *Minecraft* movie in production.

Minecraft was started by a Swedish man by the name of Markus Persson. When Persson sold *Minecraft* to Microsoft for $2.5 billion in 2014, he became, overnight, extraordinarily rich. He was on the cover of *Fortune* magazine. He started to live the sort of life a playboy billionaire is supposed to lead. He spent $70 million on a 23,000-square-foot mansion in Beverly Hills. He outbid Beyoncé and Jay-Z to buy it. It has a sixteen-car garage, a giant wine cellar, a home gym, an infinity pool with views of Los Angeles, and a wall of sweet dispensers that would make even the biggest sweet shops sick with envy. Naturally, he's been hosting wild parties there surrounded by beautiful, young and famous people ever since. He also parties in Las Vegas, Ibiza and Stockholm, where he owns the city's two most expensive apartments. He flies around the world by Learjet, or in British Airways' First Class. His status, it's reasonable to observe, has soared to stratospheric levels.

But, as he admitted in a series of tweets posted not long after selling *Minecraft*, all that success and status wasn't making him happy.

'The problem with getting everything,' Persson wrote in one tweet, 'is you run out of reasons to keep trying, and human interaction becomes impossible due to imbalance.'

In another: 'Hanging out in Ibiza with a bunch of friends and partying with famous people, able to do whatever I want, and I've never felt more isolated.'

Another: 'In Sweden, I will sit around and wait for my friends with jobs and families to have time to do shit, watching my reflection in the monitor.'

And another: 'Found a great girl, but she's afraid of me and my lifestyle and went with a normal person instead.'

Persson did marry, by the way, at one point after his riches came in, but was divorced within a year. His story, to me, sounds like a real-life, modern folk tale about the perils of excessive success, and the status that comes with it.

Compare Persson's tale with Mme C. J. Walker's. Because their stories, I think, reveal a fascinating truth: that there is a right and a wrong way to approach and enjoy status.

Status, at its core, is about being somebody who matters. You've achieved success in your field. Through luck or talent or hard work or all three, you are, or have become, someone who is recognised. But status can be empty, cold even. It's empty when it comes from the sort of success that's self-oriented, egotistic and singular. It's empty when the success is about you and for you. This sort of empty status rises you up high, yet leaves you somehow low and disconnected from others.

The solution to this problem, I think, and the way to convert success from one that's empty and lacking in meaning to one that's full and meaningful, is to upgrade from the idea of *status* to the concept of *significance*.

Significance is a type of success that isn't only about you. You are at the heart of it, yet your aim is not to achieve this only for yourself, but for others too. Significance is a form of success that is self- *and* other-oriented. It's egotistic *and* altruistic. It's plural, warm, human. Significant success is intimately connected to other people, and it connects you to other people.

If you have status, your success may well be only about you, and perhaps your immediate circle. But if you are significant, your success is our success.

This idea of significance has been present in the earliest discussions of how people should live. In Aristotle's discussion of ethics, for instance, almost two-and-a-half thousand years ago, he decided that one of the traits of the 'good man' is that he will display 'magnificence', by spending large amounts of his wealth on the city where he lives.

This idea of significance runs through the rags-to-riches story of Mme C. J. Walker. In her rise, from the ex-slaves' hut to her grand villa, she is a practical example of how we can rescue the concept of status from something embarrassing and awkward, to something we can be proud of, and be proud of wanting.

Because Walker not only used her riches for herself. As her life advanced and she achieved success, she brought others along with her. She paid the twenty thousand black women who worked for her handsomely. At a time when an unskilled white man would earn around $11 per week, her agents, all female, earned between $5 and $15 per day. One woman, who had previously earned $5 a week as a servant, earned $250 a week selling her products. To build Villa Lewaro,

Walker used one of New York's first registered black architects, Vertner Tandy.

Walker also cared about good causes and gave money to them. She used her position to make the country better for all black people – and so, of course, for all people. She helped lead a protest against lynching. She travelled to the White House with other black leaders to present a petition to Woodrow Wilson. She donated $1,000 to build a YMCA in Indianapolis. She gave $5,000 to the National Association for the Advancement of Colored People's anti-lynching fund: at the time, the largest single donation ever. She spent $10,000 a year on the education of young African-Americans. She paid for six young people to go to Tuskegee University, which was established to educate African-Americans.

Walker encouraged her employees to do good too. At a gathering of her staff in 1917, she awarded prizes not only to those who had sold the most, but to those who contributed the most to society.

When you hear all this, it's easy to see why Mme C. J. Walker is such a heroine and inspiration. She began a tradition that's inspired African-American women ever since.

Earlier, I only shared the first part of what Mo'Nique said when she thanked the Academy. I didn't mention what those white gardenias she was wearing in her hair meant. They were a reference to Hattie McDaniel. McDaniel was the first black actress to win an Academy Award, for her role as Mammy in *Gone with the Wind*. She wore gardenias in her hair when she accepted her award in 1940. Mo'Nique mentioned McDaniel in her acceptance speech too, and she also thanked America's first female self-made billionaire.

This woman's story is another rags-to-riches tale of success and significance. At one stage, she was so poor she wore overalls made from potato sacks, and the local children called her 'Sack Girl'. Sack Girl is better known today by her first name, Oprah. Oprah Winfrey is well known not only for her incredible success, but for the way she brings people along with her. Winfrey once took her staff and their families – 1,065 people in all – to Hawaii for a holiday. She has donated more than $400 million to schools and colleges. That includes more than 400 scholarships for students to study at Morehouse College, a college for African-American men in Georgia, and a school in South Africa called the Oprah Winfrey Leadership Academy for Girls.

Just as Mme C. J. Walker inspired others in the early part of the twentieth century, so Oprah Winfrey inspires people today. When Halle Berry won an Oscar in 2002, like Mo'Nique, she also thanked Winfrey, calling her 'the best role model any girl can have'. But I think Winfrey and Walker are more than just that. I think they show us all that there is a right way to approach status.

Status needn't be self-centred, awkward and embarrassing to want. It can be much more positive. When it's driven by ambition for others as well as ourselves, when it's altruistic as well as egotistic, when it's not about me but about us – that's when instead of disconnecting you from others, it connects you to others, and that's when status becomes not only something you can think about privately, but something you can talk about in public.

This sort of success is not about getting and *having*, it's more about getting and *giving*. This is the sort of success that leads not only to status, but also to its smarter, nicer, more attractive upgrade of a cousin: significance.

As it turns out, as scientists have now proved, seeking significance is not only a smart way to make meaningful, practical, inspiring sense of status, it's also one of the surest routes to genuine, lasting happiness.

Your Mum Was Right: It Is Better to Give

Growing up, every time there was a birthday approaching, or it was near Christmas, my mum would always tell my brother, Rob, and me, 'It's better to give than receive.' We didn't believe her for a minute.

How on earth could giving a calendar to Nana and Grandad, or a pair of socks to Dad, compare with receiving *Star Wars* toys or a BMX? I still have my Millennium Falcon, and I remember the Christmas Day that Rob and I rode out on our shiny new BMXs: him on a black-and-gold Ultra Burner, and me on a yellow-and-blue Mag Burner.

But it turns out that, as a pair of psychologists called Liz Dunn and Mike Norton have shown, Mum was right. Of the key take-outs from Dunn and Norton's 2014 book *Happy Money*, the simplest to follow were: spend your money on experiences and on other people.

If your gut reaction to the advice about spending on others was the same as mine when I was a child, consider that the same experiment has been conducted all around the world, and it works each time. When participants are given money and told to spend it either on themselves or others, and they're tested for happiness afterwards, the results are always the same. It doesn't matter if you're rich or if you're poor, if you live in the US or if you live in South Africa or India or Uganda or Canada. If you spend your money on other people rather than yourself, it'll make you happier.

Does that work for time as well? Up till the time when *Happy Money* was published in 2014, most of the academic community of psychologists who study how people make, and how they should make, decisions were studying how people spent their money. But now, Dunn and Norton and a few others, such as Cassie Mogilner at UCLA, have introduced an innovative new approach. Now, rather than investigate how people spend their money, they are looking at how people spend, and how they think about spending, their other precious resource: time.

Their starting point is to observe that, just as with money, time can be spent, saved, wasted and given away. They want to discover if we're all spending our time well, or we're wasting it, or if giving it away is a good idea or not. This kind of research is particularly valuable because time, unlike money, is finite and short, and the most precious resource we have. If you spend money, on yourself or others, at least you can get some more. But it just isn't like that with time.

Understanding how to spend time is especially valuable today because, in lives that feel increasingly busy, people feel more time poor than ever. In the US, for instance, there's been 'a steady rise in the number of men and women who say they "always" feel rushed', according to Brigid Schulte in her book *Overwhelmed*. In the UK, three out of four Brits now feel overwhelmed.

So, since time is precious in a way that money could never be, and since we all feel like we haven't got enough of it, it seems pretty clear to me that the last thing you should do is give it away. That thought sounds sensible, practical and obvious. It's also, it turns out, completely wrong.

That strange truth was discovered by Mogilner, Norton and another psychologist called Zoë Chance through three curious experiments. Imagine, for a moment, that you'd agreed to take part. In the first experiment, which is an hour long, at the tail end of it the scientists ask you to either write a letter to someone, or to count how many 'e's are in a piece of Latin text.

In the next, they contact you on a Saturday morning and tell you either to spend ten minutes doing something for yourself – perhaps getting some admin done, or reading the paper, or playing a computer game – or doing something for someone else.

In the third experiment, fifteen minutes before the end of an hour-long exercise, they say you can either help an at-risk student improve an essay they've written, or go early.

In each case, which would you have chosen? Which choice, do you think, would have made you happier? Personally, I'd have hated the waste of time counting the 'e's, so I'd have written the letter to someone in the first one. After the Saturday-morning call, I'd have spent the extra ten minutes crossing something off my to-do list. And the third one would have been the easiest of the lot: I always love an extra bit of time. You know when a friend cancels? When I was younger, I'd have been a bit downhearted. But nowadays, I breathe a sigh of relief I've got some free time back.

Now that I've shared my answers with you, I can also reveal that, assuming I wanted to squeeze more happiness out of my time, I'd have gone wrong in two of my three choices. To maximise happiness, I did the right thing writing a letter to someone, but I should also have done something for someone else on the Saturday, and helped an at-risk student rather than slope off early.

Through this study, Mogilner, Norton and Chance proved a radical new point. Just as spending money on others is a sure strategy for more happiness, so is spending time on others.

The reason for this, they figured out, is that, while it's not possible to actually increase the time we have – though you may remember from the chapters *Outside & Offline* and *Relationships* that you can increase your chances of living longer – giving time to others makes people feel more 'time abundant', as if they have more.

It does this, they went on to show, in two ways. It makes people feel like they're better at making use of time and that they get more done with it. And it makes them feel like they have more time in the future. Those ideas are perhaps connected. If you feel like you're more efficient with your time, even if the time you have in the future is fixed, it will feel like it's more because you'll get more from it.

So thanks, Mum, you were right. The science backs you up. Giving is better than receiving, even when it comes to time. And thanks to Mogilner, Norton and Chance too, because they've not only identified that giving time is a route to happiness, they have also proposed the idea that it leads to a positive, happy loop: if you give now, next time you have the chance to give, you will remember the happiness and give more. So giving – money and time – leads to the creation of a virtuous circle that leads to increased happiness.

This brings us back, once more, to status and significance. Since an increase in status is likely to increase your happiness and the length of your life, there's really no need to be shy about wanting more. But since status is such an awkward idea, and associated so strongly with the sort of cold, selfish success that disconnects us from others, I think it's time to ask status to step aside and make way for an upgrade. Instead of simply status, we should all yearn for warm, big-hearted success that connects us to others – and is better known as significance.

If we give money and time, in big, generous acts like those of Mme C. J. Walker and Oprah Winfrey, or in small, everyday, random acts of kindness, we can get into positive, virtuous cycles that lead to increased happiness, for others and ourselves. The path to this virtuous circle is simple and clear. For longer lives, more happiness, and the sort of success we can feel proud of, we should reach out past status, and aim for significance instead.

Status vs. significance

- Self oriented
- Egoistic
- Spend time and money on self

- For self and others
- Egositic and altruistic
- Spend time and money on self and others

Status & Significance Summary

1. We need to talk about status, because people with higher status live longer, healthier, happier lives.

2. Studies show that giving money and giving time are both more likely to lead to happiness.

3. There's no need to feel embarrassed and awkward if we reposition the idea in our minds: rather than waste our time on egotistical status seeking, we should spend our time on an egoistic *and* altruistic search for significance.

BIG YOURSELF UP ... and Others Too: How to Avoid Empty Status and Be SIGNIFICANT Instead

As before, the questions in *Past Times* are about specific experiences from your past. The questions in *The Way to Happy Days* will help you think about your life in general. Both will help you bring the sort of status and significance you can be open about wanting, and proud of having, into your life.

Past Times: Did That Experience Increase Your Status & Significance?

Think about an experience you had in the past, like what you did last weekend or last holiday. Try this using experiences that were really good, ones that were just average, and ones that were downright awful. Then, ask yourself these questions, giving an answer on a scale of 0 to 5, where:

> 0 = *Not at all*
> 1 = *Very little*
> 2 = *A little*
> 3 = *Some*
> 4 = *A lot*
> 5 = *A great deal*

1. By how much did [insert experience here] increase your status?

2. How proud would you feel if you told someone about this?

3. How much would you be impressed if someone else told you they'd done this?

4. To what extent did it give you a chance to exercise control?

5. To what extent did it increase your capabilities for living?

6. To what extent did it help you participate in society?

7. To what extent did it increase your social capital?

8. To what extent did it connect you to other people?

9. To what extent were you giving your time and doing something for others?

If your answers are mostly 4s and 5s, it's clear this was a good experience. If mostly 3s or less, consider the questions below, and see if you increase the status and significance that your experiences deliver in the future.

The Way to Happy Days: How to Achieve Meaningful Status and Be Significant

Use these questions to think about how you can increase your status and be more significant.

1. How can you change this experience so that it'll be more impressive?

2. What can you add to it so that it makes you more likely to want to tell someone about it?

3. Are you giving enough of your time to others?

4. If you give money to charity or causes that matter to you, why not think about giving your time too?

5. Are you spending enough time on experiences that challenge your abilities and give you a chance to exercise control?

   This is one reason why climbing is so good for people. Climbing is hard. Holding on requires control. Conquering a climb leaves you with a sense of control.

6. How could you play a more active role in society, generally, in your profession, or in your local community?

7. Do you watch too much TV? How can you organise your life so you watch less? What will you do with your time?

SOMETHING FOR THE WEEKEND

Here's a handful of ideas you can use next weekend to increase your status and significance. On the following pages, write down three ideas of your own.

1. Host a BBQ

Invest in the community around you by hosting a big BBQ for your friends, neighbours and a few work colleagues you like.

2. Go to Glyndebourne

Or another opera or classical music event. If the cost puts you off, many tickets at the Royal Opera House in Covent Garden are £35 or less. Some tickets cost as little as £3.

3. Turn off the TV

For a whole weekend. Unplug it or else you'll switch it back on. It'll force you to do something else. Even better, figure out a way to hide your TV when you're not watching it. We're creatures of habit who follow the most obvious path, so if you can architect the design of your home so the TV doesn't dominate your social space, you'll just start watching it less. I know a person who does this well. Her TV is kept behind cupboard doors. Unless there's a specific thing to watch, for which there's some kind of ceremony and the doors are opened, you don't even notice it.

4. Progress to impress

Learn a skill that will increase your capabilities in life and, perhaps, impress a potential partner or friends. Take an RYA course to sail or get a motorboat licence: handy when you go away. Learn to tango: having two left feet impresses no one.

5. Do something for someone else

Not to get something back, but for the pure, simple, intrinsic pleasure of doing something for someone else. Tidy an elderly neighbour's garden. Connect a friend with someone you think they'll like. Suggest somewhere you think they'll like to go. Or simply ask someone you know, 'Anything I could do to help out right now?'

_____

_____

_____

_____

ETERNAL SUNSHINE FOR EVERYONE'S MINDS

'In our leisure we reveal what kind of people we are.'

OVID

We are encircled by a mighty forest, in Germania, in 180 AD. We stand at the edge of a break in the trees, as one with the legionaries, centurions, catapults and cavalry of the Roman army. Walking through, inspecting the troops, is the Roman general Maximus Decimus Meridius. His shoulders are the second-century equivalent of an American football player: beefed up by strips of leather and metal armour. A grey wolf pelt drapes from manly shoulder to manly shoulder, adding warmth, girth and the sort of bling that befits a Roman general.

Across the other side of the clearing, a white horse bursts out of the dark forest. Red blood runs down its white flanks. On its back, bolt upright, held fast, and swaying like wheat in a summer breeze, is a headless man.

His clothes are those of a Roman. He was an emissary.

From among the trees at the edge of the clearing, a barbarian emerges, holding the dead man's head by his hair. He hurls a battle cry at the Romans: *'Ihr seid verfluchte Hunde!'*

It means, 'You are damned dogs!'

Now, a horde of barbarians appear, their hair long, their faces bearded and muddy. They shake spears, bang shields and echo his battle-cry.

The scene cuts to another part of the forest. It is misty, calm, quiet. We are riding alongside General Maximus, as he steers his horse towards a gathering of his elite cavalry. It is here that, as the horses whinny and the men of the cavalry listen and laugh, Maximus delivers his first short, great speech of the movie. He begins by calling his troops '*fratres*', the Latin word for brothers. He ends by reminding them that, 'What we do in life echoes in eternity.'

And then battle commences.

This, in my opinion, is one of the greatest openings of any movie. I wasn't the only person impressed by *Gladiator*. It was one of the highest-grossing movies of 2000. At the next year's Academy Awards, it was named Best Film. Its hero, Russell Crowe who played General Maximus, won Best Actor.

My favourite part of this opening scene, besides seeing the Roman army made flesh and blood on screen, is that punch-line at the end of Maximus's speech. It's a line that captures, I think, so much.

First, it expresses a truth that's not only eternal, but especially relevant for our times: it's what we *do* that matters, not what we *have*. Because Maximus doesn't say, 'What we *have* in life echoes in eternity.' It isn't important how many furs, toys, ancient maps, watches, pairs of shoes or sets of crockery you have. It didn't matter before, and it sure doesn't matter nowadays. These days so many people have so much, stuff just isn't likely to impress anyone any more. Stuff will echo for about as long as a metal bin reverberates when you throw something in it.

Second, it isn't just a set of inspiring words written by the screenwriter, David Franzoni. It's based on a piece of wisdom that comes directly from the time the movie is set in, and the real Roman emperor at the time. The philosopher emperor Marcus Aurelius, who ruled from 161 to 180 AD, wrote in the notes that are now called his *Meditations*, 'What we do now echoes in eternity.'

Third, I like the line for its simple, practical wisdom. It's a reminder that, wherever you are, whatever you do, and whenever you do it, every choice and action you take will have consequences. I'm not quite advocating butterfly theory, the idea that a flap of a butterfly's wings could, through a series of leveraged flaps, lead to a huge impact. This idea is closer to the ripples that circle a pebble when you throw it on the surface of a placid lake. The consequences of our actions run the full gamut, from small and local and barely noticeable, to large and global and unmissable, and everywhere in between. No matter what you do, it will impact your own life. It will impact the lives of those around you: your children, your partner, your friends, your family, your community.

What we do in life may not echo all the way to eternity. Hey, eternity's a long time, and, even if what we do does echo that long, there's little chance you and I'll be around to see it. But what you do now, today, as Maximus said and Marcus Aurelius wrote, will at least echo through your own life, and the lives of others around you. Knowing that, and knowing that death is hurtling towards us far faster than we'd like, we may as well do something that matters. We may as well do things that create a positive echo and impact, today and for all our days.

You Probably Think this Book Is About You

I've come in for some criticism for the ideas I've written and talked about in recent years, about how people have too much stuff, how experiences are better than material goods and how, if you care about yourself, your friends and family, you should focus on experiences.

'It's so elitist!' they say. 'It's just for rich people! This doesn't apply to poor people! All those experiences you talk about, like skiing, cost a lot of money. This is just for rich, white, middle-class people. What about the millions struggling to get by?'

These comments really make me angry. Because, no, it's not just for rich people. It applies to everyone. And if those people listened or read carefully, they'd notice I talk about experiences of all price points, from snow-sports, to praying, having lunch with a friend, singing, and walking by the sea. Because this is for everybody, whatever your colour or class, including the millions still struggling to get by.

And the message in this book isn't only good for you and yours. Sure, if you take inspiration from Kurt Vonnegut and Joseph Campbell and the mud map, you will say, 'Yes!' and cross the threshold to adventure more often, you will walk life's inevitable road of trials like a resilient hero – and your life will take the shape of an exciting, positive, fascinating *Story*.

If you don't compromise yourself, if to thine own self you stay true, and if you follow your dream as Bruce and Caitlyn Jenner did, it won't always be easy, but you'll paint your life with the benefits of autonomy, self-actualisation, growth, and all the other stripes on the flag of *Transformation*.

If you agree with Tristan Harris and Romesh Ranganathan that the wizards in Silicon Valley have made these phones just too good, and you want to escape the ranks of the unhappy 'rat people' – like Essena, Danny and Darlene – remember the findings from the island of Yakushima and the app that maps where we're happiest, and you'll find yourself spending more time *Outside & Offline*.

If you remember Marina Keegan, and her *cri de coeur* about the opposite of loneliness, and the terrible consequences of social isolation, you'll put the effort into creating good, meaningful *Relationships*.

If you're prepared to come out of the shadows, to be knocked down again and again, like Scott Keneally and all the people you know who strive valiantly and dare greatly in the mud and dust of life, you'll seek 'real flow' and a life of *Intensity*.

If you see, in your mind's eye, the sun setting over Rishikesh and the foothills of the Himalayas, then remember how much hides behind our rose-tinted memories, and recall the new peak-end rules – you'll craft your own masterpiece of a life from the right chiaroscuro mix of experiences and snapshots that are both ordinary and *Extraordinary*.

If you picture, on stage at the Oscars, Mo'Nique thanking the Academy and seventy-three-year-old Jack Palance doing one-handed push-ups, and accept the deeply awkward but inescapable fact that status is good for health and happiness – you'll be more likely to follow the inspiring example of Mme C. J. Walker, and live a life of *Status & Significance*.

If you do all this, then, as the science says, you'll have far better free time, and more health, wealth and happiness.

But this isn't only about you.

If you follow these principles, it'll be good for all of us, including the millions struggling to get by, including your children and their descendants. Because if more people stop being materialistic, and become experientialists instead, it'll be good for three of the most worrying problems we face today: the environment, the happiness deficit, and inequality. It may also lead to a change in one of the fundamental aspects of our society.

Experientialism won't solve our environmental issues at a stroke. Flying to Borneo or Buenos Aires will still be far from ideal. But, given the waste and impact of material goods, both upstream and downstream, if more people spend less on stuff and more on experiences, we have a real opportunity to reduce environmental impact – while maintaining economic growth. (Note also that flying's footprint has reduced dramatically in recent years, and I believe it'll reduce still further in the years to come. A plane named *Solar Impulse 2* has flown around the world using nothing but solar energy.)

Since science has shown that experientialism is better than materialism at making people happy – because it brings us closer to others and gives us better stories, for instance – it will reduce the anxiety, loneliness, stress and depression that comes with our consumer-driven capitalist system. It is also likely to improve community relations, as research shows that experientialists are more likely to be prosocial, that is, they're more likely to think of others and do things for them too.

One of the most interesting, and almost always over-looked, aspects of why inequality is bad for societies is that the most important factor that leads to differences in health, happiness and longevity isn't material abundance. It's differences in status.

At present, in a mostly materialistic society, status is largely defined in material terms. If more people move to experientialism, status will be defined in experience terms. Of course, this is obvious. But it's also crucial, because one of the reasons why experiences are better than material goods at making us happy is that they're harder to compare and we're less inclined to compare them – that means the status they carry is less clear-cut. If more people become experientialists, in other words, and think of themselves, and others, in experiential rather than material terms, their differences in status will be fuzzier. The result will be a society that not only thinks about status in a different way, but also perceives inequality in a different, healthier way.

To show you what I mean, meet Sean. Sean earns £600,000 a year. He works in private equity and lives in a four-bedroom house in Notting Hill, which he bought with cash. He drives an Audi, holidays in a villa just outside of Juan-les-Pins on the French Riviera.

Now, say hello to Sarah. Sarah earns £30,000 a year. She works in publishing. She rents a two-up, two-down house in Bristol. She doesn't own a car, but has a bicycle. She goes on camping holidays.

Think about these two people for a moment. It's obvious who's winning the social-status game. But who's happier?

A few more details to help you decide. Sean works fourteen-hour days, and many weekends. He sleeps in a separate bedroom from his wife, who is semi-estranged from him. He doesn't have much time for his friends. He rarely sees his family. When he does he is constantly on at least one of his mobile phones. Sarah finishes work by 6 p.m., and has time for friends and family, and hobbies like tennis and rock climbing.

If you think about these two from a materialistic point of view, it's clear who the winner is. These people reflect some of the inequality in our society. But consider them from an experientialist point of view. Now, who's in front?

Of course, there are still differences. There always will be. Sean's villa versus Sarah's tent. But the comparisons we make between experiences are far fuzzier than with material goods. So the difference in status that comes with them is blurred, and the impact that has on people's perception of themselves and where they sit in the status hierarchy blurs.

As with the rest of this book, this idea is backed by science. In one experiment, for instance, a researcher investigated how likely people said they would be to swap their material or experiential goods for a 'better' one. With material goods, people were far more likely to say they would switch for an upgrade. That makes sense to me. I like my Nissan, for instance, but I'd swap it in a heartbeat for my neighbour's BMW. But when people were asked if they'd swap their experience – a three-star holiday in the Bahamas, say, for a five-star trip there – they were far less likely to. Asked why not, most people replied that their experience was uniquely theirs. The story I like to compare is if your neighbour goes on a five-star holiday in the Indian Ocean and drinks chilled champagne on the beach, while you go to Sagres in Portugal, surf in the waves and drink the local beer on the beach. It's clear who's had the fancier holiday. But who's happier? Who's had the better time? With experiences, as you can see, better is less clearly defined.

If our dominant world view shifts from materialism to experientialism, it will have a positive impact on inequality, and all the issues that come with inequality – especially its nasty, negative effect on the health and happiness of millions, and especially on poorer people who currently spend a higher proportion of their income trying to keep up with the arms race of consumerism.

So, this will impact people who are poorer directly. Also, if you study social change, as I do, you'll know that societies evolve through a mix of innovation and imitation. That is, a few people try something new, and then others copy them.

Here's how this typically works. As sociologists have shown, new ideas are first tried out and picked up by a few influential people. Called 'innovators' and 'early adopters', they tend to be wealthier, more educated and better connected. They get out more, they travel more often, and they read more. Then, other people notice what these innovators and early adopters are doing, realise the benefits of the innovation they've adopted, and copy it. You can see this in action if you think of typical innovations from the past decades, like holidays abroad, VHS video recorders, ABS brakes, mobile phones, joining a gym and electric cars. Even consumerism began this way. First, the richest people became avid consumers, buying toasters and washing machines and the latest cars, and then the others followed. I believe the adoption of experientialism will follow a similar pattern.

How ideas catch on:
the diffusion of innovations curve

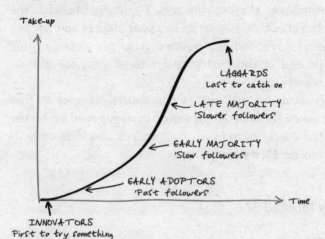

Take-up

LAGGARDS
Last to catch on

LATE MAJORITY
'Slower followers'

EARLY MAJORITY
'Slow followers'

EARLY ADOPTORS
'Fast followers'

Time

INNOVATORS
First to try something

How experentialism is catching on

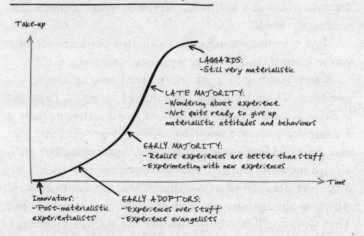

Take-up

LAGGARDS:
-Still very materialistic

LATE MAJORITY:
-Wondering about experience.
-Not quite ready to give up
materialistic attitudes and behaviours

EARLY MAJORITY:
-Realise experiences are better than stuff
-Experimenting with new experiences

Time

Innovators:
-'Post-materialistic
experientialists'

EARLY ADOPTORS:
-'Experiences over stuff'
-Experience evangelists

So the more you, as one of these innovators and early adopters, discover a happier, more successful life through experience, the more others will operate this way too. By looking at life through an experiential lens, you will help others get the benefits too. By living life with the STORIES checklist as your guide, your choices and actions will have a resounding, positive echo not only in your own life and in those of people around you, but also in wider society.

This assumes two things, of course. Not only that you've taken the wisdom presented here, summed up by the STORIES checklist, to heart, but that you also start using it. Let's consider each point in turn.

What's Your ExQ 2?

Time for a second test. Remember at the beginning of the book, you took the test on page 31 to get a sense of your current Experience Quotient? How did you score? Go back and take a look at it again. Would you have scored better after reading the book?

Now, take this second test. It's another chance to see what you've learned, and if you've increased your ExQ.

Before you begin, a reminder about how to answer the questions. Though you may be tempted to say, 'It depends,' because circumstances vary and we're all different, there is a generally correct answer to each of these questions. We may be as individual as snowflakes, remember, but we're all still snow. As you give your answers, notice if there's any difference between what you think the correct answer is and which of the options you'd most likely choose in real life. That way, you'll not only discover the level of your experience intelligence, you'll also find out if you're actually applying your experience intelligence to improve your experiences and your life.

1. Which of these is more likely to be a bullshit/empty/junk experience?
   a. Dinner with your relatives.
   b. Watching TV.

2. Which is more likely?
   a. If you become successful, you'll become happy.
   b. If you become happy, you'll become successful.

3. Which is likely to bring more happiness?
   a. A long weekend of adventures, with a relaxing finale.
   b. A long weekend packed with adventures, right to the very end.

4. The best way to approach life is:
   a. Like a gifted author, aware of the past, present and future.
   b. Like a brilliant actor, always in the present.

5. The best way to achieve the opposite of loneliness is to:
   a. Make sure every experience includes other people.
   b. Be happy to have some experiences on your own.

6. It's Friday, 4 p.m., your work is done, your boss is away. Which of these will lead to more happiness?
   a. Help a colleague finish up a piece of work.
   b. Go home early.

7. If you get so immersed in an experience that you forget yourself and lose track of who you are, that's:
   a. Good – you're in the moment.
   b. Bad – what's the point if you don't remember and you're not present?

8. You're more likely to find flow:
   a. On your own doing something you enjoy.
   b. Having a chat with old friends in the pub.

9. What happens at the beginning of an experience …
   a. Doesn't matter, after all, it's the end that counts more.
   b. Matters a lot, maybe as much as the end.

10. Older people prefer 'calm happiness' to 'excited happiness'.
    a. True.
    b. False.

Answers are at the back, on page 360.

How to Train Your Elephant

As you read this, try to do one simple thing. Don't think about pink elephants. Do not picture them. Repeat: do not let images of pink elephants come into your head.

Sometimes it's hard to point your mind in the direction you want it to go, isn't it?

People have been thinking about, and taming and riding, elephants – though usually grey ones, not pink ones – for thousands of years. Through the ages, smart people have often used elephants to talk about how we think and what we do. Around 2,500 years ago, for instance, in what is India today, Gautama Buddha used an image of an elephant to talk about how enlightened he was.

'In days gone by this mind of mine used to stray wherever selfish desire or lust or pleasure would lead it,' he said. 'Today this mind does not stray and is under the harmony of control, even as a wild elephant is controlled by the trainer.'

It's a brilliant, vivid image, and prescient too. Because it reflects what modern psychologists say about the conscious and subconscious minds. When a prominent American psychologist by the name of Jonathan Haidt – which is pronounced 'height' – spent time thinking about how the mind works, he pictured it in a similar way, but with an interesting twist.

'I was a rider on the back of an elephant,' Haidt wrote in his book *The Happiness Hypothesis*. 'I'm holding the reins in my hands, and by pulling one way or the other I can tell the elephant to turn, to stop, or to go. I can direct things, but only when the elephant doesn't have desires of his own. When the elephant really wants to do something, I'm no match for him.'

And when a man named Cass Sunstein and a now Nobel prize-winner named Richard Thaler looked for an illustration for the cover of their book about behavioural economics, *Nudge*, they chose a mother elephant gently nudging a baby elephant.

In the book – like Haidt and the Buddha before them, and like fellow Nobel prize-winner Daniel Kahneman – Thaler and Sunstein distinguish between the conscious and subconscious minds. They call the conscious mind, because it acts a lot like the calculating, rational perspective of classical economics, *Homo economicus*. This is the rider on the elephant, the one who can see what's coming, who gathers information and works out where to go next. They call the subconscious mind *Homer economicus,* in honour of the *Simpsons* cartoon character who says, 'Doh!' a lot, often at his own elephantine stupidity.

We'd all like to think that we're not nearly as dozy as Homer Simpson, and that it's the smart, sensible rider who decides which way we go. But, as psychologists have shown time and again, it's the elephant who chooses.

Which means that, even if you've been inspired by the science you've read about in this book, and you can see how the STORIES checklist will improve the quality of your experiences, and even if your ExQ has increased as a result, you could still be stuck in the ruts of your old habits. Old elephant tracks are hard to walk away from.

So, it's important to think about how you're going to get your wild elephant to follow a new path. Luckily for us, there's a guy who can help, a man who, by his own admission, is 'obsessed with how behaviour works'.

We met him earlier. His name's BJ Fogg. Fogg's methods may be used by some of his former students to hook millions into addictive habits that may not be very healthy, but that was never Fogg's intention.

'I look at some of my former students and I wonder if they're really trying to make the world better, or just make money,' Fogg once said. 'What I always wanted to do was un-enslave people from technology.'

Fogg, in fact, has spent the past few decades, from his base at Stanford University, trying to figure out how to help people train their inner elephants, and how to get them to go where the rider wants them to go.

As a result of that work, Fogg has figured out a simple and very useful model for how behaviour works. Don't be fooled by its simplicity, though. It's one of the primary tools that designers use to make many of Silicon Valley's most engaging and successful services. If they can use this to design services millions can't help but use from the moment they wake up to when they go to sleep, there's every chance the same techniques will be useful for steering your elephant along the path to happiness and success.

Here's the model:

$B = MAP$ ... at the same time, where:

B = behaviour
M = motivation
A = ability
P = prompt

Another way of putting this: people do things when they want to do them, when they can do them, and when there's some sort of prompt that nudges them to do them right now. If any of those are missing, so Fogg has observed, the behaviour doesn't happen.

The starting point for all of this is the 'M' for motivation. Because, of course, if you're not bothered, you won't bother. If someone doesn't care about being healthy and eating fruit rather than processed foods, for instance, it doesn't matter how red and shiny the apples in the bowl are, or how cheap they are, or how close the bowl is. They'll probably just grab the crisps instead.

Fogg sometimes calls the 'A' for ability by another name: 'S' for simplicity. It's about how easy the thing is for a person to do. The fewer hurdles a person has to get over, the more likely they are to do something.

Fogg has identified six of these hurdles: physical effort, mental effort, cost, time, if something's socially deviant, and if it's 'non-routine'. Knowing about these six barriers is useful if you want to change your behaviour. They not only suggest six potential roadblocks between you and your new target behaviour – it's too hard, too awkward, too expensive, it'll take too long and, anyway, it's weird and 'We don't do it like that around here'. But by flagging these up, they also suggest six ways you can move those roadblocks to one side, and give yourself a better chance of achieving your target behaviour. You can make it easier, simplify the steps, keep the cost down, reduce the time required, choose your social circle more carefully, and try to make the new action ever closer to a habit. We'll come to a smart idea about that last point in a minute.

The 'P' for prompts are one of Fogg's smartest observations. If someone is motivated and able to do something, they often don't. They still need a final nudge at the right time to make the behaviour happen.

How many times have you found yourself wanting to do something, but then not doing it, and saying, 'I can't be bothered right now'? Whatever the reason, you needed a prompt to get you over the barriers between you and your target behaviour. At other times, you're motivated and there's nothing in your way, but you just forget. What you need then is a reminder, a signal of some sort. And at other times, you're partially motivated and it's not hard to do, but you need some sort of spark to get you off your butt and into the gym.

The best kind of prompts are internalised. Think of the chocolate ad, 'Have a break, have a KitKat.' Genius. Every time people thought of having a break, the advertisers had drummed into their minds the connection that they should have a KitKat. Or, think what happens nowadays when people see a sunset or a concert or their child in a school play. Now they all have smartphones, they've internalised the idea that the most natural thing in the world is no longer to just watch and enjoy it, but to record it for posterity – where posterity really means they'll never look at it again.

So, let's look at using B = MAP here, where our target behaviour is to use the STORIES checklist. Let's assume you're motivated to use it, so you've got the 'M'. How can we increase the 'A' and create a 'P' that'll work every time you need it to?

Beginning with 'A', then, is there anything in the way of you using it? Let's consider the six simplicity factors.

One: it takes no physical effort.

But, two: I guess it does take a bit of mental effort. You do have to think.

Three: it costs the price of this book, which you've already bought, so the good news is, it's free from now on. And, even better news, it'll save you money, and give you more value for money, by helping you avoid wasting your money on rubbish experiences, and spend it on better ones instead.

Four: it doesn't need to take long – a few moments or a bit longer, depending on how deep you dig. You can check the overall idea with the one pivotal question: Will this experience give me STORIES?

Then, if you've time and inclination, you could follow all seven branches:

S: Will this experience give you a story to tell others, or that tells you who you are?

T: Will it help you develop, grow, transform?

O: Will you be outside and offline?

R: Will it bring you closer to others, and enhance your relationships?

I: Will it be intense, and launch you into the zone of flow?

E: Will it be new, awesome and extraordinary in some way?

S: Will it raise your status, connect you to others and help you be significant?

Five: you might think that specifically referring to a checklist is socially awkward, as bad as getting a whiteboard out to make a point during dinner. If you think back to the introduction, though, and in particular the section called *The Snowflakes, the Snow and the Experience Manifesto* on page 36, you may remember that many doctors were reticent to use a checklist at first. But when they saw how a nineteen-point checklist dramatically improved results, with no increase in skill and only a tiny input of time and effort required, even they adopted the idea.

Six: is asking if an experience will be good or not 'non-routine'? I don't think so. It isn't in our house. It's never been like that in my life either. Before anyone agrees to do anything or go anywhere, they consider if it'll be a waste of time or time well spent, don't they? And just think of the endless conversations you've had with your more annoying friends and family members about what to do tonight, or this weekend, or this summer.

So, trying to figure out what to do is as routine as cleaning your teeth before you leave home in the morning. And what the STORIES checklist does is make those 'What are we going to do?' conversations more productive, because it gives them a shape and a score card. Now, instead of long discussions that go nowhere, you have a set of criteria to judge experiences against.

Today, there are more options available than ever before. But many of them are like processed food. The STORIES checklist can act as a scorecard that separates the empty, junk, bullshit experiences from the compelling, exciting, awesome ones. It'll simplify your decision-making. It'll help you choose better, more often.

Use it a few times, see how it improves your decision-making and your experiences, and it'll soon become routine.

So, to achieve the 'B' – the behaviour of using the STORIES checklist – we have 'M' and 'A', the motivation and the ability. How about that all-important 'P', the prompt?

Here, Fogg has another simple, yet inspiring, solution. It's wrapped up inside an idea he calls 'Tiny Habits'. The best way to create new long-term habits, Fogg has discovered, is to do two things. First, so that it's incredibly easy to do and repeat, make the new behaviour you want as tiny as possible. And then, use an existing behaviour as your 'P'. There's a practical way to formulate and remember this idea: 'After I [insert existing behaviour], I will [insert new habit].'

Fogg gives a comedy example of how he's used this method. Once, he wanted to get fitter, so he set himself the tiny target of doing two press-ups, and used going for a pee as his prompt. He formulated this as, 'After I pee, I will do two push-ups.' It worked. Doing the press-ups soon became such a regular habit, he ended up doing between eight and twelve every time, totalling between fifty and seventy a day. At the least, we now know how often he goes to the loo. But far more useful is, of course, this revelation about how every one of us can use existing behaviours as prompts to create new paths for our elephants to follow.

So, if you want to get the benefits of the STORIES checklist, the best way is to identify your own relevant existing behaviour, and add the new super small habit of asking, 'Will this give me STORIES?'

For me, the best time is whenever someone asks if I'm doing something or going anywhere, and I start wondering about an experience. So my 'After I ..., I will ...' looks like this:

'After I start thinking about any experience, I will ask, "Is this going to give me STORIES?"'

What would your 'After I ..., I will ...' look like? Maybe your prompt will be, 'After I start thinking about the weekend or tonight.' Or, 'After I start reading the What's On section of the paper.' Or, 'After I check my favourite travel or going-out app or website.' Or, 'After I see someone posting about an experience on Facebook.' No matter your 'After I ...' prompt, it's key that you add in your new target behaviour. So maybe your complete 'After I ..., I will ...' will look something like this:

'After I open up the *Time Out* app, I will look for events that'll give STORIES.'

Whatever it is, the more you say, 'After I ...,' followed by, 'I will use the STORIES checklist,' in some way, not only will you be more likely to ride your elephant, whether it's grey, pink or any other colour, in the direction you want it to go, but you'll also get more out of your time. Just as a checklist transforms the outcome for already brilliant, educated people like pilots and surgeons in life-threatening situations like flying and surgery – so it'll help you in the most exciting and dangerous and precious thing you'll ever come across: your life.

How to steer your elephant to happiness

After I wonder what to do next weekend, I will ask...

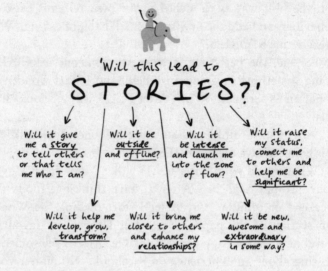

'Will this lead to
STORIES?'

Will it give me a **story** to tell others or that tells me who I am?

Will it be **outside** and **offline**?

Will it be **intense** and launch me into the zone of flow?

Will it raise my status, connect me to others and help me be **significant**?

Will it help me develop, grow, **transform**?

Will it bring me closer to others and enhance my **relationships**?

Will it be new, awesome and **extraordinary** in some way?

Do this, and not only will the STORIES manifesto transform your life, but you'll also be contributing to a radical, exciting and positive change in our culture.

Viva the New Cultural Revolution!

Warren Susman was a curious figure. A cultural historian at Rutgers University in New Jersey in the US, who sometimes wore bright red blazers when giving lectures, he viewed history in a different way from most of his colleagues. He wasn't interested in piecing together the dates of battles and the achievements of politicians. He thought history was better seen through the everyday lives of normal people and cultural artefacts so common no one would think to notice them. He thought Mickey Mouse revealed more about the 1930s than the US president Franklin D. Roosevelt, for instance.

Many thought Susman was on to something in the way he approached history. Regrettably, he published very little, and what little he did publish was often obscure, and in relatively obscure journals and anthologies. 'His essays are always too brief,' a fellow historian by the name of Robert Westbrook once wrote. 'They inevitably end just as the reader thinks Susman has got up to speed.'

Susman died in 1985, aged fifty-eight, of a heart attack while addressing the Organization of American Historians' annual convention. He is best remembered for his third and final book, published the year before, *Culture as History: The Transformation of American Society in the Twentieth Century*. I think the insights it contains provide a clue about how the culture in the US, the UK and other consumer societies is changing as more people move away from materialism and become experientialists in the twenty-first century.

If you're worried that I think American culture and history is everyone's culture and history, let me be clear. I don't think British or any other society was, is, or will be the same as American society. We don't have guns, the story of the West, exceptionalism, baseball, Silicon Valley, Fox News, a history of segregation or Donald Trump – at least, not the way they do.

But we still have capitalism, consumerism, bankers, open culture, entrepreneurs, democracy, sensible and crazy news outlets, and a general, if imperfect, respect for the rule of law. And America, because of its enviable economic power, rises in living standards, and culture of creativity and innovation, and as guarantor of freedom for the best part of the twentieth century, has become a beacon – for individuals, cultures and nation states.

We may not slavishly and precisely follow American culture, but you don't have to look too hard to see how cultural changes that have happened in the world's great innovator have also been imitated in the world's early adopting fast followers, like the UK and Australia, and then slower followers too. Often waves that begin in the US, especially in the hotbeds of invention on the coasts, soon ripple out to the rest of the world: from the consumer revolution to Elvis Presley, hippies, hip hop, skateboards, Google and Facebook.

Sometimes, the direction isn't so clear-cut, and rather than follow, our cultures evolve at a similar time. You can clearly see, for instance, the problem of 'stuffocation' and the rise of the experience economy in the UK as much as in the US. They're being charted by US institutions like Bloomberg News and *Forbes*, just as they're being reported by British newspapers like the *Guardian* and the *Financial Times*. So Susman's observations, I believe, are relevant over here too.

In one of the essays in *Culture as History*, Susman described how American society fundamentally changed from the nineteenth to the twentieth centuries, from what he called a 'culture of character' to a 'culture of personality'.

In the nineteenth century, he observed, people were concerned with having a good character above all else. It was the cornerstone for their identity, an essential building block for life. Susman reviewed literature, art, music, books and pamphlets from the era. After reviewing more than 200 pieces of work, he listed the words most closely associated with character: 'citizenship, duty, democracy, work, building, golden deeds, outdoor life, conquest, honor, reputation, morals, manners, integrity, and above all, manhood.'

If you think about how people lived then, in small, close-knit communities, this makes sense. If you weren't honourable or a good citizen, if you didn't have good morals and manners and integrity, people would find out. So, if you wanted to get on in the society, it would make sense to think about your duty, citizenship and doing 'golden deeds'.

Then, as the nineteenth century turned to the twentieth, so Susman noted, a radical change took place in American culture. This was a time, it's worth remembering, when the American people were moving from village communities where everyone knew everyone else, to the relative anonymity of the city. Before, most people in the US lived a simple country life based around agriculture. Now, as the industrial and consumer revolutions gathered steam, the nation shifted its focus from farming to the production and consumption of industrial goods like cars, radios and toasters. As the people of America physically moved, and as what they did with their days changed, so society transformed, and the underlying culture did too.

Whereas in the nineteenth century, people had been concerned with what you might call 'internal values', and who they really were inside, in the twentieth century, they became fascinated with what you might call 'external values', and how they appeared on the outside, to others. Who you really were, in private, no longer mattered so much. What mattered now was how you presented yourself in public.

This was especially visible, as Susman noted, in a 'radical shift in the kinds of advice manuals that appeared after the turn of the century'. In this new world, instead of admiring self-sacrifice, people sought self-realisation. Suddenly, there was a new set of words to describe this new culture of personality: instead of being concerned with duty, morals and integrity, people now wanted to have the 'most glowing personality' and appear to be 'fascinating, stunning, attractive, magnetic, glowing, masterful, creative, dominant, forceful'.

Two books, in particular, sum up Susman's point. They were written by the same person, a popular author by the name of Orison Swett Marden, who also founded and edited a magazine called *Success*. In 1899, Marden published *Character: The Grandest Thing in the World*. It is filled with studies of historical heroes who have 'high ideals', who are 'true Christian gentlemen, pure, upright, intelligent, strong, and brave, possessing a sense of duty, having benevolence, moral courage, personal integrity'. In 1921, he published *Masterful Personality*. Its focus was on how the reader could develop 'personal charm', the sort of aura and power of personality that could 'sway great masses', and 'to know what to say and how to say it'.

'You can compel people to like you,' Marden wrote in *Masterful Personality*. 'So much of our success in life depends upon what others think of us.'

It's no accident that this culture of personality emerged at the dawn of our materialistic consumer culture. As people began to think, according to this new culture of personality, of personal success as something external and distinct from their inner selves, as something to present to others – so they began to think, in line with the ethos of the new materialistic consumer culture, of their happiness and identity as external, distinct, and separate from themselves too. This new culture of personality, materialism and consumerism was resolute. Success, happiness and identity were only real if you presented them to others. They were only true as others perceived them. And they were now available to all, for sale, out there, in objects you bought.

There's something radically undermining about this idea. Why should we look for happiness outside ourselves? Why is success separate from who we are? Why should we look for identity in how we are perceived by others?

And yet, as well as subverting the fundamental building block that our previous society was built on, this culture of personality, materialism and consumerism was a force for good. It drove capitalism, the much maligned yet magical system that's hauled billions out of poverty, and enabled what Susman called our 'culture of abundance'. But it's also left us where are today: rich but empty, well but worried, happy but depressed. Despite fancier toys that pack in ever more func-tions and fun, we are more depressed today than ever before. With so much stuff, we are the first humans ever to want less, not more. With so many options, we need help filtering the infinite choice into activities that are worth our time, and those that aren't.

And so now, in the twenty-first century, the foundations which gave rise to the culture of personality and material-ism and consumerism are, I believe, fundamentally shifting. We're tiring of materialism and consumerism. We're happy that we have such abundance, but we're unhappy about materialistic consumerism's impact on the environment and our mental well-being. We want fewer material things. We want less stress and depression. We want more happiness instead.

We are still consumers. But we are moving away from materialism and towards experientialism. We now look for happiness, and project our success ever less in the material things we have, and ever more through the experiences we do.

We are still consumers. But now we are digital consum-ers, connected to each other via our mobile devices and social media. As we share much more of our lives through these chan-nels, the distinction between private and public is blurring.

Think about the impact this has on the culture of person-ality. Consider the difference between defining a person by things they own, compared to the activities they do, or the places they go, or between a person who deliberately manages and projects a public image, compared to someone who simply shares their inner thoughts. Compare the sense of identity from buying and wearing branded shoes, compared to the sense of identity that accompanies completing a Tough Guy, or tough-girl, obstacle-course race. What does a designer watch tell you about yourself, even if its fancy adverts assure you the owner is merely looking after it for the next generation? Compare that with the sense of identity that comes from spending more time outside and offline, or going through a process of transformation.

If you think of all the items on the STORIES checklist, it's clear that each is far less about painting a personality to show to others, and far more about developing your own, internal character. You can't show character unless you're tested. You need tension to push against. You need hurdles to overcome. Without those, there is no opportunity to discover your own personality. So, we need the challenge and struggle, the road of trials, inherent in *Story*, in *Transformation, Intensity* and *Extraordinary*, and likely to be available when you're *Outside & Offline*, in *Relationships*, and when you're working to increase your *Status & Significance*.

Each of the items on the STORIES checklist is about challenges that develop resilience. Each is about opportunities to test, develop and grow your experience intelligence. Each item offers a chance to make a choice, to take an action, to develop habits that, rather than enhance your external, this-is-me, look-how-great-I-am, *Keeping Up with the Kardashians* personality, to test and grow and develop your character instead. Or, perhaps, to be more accurate, *as well as* enhance how you appear, externally, to others, each will also develop your character – and character is where the focus is.

I don't think we'll go back to the culture of character of the nineteenth century. The digital and social and consumer horse has bolted. Instead, we'll move forward, away from the culture of personality of the twentieth century, and forward to a new, digitally mediated, shared and enhanced culture of character.

What will that look like? A few things are for sure: less stuff, less stress, less status-related issues of inequality, more experiences, better experiences, and happier people living more fulfilled lives. That, I believe, is the promise that's possible as capitalism evolves from being based on materialistic consumerism to experientialist consumerism, and as more people get better at making the most of their time. And if you want to keep up today, and get ahead tomorrow, then you should aim to increase your ExQ and become an expert at how you spend your time.

Thanks to the laws of imitation and the diffusion of innovation, upgrading your own life is the most ethically responsible thing you can do. Use the STORIES checklist, and the impact will not only echo through your own life, and the lives of your friends and family and descendants – it will also echo through the rest of society.

As more of us do this, we'll improve our chances of solving our local and global environmental issues. We'll flatten the social gradient and reduce the negative impacts of status-oriented society. We'll solve other problems of the well-being deficit. We'll reduce loneliness, increase exercise, improve joy, and increase life satisfaction. As we take on board the latest findings from the science of success, we'll evolve capitalism so that it's fit for purpose for human society in the twenty-first century. We'll discover that, as well as solving the age-old problems of scarcity, capitalism can now solve today and tomorrow's problems of abundance.

As more of us agree that learning how to spend our leisure time is vital for making the most of our exciting, complicated twenty-first-century lives, and as more of us make it a habit to use the seven science-backed rules of the STORIES checklist, we'll feel more alive, and help everyone in society enjoy richer, happier days.

Conclusion Summary

1. Seeking richer, happier days for yourself and your family sounds selfish, but it isn't.

2. We now live in a materialistic culture of personality. People expect to find happiness outside of themselves: in the things they own and how they appear to others.

3. This culture is bad for the environment, inequality and well-being.

4. Experientialism addresses each of these problems.

5. If you choose experientialism rather than materialism as your guiding star, you'll be part of the solution to today's materialistic culture of personality.

6. By increasing your experience intelligence and applying it via the STORIES checklist, you'll have richer, happier days, and help create a better, happier society for all.

The Way to Happy Days: How to Steer Your Elephant to the STORIES Checklist

The most likely way to turn using the STORIES checklist from a one-time action into a long-term habit is to use BJ Fogg's Tiny Habits formula. Yours should look a little like this:

'*After I* [add existing behaviour here], *I will* ask, "Will this experience lead to STORIES?"'

If that's all you do, that's enough. To make this habit stick, remember, you have to keep it super tiny. This is the question equivalent of two press-ups after peeing.

If you do this often enough that it becomes a habit, you're welcome to go up a level and follow as few or as many of the seven branches as you have time for. Asking these is like doing between eight and twelve press-ups: impressive but optional, and only possible once the very simple habit of two press-ups becomes so routine you barely even think about it. These questions will most likely run in a sequence:

1. '*After I* ask, "Will this experience lead to STORIES?", *I will* ask about the "S" for story: Will this experience give me a *story* to tell others, or that tells me who I am?'

2. '*After I* ask about the "S" for story, *I will* ask about the "T" for transformation: Will this experience help me to develop, grow, *transform*?'

3. '*After I* ask about the "T" for transformation, *I will* ask about the "O" for outside and offline: Will this experience take me *outside & offline*?'

4. '*After I* ask about the "O" for outside and offline, *I will* ask about the "R" for relationships: Will this experience bring me closer to others, and enhance my *relationships*?'

5. *'After I* ask about the "R" for relationships, *I will* ask about the "I" for intensity: Will this experience be *intense*, and launch me into the zone of flow?'

6. *'After I* ask about the "I" for intensity, *I will* ask about the "E" for extraordinary: Will this experience be new, awesome and *extraordinary* in some way?'

7. *'After I* ask about the "E" for extraordinary, *I will* ask about the "S" for status and significance: Will this experience raise my *status*, connect me to others, and help me be *significant?'*

8. Then, *after I* have asked about status and significance, or *whenever I* stop asking about the experience, *I will* do a small dance of joy, knowing that I have a much clearer idea of whether the experience is worth my time or not.

ENDNOTES

There weren't enough pages for all the endnotes. For the full list plus additional insights from science papers on similar areas, visit www.timeand howtospendit.com/endnotes.

INTRODUCTION

Eternal Sunshine for Your Spotless Mind

Pierre Bismuth's comments are based on a telephone interview conducted in 2018, and various articles, including Jessica Lack, 'Eraserhead'. *The Guardian*, 6 Sep 2008.

'The Experience Machine'
Robert Nozick, *Anarchy, State, and Utopia* (London: Blackwell Publishers, 1974).

We have more leisure time today than ever
Overall, we have more leisure time than ever, and our leisure time has remained fairly stable in recent decades. See:

'Men enjoy five hours more leisure time per week than women', *Office for National Statistics*, 9 January 2018.
Derek Thomson, 'The Myth That Americans Are Busier Than Ever', *The Atlantic*, 21 May 2014.
Oliver Burkeman, 'Why you feel busy all the time (when you're actually not)', *BBC.co.uk*, 12 September 2016.

Americans get five hours and fourteen minutes
Source: Bureau of Labor Statistics, American Time Use Survey 2017.

Britons get five hours, forty-nine minutes
Source: 'Leisure time in the UK: 2015', *Office for National Statistics*, 24 October 2017.

how come so many of us don't feel time-rich?
Or why else would there be so much coverage of this topic? For instance:

Oliver Burkeman, 'Why you feel busy all the time (when you're actually not), *BBC.co.uk*, 12 September 2016
Tony Crabbe, *Busy: How to thrive in a world of too much* (London: Piatkus, 2014).
Brigid Schulte, *Overwhelmed: Work, Love, and Play When No One Has the Time* (Toronto: Harpercollins Canada, 2015).

we earn more, so time feels more expensive and scarce
'In search of lost time: 'Why is everyone so busy?', *The Economist*, 20 December 2014.

busyness is a status symbol … conspicuous consumption of leisure has been replaced by conspicuous busyness
Silvia Bellezza, Neeru Paharia, and Anat Keinan (2017) 'Conspicuous Consumption of Time: When Busyness and Lack of Leisure Time Become a Status Symbol'. *Journal of Consumer Research*, Vol. 44, No 1, pp. 118–138.
Jake Knapp and John Zeratsky, *Make Time: How to focus on what matters every day* (London: Bantam Press, 2018).
'In search of lost time: Why is everyone so busy?', *The Economist*, 20 December 2014.

More things than ever to keep up with and visit and try out – new festivals, restaurants, pop-up bars, and cities that are now only a short flight away
For instance, new festivals: the number of festivals listed on festival website eFestivals more than doubled between 2007 and 2015, jumping from 496 to 1,070.

Multitasking. This fools us into thinking we're being more productive and efficient with our work time, so we start to multitask in our leisure time too
Brigid Schulte, *Overwhelmed: Work, Love, and Play When No One Has the Time* (Toronto: Harpercollins Canada, 2015).
'In search of lost time: Why is everyone so busy?', *The Economist*, 20 December 2014.

Sociologists even have a nasty name for the thing you get if you multitask: 'contaminated time'.
Brigid Schulte, *Overwhelmed: Work, Love, and Play When No One Has the Time* (Toronto: Harpercollins Canada, 2015).

we're addicted to the Internet via devices like our smartphones
UK Office of Communications: '15m digital detoxes are ditching their device', Ofcom, 4 August 2016.

As recently as 2007, the amount of leisure time that we spent on [devices] could be measured in minutes.
Because that was before the iPhone launched and the smartphone era began.

We now spend, on average, three and a half hours a day online.
'15m digital detoxes are ditching their device', Ofcom, 4 August 2016.

We're spending way more than half of it glued to our screens. Once we've unhooked from our devices, we've only got about two hours of leisure time left.
I calculated by taking the five or so hours we get free each, and subtracting the three and a half hours we spend on our devices.

People say they're too busy to make friends out of work … date … sleep … to eat dessert … four out of ten say dessert is better than sex
Brigid Schulte, *Overwhelmed: Work, Love, and Play When No One Has the Time* (Toronto: Harpercollins Canada, 2015).
Also, we now spend less time socialising. In 2015, people spent an average of around six hours per week socialising. That's a fall of 12.7% since 2000. Source: Office for National Statistics (ONS)

we all end up thinking that leisure is trivial and doesn't require any special training.

Brigid Schulte, 'From leisure society to shopping on the toilet, where did we go wrong?', *Sydney Morning Herald*, 20 March 2014.

As Warren Buffett, the world's third-richest man with a net worth of more than $80 billion, once said, 'I can buy anything I want, basically, but I can't buy time.' Source: 'Q&A with Bill Gates and Warren Buffett, Moderated by Charlie Rose', *Columbia Business School*, 27 January 2017.

What if I said you'll have fewer disappointing, waste-of-time experiences, and instead more of the sort of meaningful, exciting, share-worthy experiences that lead not only to more joy, but a more *enduring* sort of happiness?
By 'enduring sort of happiness', I'm referring to the Aristotelian concept of 'eudaimonia'. Built out of two concepts, 'eu' meaning good, and 'daimon' meaning spirit, if you live a eudaimonic life that means you're reflecting who you really are. See:

Aristotle, *Nicomachean Ethics* (Cambridge: Hackett, trans. by Terence Irwin, 1985).
Edward L. Deci and Richard M. Ryan (2008) 'Hedonia, Eudaimonia, and Well-Being: An Introduction.' *Journal of Happiness Studies*, Vol. 9, No. 1, pp. 1–11.

three out of every five Brits say they've bought something [because it's a superfood]
Kyrsty Hazell, 'Study: One In 10 Wrongly Believe That Superfood Helps Prevent Cancer', *Huffington Post*, 20 October 2011.

Michael van Straten. He wrote about the 'four-star superfoods'
Michael van Straten and Barbara Griggs, *Superfoods* (London: DK, 1990).

Next, the term was adopted by journalists trying to add spice to their headlines and marketers trying to sell more of their products.
Marion Nestle, 'Superfoods Are a Marketing Ploy', *The Atlantic*, 23 October 2018

Since 2007, the EU has banned anyone using the term unless they have specific evidence of health benefits.
Amy Fleming, 'Do 'superfoods' really exist?', *The Guardian*, 16 January 2014.

... typing 'superfood' into Google and searching for it more than 250,000 times a month.
Allison Fox, 'These Are The 10 Most Popular Superfoods In The U.S.', *Huffington Post*, 26 October 2016.

... superfoods ... do at least have nutrients in them.
'Superfoods or Superhype?', The Nutrition Source from the Harvard T. H. Chan School of Public Health's Department of Nutrition (View at: www.hsph.harvard.edu/nutritionsource/superfoods).

'I took a dog of three years old, fat, and in good health,' wrote Magendie, 'and put it to feed upon sugar alone ... It expired the 32nd day of the experiment.'
Ira Wolinsky, *'Nutrition in Exercise and Sport'*, Third Edition (Boca Raton, Florida: CRC Press, 1997).

David Graeber ... says modern life has thrown up all sorts of meaningless jobs ...
David Graeber, 'On the Phenomenon of Bullshit Jobs: A Work Rant', *STRIKE! Magazine*, August 2013.
David Graeber, *Bullshit Jobs: A Theory* (London: Allen Lane, 2018).

brevis lux, our 'brief light', and that afterwards all we had to look forward to was *nox est perpetua una dormienda*, 'a night that's never ending and in which we'll always be asleep'.
From 'Catullus 5', an ode from a Roman poet named Catullus to his lover Lesbia.

Dylan Thomas had an answer: 'Rage, rage against the dying of the light.'
From Dylan Thomas, *Do Not Gentle Into That Good Night*.

'The popular assumption is that no skills are involved in enjoying free time, and that anybody can do it. Yet the evidence suggests the opposite: free time is more difficult to enjoy than work ... '
Mihaly Csikszentmihalyi, *Finding Flow* (New York: Basic Books, 1997).

People are often no happier after a holiday than if they hadn't taken one at all: Jeroen Nawijn, Miquelle Marchand, Ruut Veenhoven and Ad Vingerhoets (2010) 'Vacationers Happier, but Most not Happier After a Holiday.' *Applied Research Quality Life*, Vol. 5, No. 1, pp. 35–47.

Almost all of us – 96 per cent, in fact – admit to living much of our lives on 'autopilot', doing things without even thinking whether they'll be good or bad for us.
Mark Williamson and Renata Saleci, *Autopilot Britain*, 2017 (a report for UK retailer Marks and Spencer, based on an online survey of 3,000 people).
In particular, this:
'People recognise that the choices they are making don't add up to the life they want to live.'

Despite more free time and more money to spend during that free time, Americans are becoming unhappier.
Ashley Whillans, 'Time for Happiness', *Harvard Business Review*, January 2019.
Laura Paddison, 'The U.S. Is Getting Richer But Americans Are Unhappier', *Huffington Post*, 18 October 2018 (based on World Economic Forum data).
Richard Florida, 'The Unhappy States of America', *CityLab*, 20 March 2018 (based on Gallup polling data).

Three out of four Britons now openly admit they're not getting the most out of their time.
Mark Williamson and Renata Saleci, *'Autopilot Britain'*, 2017.

When people all across Europe were asked if they were happy with how they were spending their time back in 2013 ... three in ten said they weren't.
'Satisfaction with time use, by country, 2013', Eurostat.

And so it sounds to me like there are millions of people in the UK, the US and Europe who aren't getting the most from their time
After all, if 75% of Britons don't think they're getting the most from their time, that's 50m people. If 28% of the EU aren't satisfied, that's 128m people. I suspect there are more people in all parts of the world who would get more from their time if they designed it better.

The Old Testament story of Job;
This version of the story of Job comes from a mix of the Bible and Hayley Shepherd. She tells it much funnier than me.

IQ ... the standard way to determine a person's potential.
Kendra Cherry, 'Alfred Binet and the History of IQ Testing', *VeryWellMind. com*, 18 November 2018.

Clinton is often cited as the charismatic, charming, smiling poster boy for the revolution which was discovered by a pair of psychologists ... and popularised by the writer Daniel Goleman.
On Clinton:
Fred Greenstein (2000) 'The Qualities of Effective Presidents: An Overview from FDR to Bill Clinton.' *Presidential Studies Quarterly*, Vol. 30, No. 1, pp. 178–185.

On emotional intelligence:
Peter Salovey and John D. Mayer (1990) 'Emotional Intelligence'. *Imagination, Cognition and Personality*, Vol. 9, No. 3, pp. 185–211.
John D. Mayer, David R. Caruso and Peter Salovey (1999) 'Emotional intelligence meets traditional standards for an intelligence.' *Intelligence*, Vol. 27, No. 4, pp. 267–298.
Daniel Goleman, *Emotional Intelligence* (New York : Bantam Books, 1995).

'General intelligence' ... standard definition ... the 'capacity of the individual to act purposefully, to think rationally, an
d to deal effectively with [their] environment'.
David Wechsler, *The measurement of adult intelligence* (Baltimore, MD, US: Williams & Wilkins, 1944).

'[Emotional intelligence is the] ability to monitor one's own and others' feelings and emotions, to discriminate among them and to use this information to guide one's thinking and actions'.
Peter Salovey and John D. Mayer (1990) 'Emotional Intelligence'. *Imagination, Cognition and Personality*, Vol. 9, No. 3, pp. 185–211.

Evidence has emerged ... that strongly suggests a causal link between happiness and success.
Sonja Lyubomirsky, Laura King and Ed Diener (2005) 'The Benefits of Frequent Positive Affect: Does Happiness Lead to Success?.' *Psychological Bulletin*, Vol. 131, No. 6, pp. 803– 855.
Julia Boehm and Sonja Lyubomirsky (2008) 'Does Happiness Promote Career Success?.' *Journal Of Career Assessment*, Vol. 6, No. 1, pp. 101–116.
Lisa Walsh, Julia Boehm, and Sonja Lyubomirsky (2018) 'Does Happiness Promote Career Success? Revisiting the Evidence.' *Journal of Career Assessment*, Vol. 26, No.2, pp. 199–219.
Sonja Lyubomirsky, Julia Boehm, Lisa Walsh, 'The relationship between happiness and career success isn't as clear as you might think', *World Economic Forum (weforum.org)*, 15 August 2018.
Shawn Achor (2012) 'Positive Intelligence.' *Harvard Business Review*, Vol. 90, No. 1–2, pp.100–102.
Shawn Achor, *The Happiness Advantage: the seven principles that fuel success and performance at work* (London : Virgin Books, 2011).

Then, there's a growing body of other research ... that has shown conclusively that, if you want to be happy, you should spend more of your focus and money on experiences.
For example:

James Wallman, *Stuffocation* (London: Penguin, 2015).

James Wallman (2017) 'How to spend it.' *New Scientist*, Vol. 235. (online as 'Experience or Stuff, What's the Best Buy For a Happiness Boost?').

Elizabeth Dunn and Michael Norton, *Happy Money: The Science of Spending* (New York: Simon & Schuster, 2013).

Tom Gilovich and Leaf van Boven (2003) 'To Do or to Have? That is the Question.' *Journal of Personality and Social Psychology*, Vol. 85, No. 6, pp. 1193–1202.

Leonardo Nicolao, Julie R. Irwin, and Joseph K. Goodman (2009) 'Happiness for Sale: Do Experiential Purchases Make Consumers Happier than Material Purchases?.' *Journal of Consumer Research*, Vol. 36, pp. 188, 198.

Elizabeth W. Dunn, Daniel T. Gilbert, Timothy D. Wilson (2011) 'If Money Doesn't Make You Happy, Then You Probably Aren't Spending It Right.' *Journal of Consumer Psychology*, Vol. 21, No. 2, pp. 155–125.

Another wave of research ... has shown that being able to handle tough times and bounce back is not only essential for happiness, it's also key for success.

Sheryl Sandberg and Adam Grant, *Option B : facing adversity, building resilience and finding joy* (London: WH Allen, 2017).

Shawn Achor and Michelle Gielan, 'Resilience Is About How You Recharge, Not How You Endure', *Harvard Business Review*, 24 June 2016.

Ephrat Livni, 'To be resilient, start by avoiding the word "happiness"', *Quartz (qz.com)*, 7 November 2017.

Andrea Ovans, 'What Resilience Means, and Why It Matters', *Harvard Business Review*, 5 January 2015.

Diane Coutu (2002) 'How Resilience Works', *Harvard Business Review*, Vol. 80, No.5, pp. 46–50, 52, 55.

Johanna Leggatt, 'School marks are important. But resilience is the real indicator of success', *The Guardian*, 10 January 2018.

A headline in business publication *Forbes* captures this idea: 'How successful are you? Answer: how resilient are you?'

Jan Bruce, 'How Successful Are You? Answer: How Resilient Are You?', *Forbes*, 6 February 2013.

American Psychological Association (APA)'s advice on the ten ways to increase your resilience

For the full list, visit 'The Road To Resilience' on the APA's website: www.apa.org/helpcenter/road-resilience.aspx

Psychologist Ann Masten calls the 'ordinary magic' of resilience

Ann Masten, *Ordinary Magic: resilience in development* (New York: Guilford Press, 2015).

Society's success was measured – some would say 'mismeasured' – in terms of economic success, and defined by GDP.

For more, read my *Stuffocation* (London: Penguin, 2015), and Joseph E Stiglitz, Amartya Sen and Jean-Paul Fitoussi, *Mismeasuring Our Lives* (New York: New Press, 2010).

The Athenian wise man Solon captured this when he said to the richest man in the world, King Croesus, 'Never call a man happy till he's dead.' From Herodotus, *The Histories* (London: Penguin, trans. by Aubrey de Sélincourt, 1972).

I've discussed this idea with a number of leading social scientists ...
These conversations took place in 2017 and 2018.

The Plane that was Too Much for One Man to Fly

This story is based on numerous sources, especially:
Atul Gawande, *The Checklist Manifesto: how to get things right* (London: Profile Books 2011).
Yisrael M. Safeek (2010) 'Protocols, prompters, bundles, checklists, and triggers.'
Healthcare Financial Management, pp. 70–75.
Atul Gawande et al. (2009) 'A Surgical Safety Checklist to Reduce Morbidity and Mortality in a Global Population.' *New England Journal of Medicine*, Vol. 360, No. 5, pp. 491–499.

while, at a detailed level, we're all as individual as snowflakes, at a basic level, we're all snow.
This phrase comes from an awesome acting and speaking coach by the name of Ewa Kolodziejska. She says it simpler: 'We're all snowflakes, but we're all snow.'

checklist with nineteen points
Look it up! See https://www.rcophth.ac.uk/wp-content/uploads/2015/01/WHO_-_NPSA_generic_checklist.pdf

It was, as a newspaper at the time put it, just 'too much plane for one man to fly'.
Michael R. Grüninger, Markus Kohler and Capt. Giancarlo Buono (2010) 'Too Much Plane for One Man to Fly'. *Bart*, pp.78–79.

experiences give us a sense of identity that's both inward- and outward-facing. They tell each one of us who we are, and they enable us to tell others too 'tell us who we are':
Travis Carter and Thomas Gilovich (2012) 'I Am What I Do, not What I Have: The Centrality of Experiential Purchases to the Self-Concept.' *Journal of Personality and Social Psychology*, Vol. 102, No. 6, pp. 1304–1317.

'sense of identity that's inward-facing'—in other words, intrinsic motivation:
Edward L. Deci, Richard M. Ryan, *Intrinsic Motivation and Self-Determination in Human Behavior* (New York: Springer Science & Business Media, 1985). Also, see www.selfdeterminationtheory.org.

When you have a story, you set in motion a domino line of positivity that almost inevitably leads to happiness ...
I suppose not all experiences lead to the best stories, but if you do something you should find something to say, at least. For more on this:

Amit Kumar and Thomas Gilovich (2013), "Talking About What You Did and What You Have: the Differential Story Utility of Experiential and Material Purchases", *Advances in Consumer Research* Volume 41, eds. Simona Botti and Aparna Labroo, Duluth, MN: Association for Consumer Research.
Jonathan Gottschall, *The storytelling Animal:how stories make us human* (Boston: Mariner Books, 2012).
Paul Zak, How 'Stories Change the Brain', *Greater Good Magazine*, 17 December 2013.

Growth, purpose and becoming the person you want to be are all key for happiness.
Christine Robitschek and Corey L M Keyes (2009) 'Keyes's Model of Mental Health With Personal Growth Initiative as a Parsimonious Predict.' *Journal of Counseling Psychology,* Vol. 56, No. 2, pp. 321–329.

science is now clear that spending time in nature is good for you, lowering heart rate and blood pressure, reducing stress, and improving happiness
Jeremy Coles,'How nature is good for our health and happiness', *BBC Earth.* 20 April 2016.
Jill Suttie, 'How Nature Can Make You Kinder, Happier, and More Creative', *Greater Good Magazine.* 2 March 2016.
Simon Worrall, 'We Are Wired To Be Outside', *National Geographic.* 12 February 2017.

In an ever more complex and demanding world of digital connections and distractions – when friends, family and boss can get hold of you any time and everywhere – it's more important than ever that we tune out, turn off and drop out.
For more on this:

Adam Alter, *Irresistible* (New York: Penguin, 2017).
Tony Crabbe, *Busy: how to thrive in a world of too much* (London: Piatkus, 2014).
Alex Soojungkim-Pang, *Rest: Why You Get More Done When You Work Less Hardcover* (London: Penguin, 2016).

As study after study has confirmed, including a seventy-five-year-long study at Harvard University Medical School, our friends, family, neighbours and community are key to well-being.
Harvard Study of Adult Development: https://www.adultdevelopmentstudy.org/

Experiences that engage and challenge us give us a chance to be good at something, and get us into what psychologists call a state of 'flow' ... it isn't *what* you do, but *how* you do it that matters most.
Mihaly Csikszentmihalyi, Flow: *The Psychology of Optimal Experience* (New York: Harper Perennial Modern Classics; 2008).

One of the magical reasons why experiences bring us so much happiness is that we not only get to enjoy them in the moment, we also get to look forward to them and remember them afterwards.
James Wallman. *Stuffocation* (London: Penguin, 2015).
Martha Roberts, 'The joy of anticipation', *Psychologies*, 8 April 2014.
Gal Zauberman, Rebecca K. Ratner and B. Kyu Kim (2008) 'Memories as Assets: Strategic Memory Protection in Choice over Time.' *Journal Of Consumer Research,Inc.*, Vol. 35, Issue No. 5, pp. 715–728.
Carey Morewedge (2016) 'Utility: Anticipated, Experienced, and Remembered'. In G. Keren and G. Wu (Eds.), *Wiley Blackwell Handbook of Judgment and Decision Making* (pp. 295–330). (Malden, MA: Blackwell Press, 2016).

Those were most likely to look forward to and remember feature moments that are out of the ordinary and give us a sense of awe
Out of the ordinary:

Chip Heath and Dan Heath, *The Power of Moments* (London: Bantam Press, 2017).
Simon Kemp, Christopher D.B Burt and Laura Furneaux (2008) 'A test of the Peak-End rule with extended autobiographical events.' *Memory & Cognition*, Vol. 36, No. 1, pp. 132–138.

Awe:
Dacher Keltner and Jonathan Haidt (2003) 'Approaching awe, a moral, spiritual, and aesthetic emotion.' *Cognition and Emotion*, Vol. 17, No. 2, pp. 297–314.

There's an important place for ordinary experiences too.
Amit Bhattacharjee and Cassie Mogilner (2014) 'Happiness from ordinary and extraordinary experiences.' *Journal of Consumer Research*, Vol. 41, No. 1, pp. 1–17.

Although we don't like to talk about status, who we are, what we are, and where we are in society does matter
For more on status:

Thorstein Veblen, *A Theory of the Leisure Class* (New York: Macmillan, 1899).
Alain de Botton, *Status Anxiety* (London: Hamish Hamilton, 2004)
Ahmed Riahi-Belkaoui, Social Status Matters (Charleston: BookSurge Publishing, 2009)
Geoffrey Miller, *Spent: Sex, Evolution and the Secrets of Consumerism* (New York: William Heinemann, 2009)
Alice Park, "Study: Money Isn't Everything—But Status Is!", *Time*, 23 March 2010.
Kate Pickett and Richard Wilkinson, *The spirit level: why greater equality makes societies stronger* (New York, Bloomsbury Press, 2010)
Christopher von Rueden, Michael Gurven and Hillard Kaplan (2011) 'Why do men seek status? Fitness payoffs to dominance and Prestige.' *Proceedings of the Biological Society B: Biological Sciences*, Vol. 278, No. 1715, pp. 2223–2232.
Yajin Wang and Vladas Griskevicius (2014) 'Conspicuous Consumption, Relationships, and Rivals: Women's Luxury Products as Signals to Other Women.' *Journal of Consumer Research,* Vol. 40, No. 5, pp. 834–854.

The psychological studies that show the exceptional satisfaction that comes from giving.

Re giving money, see Elizabeth Dunn and Michael Norton, *Happy Money: The Science of Spending* (New York: Simon & Schuster, 2013).

Re giving time, see:
Cassie Mogilner, Zoë Chance, and Michael Norton (2012) 'Giving Time Gives You Time.' *Psychological Science*, Vol. 23, No. 10, pp. 1233–1238.

You shouldn't think of this STORIES guide like a set of train tracks. It's not a straitjacket. It's a tool, designed to help you get the basics right.
As seen in Atul Gawande, *The Checklist Manifesto: how to get things right* (London: Profile Books, 2011).

... after reading *Stuffocation*, [Daniele] reduced the amount he was spending on stuff ... it helped [Michelle] be more present and get more enjoyment from the time she spends with her kids.
Daniele told me this in 2016, Michelle in 2015.

1. STORY

Kurt Vonnegut and the Shape of Stories

Kurt Vonnegut ...
This section is based on:

Kurt Vonnegut, 'At the Blackboard', *Lapham's Quarterly*, 13 June 2005.
a student lecture Vonnegut gave in 1995. It's titled 'Kurt Vonnegut on the Shapes of Stories' and is available at https://youtu.be/oP3c1h8v2ZQ
Kurt Vonnegut, *Palm Sunday* (New York: Dial Press, 1981).

As data analysis would later show, the shapes of stories could be drawn on a graph.
See Andrew Reagan et al (2016) 'The emotional arcs of stories are dominated by six basic shapes.' *EPJ Data Science,* Vol. 5, p. 31.

The 'Hero's Journey'

Joseph Campbell, *The Hero With A Thousand Faces* (Princeton, N.J. : Princeton University Press, 1968).
Christopher Vogler, *The Writer's Journey, third edition.* (Chelsea, Michigan: Sheridan Books, 2007).

Monkeys Don't Believe in Heaven

This section is informed by Yuval Noah Harari, *Sapiens – A Brief History of Humankind* (London: Penguin Random House, 2014).

The Stories of Our Lives, and the Domino Line to Happiness

This section on narrative psychology is informed by:

Dan McAdams (2013) 'The Psychological Self as Actor, Agent, and Author.' *Perspectives on Psychological Science*, Vol. 8, No. 3, pp. 272–295.
Dan McAdams (2008) 'Personal Natives and the Life Story.'Guilford Press, pp. 242–262.
Jack Bauer and Dan McAdams (2004) 'Personal Growth in Adults' Stories of Life Transitions.' *Journal of Personality*, Vol. 72, No. 3, pp. 573–602.
Jack Bauer, Dan Mcadams and Jennifer Pals (2008) 'Narrative Identity and Eudaimonic Well-Being.' *Journal of Happiness Studies*, Vol. 9, No. 1, pp. 81–104.
Dan McAdams and Kate McLean (2013) 'Narrative Identity.' *Current Directions in Psychological Science*, Vol. 22, No.3, pp. 233–238.
Julie Beck, 'Life's Stories: How you arrange the plot points of your life into a narrative can shape who you are—and is a fundamental part of being human.' *The Atlantic*, 10 August 2015.
Leo Widrich, 'The Science of Storytelling: Why Telling a Story is the Most Powerful Way to Activate Our Brains'. *LifeHacker*, 5 December 2012.

Paul Zak, How 'Stories Change the Brain', *Greater Good Magazine*, 17 December 2013.
Laura A. King (2001) 'The Hard Road to the Good Life: The Happy, Mature Person.' *Journal of Humanistic Psychology*, Vol. 41 No. 1, pp. 51–72.
Michael Inzlicht, Amitai Shenhav and Christopher Y. Olivola (2018) 'The Effort Paradox: Effort Is Both Costly and Valued.' *Trends in Cognitive Sciences*, Vol. 22, No. 4, pp. 337–349.

These personal stories are critical for happiness because, so psychologists have found, they provide unity, purpose and meaning to your life. And while you can get away with not having these and still experience moments of joy, they're critical for achieving what the philosopher Aristotle called *eudaimonia*, and what psychologists today call a 'more enduring sort of happiness'.
See note on eudaimonia above.
Richard Ryan, Veronika Huta, and Edward Deci (2008) 'Living well: A self-determination theory perspective on eudaimonia.' *Journal of Happiness Studies,* Vol. 9, No. 1, pp. 139–170.

As well as more enduring well-being for individuals, stories also create happiness by bringing us closer to other people – through a mechanism in our brains that neuroscientists have discovered called 'mirror neurons'.
Lea Winerman (2005) 'The mind's mirror.' *Monitor On Psychology*, Vol 36, No. 9, page 48.
Liz Jacobs, 'What are mirror neurons? Further reading on the neurotherapy described in today's talk', *TED.com*, 24 July 2013.

And now for the historians, who've concluded that we're hard-wired to enjoy stories because they've made us successful as a species.
Yuval Noah Harari, *Sapiens – A Brief History of Humankind* (London: Penguin Random House, 2014).
Michael Gazzaniga, *Human: The Science Behind What Makes Us Unique* (New York: Harper Collins, 2008).
Lisa Cron, *Wired for Story* (Berkeley: Ten Speed Press, 2012).

The air there would have been fragrant with hints of hibiscus and rose, and the sort of sweet, jasmine-y aroma that coffee plants give off.
I've been in touch with an archaeobotanist about this. Because of changes in climate, it's hard to be certain exactly what plants were there. But these are reasonable suggestions.

black, white and red, with splashes of blue here, flashes of orange there.
These colours are based on the colours of feathers from birds that are there now.

... the brains of our ancestors would expand to three times the size of our nearest relatives. And while our brains got bigger, our muscles got smaller.
For a great summary, see 'Bigger Brains: Complex Brains for a Complex World' on the Smithsonian National Museum of Natural History's website. (http://humanorigins.si.edu/human-characteristics/brains)

... around two hundred thousand years ago or so, a few made the decision to boldly go where no *Homo sapiens* had been before.
Two hundred thousand years ago? Might be older. The date seems to keep moving.

Ewen Callaway, 'Oldest Homo sapiens fossil claim rewrites our species' history', *Nature*, 7 June 2017.

The transformative power of stories comes from the way they enable us to talk about things that *don't* exist.
Yuval Noah Harari, *Sapiens – A Brief History of Humankind* (London: Penguin Random House, 2014).

evolutionary psychologists ... call us the 'storytelling animal', and say that we're 'hard-wired for story'.
Jonathan Gottschall, *The storytelling Animal:how stories make us human* (Boston: Mariner Books, 2012).

Better Shape Up ... 'Cause I Need a Man in a Hole

And it's true that tragedies are enduringly popular.
Andrew J. Reagan, Lewis Mitchell, Dilan Kiley, Christopher M. Danforth and Peter Sheridan Dodds (2016) 'The emotional arcs of stories are dominated by six basic shapes.' *EPJ Data Science*, Vol. 5, p. 31.

... people who tend to describe their life through contaminated stories are more likely to be depressed, have lower levels of life satisfaction, and feel that they can't make a positive contribution to others. But people who tend to tell redemptive stories are more likely to be happy.
See note on narrative psychology above.

Why this shape?
In addition, consider:
Paul Zak, How 'Stories Change the Brain', *Greater Good Magazine*, 17 December 2013.

We Can Be Heroes

Achilles and Batwoman and T'challa
Just in case ... Achilles was the hero of the ancient Greek story, the Iliad. Batwoman and T'challa from *Black Panther* are late 20th century comic book creations.

Clive Williams – based on a mix of interviews with Clive Williams, & reading his book
I spoke with Williams by video in 2017 and 2018. See also:

Clive Williams (2017) 'The Hero's Journey: A Mud map for Change.' *Journal of Humanistic Psychology*, pp. 1–18.
Clive Williams, *A Mud map for Living: A practical guide to daily living based on Joseph Campbell's The Hero Journey* (Brisbane: self-published, 2016).

Five Ways to Be a Hero

But, as *Dilbert* author Scott Adams once wisely pointed out, we're probably wrong about a lot of things, so why not choose an illusion that puts you in a positive light?
Scott Adams, *How To Fail At Almost Everything And Still Win Big* (London: Portfolio Penguin, 2013).

2. Get stuck into an escape room
E.g., Handmade Mysteries' rooms in London or the Escapement's Egypt Room in Margate.

Visit www.handmademysteries.com and www.escapementmargate.co.uk

3. Go to immersive theatre
E.g., Secret Cinema or Punchdrunk.
www.secretcinema.com and www.punchdrunk.com.

2. TRANSFORMATION

How to Live the Dream We All Dream

Some events can change a man's life, and a woman's too ...
Based on numerous sources, including:

Official Report of the Games of the XXI Olympiad Montréal 1976, Volume III Results.
Montreal 1976 Official Olympic Film – Part 4 | Olympic History, available at: https://youtu.be/8_zrPBYEbeI
Phil Pepe, 'Bruce Jenner crushes world record, wins decathlon gold in 1976 Olympics', *New York Daily News*, 31 July 31 1976.
'Bruce Jenner: Track and Field Sports Documentary', available at: https://youtu.be/-mTDB2jdKsU

Keeping Up with the Jenners

James Truslow Adams, *The Epic of America* (New York: Little, Brown and company, 1931).

If anyone is ever fool enough to mention 'the British Dream', everyone laughs – because it sounds artificial, copycat, crass.
For instance, see 'What is the British Dream? Twitter has some ideas ...', *TheWeek.co.uk*, 4 October 2017 (www.theweek.co.uk/88803/what-is-the-british-dream-twitter-has-some-ideas)

Aristotle thought personal development was key to achieving the sort of practical wisdom a person needed to make the smart decisions that would lead to a good life.
Aristotle, *Nicomachean Ethics* (Cambridge: Hackett, trans. by Terence Irwin, 1985).

Confucius believed learning and self-improvement were essential.
Rita Mei-Ching Ng (2009) 'College and Character: What Did Confucius Teach Us About The Importance of Integrating Ethics, Character, Learning, and Education?', *Journal of College and Character*, Vol. 10, No. 4.

Growth is named as a key ingredient, for instance, in Corey Keyes's tripartite model for flourishing rather than languishing.
Christine Robitschek and Corey Keyes (2009) 'Keyes's Model of Mental Health With Personal Growth Initiative as a Parsimonious Predict.' *Journal of Counseling Psychology*, Vol. 56, No. 2, pp. 321–329.

Doing what you want to do – also known as autonomy – is fundamental to Edward Deci and Richard Ryan's Self-Determination Theory.

Richard Ryan and Edward Deci (2000) 'Self-Determination Theory and the Facilitation of Intrinsic Motivation, Social Development, and Well-Being.' *American Psychological Association*, Vol. 55, No. 1, pp. 68–78.
Richard Ryan, Veronika Huta, and Edward Deci (2008) 'Living well: A self-determination theory perspective on eudaimonia.' *Journal of Happiness Studies*, Vol. 9, No. 1, pp. 139–170.

Meaning and accomplishments are essential for Martin Seligman's PERMA model.
Martin E.P Seligman, *Flourish: a new understanding of happiness, well-being – and how to achieve them* (London: Nicholas Brealey, 2011).

Personal growth and self-acceptance are core for Carol Ryff's six-factor model.
Carol Ryff and Corey Keyes (1995) 'The Structure of Psychological Well-Being Revisited.' *Journal of Personality and Social Psychology*, Vol. 69, No. 4, pp. 719–727.
Carol Ryff and Burton Singer (2006) ' Best news yet on the six-factor model of well-being.' *Social Science Research*, Vol. 35, No. 4, pp.1103–1119.

'self-actualization': 'the desire for self-fulfillment ... to become more and more what one is, to become everything that one is capable of becoming'.
Abraham Maslow (1943) 'A Theory of Human Motivation', *Psychological Review*, Vol. 50, No. 4, pp. 370–396.

'You better not compromise yourself. It's all you got.'
Derek Norcross, 'Youth Notes: The Little Girl Can Sing', *The Orlando Sentinel*, 6 April 1969. (With thanks to Garson O'Toole, the Quote Investigator. See O'Toole's investigation into the origin of this quote at www.quoteinvestigator.com/2017/11/06/compromise).

Sir Ian McKellen ... 'the best thing I ever did' ... 'Life at last begins to make sense, when you are open and honest.'
Tomasz Frymorgen, 'It's 30 years since Ian McKellen came out and the internet is celebrating', *BBC.co.uk*, 29 January 2018.

'If I was lying on my deathbed and I had kept this secret and never ever did anything about it, I would be lying there saying, "You just blew your entire life,"' she said.
Buzz Bissinger, 'Caitlyn Jenner: The Full Story', *Vanity Fair*, 26 July 2015.

'Bruce was one of the best athletes who ever existed,'Fred Dixon once remarked. 'Now, to see that photo ... somehow it doesn't compute.'
'Bruce Jenner's Olympic Teammate – "It's Courageous ... But I Don't Get It"', *TMZ.com*, 1 June 2015.

The 'end of history' illusion.
Jordi Quoidbach, Daniel Gilbert, and Timothy Wilson (2013) 'The End of History Illusion'. *Science*, Vol. 339, No. 6115, pp. 96–98.

How to Holiday: Three Degrees of Transformation
This is one of the few parts of the book not based on science. It's my own theory.

Variety is ... the 'spice of happiness'.
Kennon Sheldon, Julia Boehm, and Sonja Lyubomirsky (2013) 'Variety is the Spice of Happiness: The Hedonic Adaptation Prevention Model.' *Oxford Handbook of Happiness*, pp. 1–18.

Something for the Weekend

Humans have enjoyed [altered states] since anyone can remember.
Yulia Ustinova (2011) 'Consciousness alteration practices in the West from prehistory to late antiquity'. *Altering consciousness: Multidisciplinary perspectives: History, culture, and the humanities; Biological and Psychological Perspectives,* E. Cardeña & M. Winkelman (Eds.). Vol. 1, pp. 45–72 (Santa Barbara, CA, US: Praeger/ABC-CLIO).

... people are happier at the moment of drinking, but there are only small overspills of that happiness into the rest of your life ... Also note that drinking does not lead to higher life satisfaction.
Ben Geiger and George Mackerron (2016) 'Can alcohol make you happy? A subjective wellbeing approach.' *Social Science & Medicine*, Vol. 156, pp. 184–91.

Sign up for comedy improv
I studied a course with Logan Murray in London (www.loganmurray.com). Or, read his awesome book: Logan Murray, *Get Started in Stand-Up Comedy* (Teach Yourself, 2015).

3. OUTSIDE & OFFLINE

Outside: Oh, We Do Like to be Beside the Seaside

Thirty-seven miles adrift of Kyushu, the most southerly of Japan's four main islands, is a tiny island called Yakushima ...
This comes from various sources, including an interview with Yoshifumi Miyazaki conducted both directly and via a translator.

Trees Are Good

Based on various sources, including:

Florence Williams,'To Fight the Winter Blues, Try a Dose of Nature', *The Wall Street Journal,* 27 January 2017.
Christopher Gidlow et al. (2016) 'Where to put your best foot forward: Psycho-physiological responses to walking in natural and urban environments.' *Journal Of Environmental Psychology*, Vol. 45, pp. 22–29.
Terry Hartiget al. (2003) 'Tracking restoration in natural and urban field settings.' *Journal of Environmental Psychology*, Vol. 23, pp. 109–123.
Gregory Bratman et al. (2015) 'The benefits of nature experience: Improved affect and cognition.' *Landscape and Urban Planning,* Vol. 138, pp. 41–50.
Alison Greenwood, Birgitta Gatersleben (2016) 'Let's go outside! Environmental restoration amongst adolescents and the impact of friends and phones.' *Journal of Environmental Psychology*, Vol. 48, pp. 131–139.

Matthew White et al. (2013) 'Feelings of restoration from recent nature visits.' *Journal of Environmental Psychology*, Vol. 35, pp. 40–51.

Folk tales, woods have been painted as dark and dangerous, places to stay away from, unless you're an outlaw
For instance, Little Red Riding Hood. And the Teddy Bears' Picnic, which begins with the line, 'If you go down to the woods today … '

Our culture doesn't seem to value forests much …
We're becoming increasingly bothered about *other people* cutting down their forests, but we have little problem cutting our own down: witness the ongoing attack on green belt land, the building of HS2 in the UK.

The medical profession thought smoking was a good idea …
Robert Klara, 'Throwback Thursday: When Doctors Prescribed 'Healthy' Cigarette Brands', *Adweek*, 18 June 18 2015.
Simon Garfield, 'The man who saved a million lives', *The Guardian*, 24 April 2005.

We Really Do Like to be Beside the Seaside

'Oh, I do like to be beside the seaside …
For the full lyrics, see Wikipedia entry: en.wikipedia.org/wiki/I_Do_Like_To_be_Beside_the_Seaside

Mappiness
The Mappiness app relaunches summer 2019.

as MacKerron and Mourato said in their scientific paper, that's the difference between attending an exhibition and cleaning the bathroom.
MacKerron and Mourato actually wrote that it was the difference between going to an exhibition and *doing the housework*—but I'm a writer, and wanted to make it easier to picture.
George MacKerron and Susana Mourato (2013) 'Happiness is greater in natural environments'. *Global Environmental Change*, Vol. 23, No. 5, pp. 992–1000.

Biophilia
Edward Wilson and Stephen Kellert (1993) 'Biophilia and the conservation ethic, in Stephen Kellert and Edward Wilson (Eds.).' *The Biophilia Hypothesis* (Washington, DC: Island Press, 1993), pp. 31–41.

If we like natural sounds because we're used to them, there's the stress of city living, the 'environmental bads' that come with modern life, like the noise and air pollution in cities.
George MacKerron and Susana Mourato (2013) 'Happiness is greater in natural environments'. *Global Environmental Change*, Vol. 23, No. 5, pp. 992–1000.

Phytoncides
Qing Li, Yoshifumi Miyazaki, et al. (2009) 'Effect of phytoncide from trees on human natural killer cell function'. *International Journal of Immunopathology & Pharmacology*, Vol. 22, No. 4, pp. 951–9.
Qing Li (2010) 'Effect of forest bathing trips on human immune function'. *Environmental Health And Preventive Medicine*, Vol. 15, No. 1, pp. 9–17.

ENDNOTES

A Very Strange Man on Hampstead Heath

Sources for this story include:

J. A. Heady and Jeremiah Morris (1953) 'Coronary Heart-Disease And Physical Activity Of Work.' *The Lancet*, Vol. 265, No. 1953, pp. 1053–1057.
Simon Kuper,'The man who invented exercise', *Financial Times*, 12 September 2009.
Dennis Hevesi, 'Jeremy Morris, Who Proved Exercise Is Heart-Healthy, Dies at 99½', *New York Times*, 7 November 2009.
And an interview with Jerry Morris's son, David.

Can You Run to Success and Happiness?

Daily Mile
The Daily Mile encourages primary and nursery schools to have their children run or jog for 15 minutes every day.

'park run'
Visit www.parkrun.com.

researchers at the University of Cambridge ... found that any sort of physical activity ... can have a positive effect ...
Neal Lathia, Gillian Sandstrom, Cecilia Mascolo, Peter Rentfrow (2017) 'Happier People Live More Active Lives: Using Smartphones to Link Happiness and Physical Activity.' *Plos One*, Vol. 12, No. 1, pp. 1–13.

Mappiness team found, people are unhappiest when they're sick in bed
George MacKerron and Susana Mourato (2013) 'Happiness is greater in natural environments'. *Global Environmental Change*, Vol. 23, No. 5, pp. 992–1000.

exercise is good for your brain ... BDNF, brain-derived neurotrophic factor ... the most likely reason why, after exercising, we often feel so at ease.
Leo Widrich, 'What Happens To Our Brains When We Exercise And How It Makes Us Happier', *Fast Company*, 4 February 2014.

... there is a 'bidirectional feedback loop and upward spiral' between happiness and exercise.
Eric Kim, Laura Kubzansky, Jackie Soo, Julia Boehm (2017) 'Maintaining Healthy Behavior: a Prospective Study of Psychological Well-Being and Physical Activity'. *Annals of Behavioral Medicine*, Vol. 51, No. 3, pp. 337–347.

'solvitur ambulando'
The Spheres at Amazon ... 'a place where employees can think and work differently surrounded by plants'. Visit www.seattlespheres.com.

Offline: To Tune In, You Need to Turn Off

'We limit how much technology our kids use at home.'—*Steve Jobs*
Nick Bilton, 'Steve Jobs Was a Low-Tech Parent', *New York Times*, 10 September 2014.

Hammersmith Apollo stage that's hosted legends like David Bowie, the Beatles, Bruce Springsteen, Public Enemy, Prince and Queen,
Source: Wikipedia (en.wikipedia.org/wiki/Hammersmith_Apollo)

Romesh Ranganathan
To keep up with Ranganathan, visit www.RomeshRanganathan.co.uk.

The Girl Who Selfie-Harmed

This story is informed by various sources including:

Madison Malone Kircher, 'Where Are You, Essena O'Neill?', *New York Magazine*, 4 November 2016.
Ellie Hunt, 'Essena O'Neill quits Instagram claiming social media 'is not real life'', *The Guardian*, 3 November 2015.
Brianna Wiest, 'A Leaked Email From Essena O'Neill Answers Every Question We Had After Her Famous Video Went Viral', *Teen Vogue*, 7 January 2016.
Abby Ohlheiser, 'Essena O'Neill: What happened in the months after Instagram star quit social media', *The Independent*, 7 January 2016.
The email Essena wrote to her followers was posted on a blog post called 'I Open At The Close' (Available at: http://agirlnamedally.tumblr.com/post/136577427665/hello-can-anyone-please-make-this-email-from).

Mirror, Mirror, On the Internet ...

This story is based on numerous interviews with Danny in 2018, as well as other sources including:

Bela Shah, 'Addicted to selfies: I take 200 snaps a day', *BBC.co.uk*, 27 February 2018.
ITV Daybreak, 24 March 2014.
Wills Robinson, 'Selfies almost killed me: Schoolboy who took 200 photos of himself every day because he wanted perfection describes how addiction drove him to attempt suicide', *Daily Mail*, 24 March 2014.

Do You Text During Sex?

Eight out of ten people check their phones within fifteen minutes of getting up.
'Planet of the Phones', *The Economist*, 26 February 2015.

The average person picks up their phone 150 times a day. Extreme users check their phones 300 times a day.
Adam Alter, *Irresistible* (New York: Penguin, 2017).

Most office emails ... are answered within six seconds.
Eames Yates, 'Most work emails are opened within 6 seconds – here's how it affects your productivity', *Business Insider*, 28 March 2017.

one out of six phones actually have faecal matter on them.
London School of Hygiene & Tropical Medicine, 'One in six mobile phones in the UK is contaminated with fecal bacteria, researchers found'. *ScienceDaily*, 15 October 2011.

[One in ten] check their phones during sex.
'Planet of the Phones', *The Economist*, 26 February 2015.
Kostadin Kushlev, Jason Proulx, and Elizabeth Dunn (2016) 'Silence Your Phones": Smartphone Notifications Increase Inattention and Hyperactivity Symptoms.' *CHI '16 Proceedings of the 2016 CHI Conference on Human Factors in Computing Systems*, pp. 1011–1020.

Are You a Mobile Addict? Quiz

Kimberly Young (1998) 'Internet addiction: The emergence of a new clinical disorder.' CyberPsychology and Behavior, Vol. 1, No. 3, pp. 237–244.

spending too much time online is bad for your health and your happiness
The data is still messy on this. Probably because there are so many people online, using the internet so many different ways, and 'too much' will be different for different people. My take on it is similar to exercise and wellbeing: there's no point taking any chances.
For a good introduction:

Adam Gopnik (2018) 'How the Internet gets inside us', *The New Yorker*, 1 February 2018.

Two instructive studies:
Morten Tromholt (2016) 'The Facebook Experiment: Quitting Facebook Leads to Higher Levels of Well-Being'. *Cyberpsychology, Behavior, and Social Networking,* Vol. 19, No. 11, pp. 661–666.
Holly Shakya and Nicholas Christakis (2017) 'Association of Facebook Use With Compromised Well-Being: A Longitudinal Study'. *American Journal of Epidemiology*, Vol. 185, No. 3, pp. 203–211.

And a convincing view:
Jean Twenge, 'There's an important link between screens and happiness that you should know', *World Economic Forum (weforum.org)*, 26 February 2018. In particular, this:
'every activity that didn't involve a screen was linked to more happiness, and every activity that involved a screen was linked to less happiness. The differences were considerable: Teens who spent more than five hours a day online were twice as likely to be unhappy as those who spent less than an hour a day.'
And:
'If you wanted to give advice based on this research, it would be very simple: Put down your phone or tablet and go do something – just about anything – else.'

If you spend more time online, you're more likely to feel isolated, stressed and depressed.
UK Office of Communications, '15m digital detoxers are ditching their device', *Ofcom*, 4 August 2016. In particular, this:
'Most internet users (59%) even consider themselves 'hooked' on their connected device ... 31% [said they] had missed out on spending time with friends and family.'

You won't sleep as well.
Jessica Levenson et al. (2016) 'The association between social media use and sleep disturbance among young adults'. *Preventive Medicine*, Vol. 85, pp. 36–41.

Even checking in every now and then is bad for your ability to get things done ... when interrupted, people take an average of twenty-three minutes to return to their original task.
Gloria Mark, Daniela Gudith and Ulrich Klocke (2008) 'The cost of interrupted work: More speed and stress'. *Proceedings of the 2008 Conference on Human Factors in Computing Systems,* pp. 107–110.

If you reduce the time you spend online, so a study by the Happiness Research Institute found, you'll feel better quite quickly.
'The Facebook Experiment: Does Social Media Affect the Quality of our Lives?', *Happiness Research Institute*, 2015.

The Wizards and the WMDs in Silicon Valley

The story of Tristan Harris is based on various sources, including:

Tristan Harris, 'How Technology is Hijacking Your Mind — from a Magician and Google Design Ethicist', *Medium*, 18 May 2016.
Bianca Bosker, 'The Binge Breaker', *The Atlantic*, 11 November 2016.
Nicholas Thompson, 'Our Minds Have Been Hijacked By Our Phones. Tristan Harris Wants To Rescue Them',*Wired*, 26 July 2017.
Essays, videos, and interviews on www.tristanharris.com

Pavlov had figured out something called classical conditioning: if you ring a bell every time you bring a dog food, and then just ring a bell, the dogs salivate as if you're bringing food
Though Pavlov, actually, didn't use a bell.
Michael Specter, 'Drool', *New Yorker*, 24 November 2014.

B. F. Skinner and 'operant conditioning'
B.F Skinner, *The Behavior of Organisms: An Experimental Analysis* (New York: Appleton-Century-Crofts, 1938).

'This is actually something you can apply across species,' Skinner said. 'It applies just as well to the human as to the pigeon.'
Natasha Dow Schüll, 'The Dark Side of Habit', *Nir Eyal's Habit Summit*, 17 March 2014. View it at https://youtu.be/ak0HE8Y_UJY

fruit machines are 'the most virulent form of gambling in the history of man' … 'electronic morphine' … 'crack cocaine of gambling'.
Ibid.

computers were now being used to change people's behaviours and create new habits – and that they'd get even better at it in the future.
Fogg, BJ (1998) 'Persuasive Computers: Perspectives and Research Directions.' Proceeding of the CHI '98 Conference on Human Factors in Computing Systems. Pp. 225-232.

Thanks to simple operant conditioning that works on pigeons as well as people, the habit becomes stronger and stronger until it's almost instinctive.
Fogg has pointed out to me that operant conditioning has never interested him and has not been a subject for his research.

'Once you know how to push people's buttons, you can play them like a piano.'
Tristan Harris, 'How Technology is Hijacking Your Mind — from a Magician and Google Design Ethicist', *Medium*, 18 May 2016.

'Magicians do the same thing,' he wrote. 'You make it easier for a spectator to pick the thing you want them to pick, and harder to pick the thing you don't.'
Ibid.

Center for Humane Technology
www.humanetech.com

Steve Jobs and the Low-Tech Lifestyle

Facebook and its subsidiary Instagram, and Google, for instance, have introduced tools to help people monitor and limit how much time they're spending on their devices.

Bianca Bosker
Bianca Bosker, 'The Binge Breaker', *The Atlantic*, 11 November 2016.

Nick Bilton
Nick Bilton, 'Steve Jobs Was a Low-Tech Parent', *New York Times*, 10 September 2014.

Alastair Humphreys
Alastair Humphreys, *Microadventures: Local Discoveries for Great Escapes* (London: William Collins, 2014).

4. RELATIONSHIPS

The Girl with the Opposite of Loneliness

This story is based on various sources, including:

Marina Keegan, 'The Opposite of Loneliness', *YaleDailyNews.com*, 27 May 2012.
Marina Keegan, *The Opposite of Loneliness: Essays and Stories* (Simon and Schuster: 2015).
Jack Hitt, 'Remembering Marina Keegan', *New Yorker*, 6 June 2012.
See Marina perform her poem 'Rolling Stones' on Youtube: https://youtu.be/zDHH7N592iI

Help! We All Need Somebody

This story is based on various sources, including:

Rhian Lubin, 'Elderly couple who rang 999 because they were 'lonely' praise caring officers who called round', *Manchester Evening News*, 12 November 2015.
Lucy Clarke-Billings, 'Elderly couple call 999 because they're lonely – so police go round for a cup of tea', *Daily Telegraph*, 11 November 2015.

Loneliness strangles you slowly …
Sarah Knapton, 'Having no friends could be as deadly as smoking, Harvard University finds', *Daily Telegraph*, 24 August 2016.
Aparna Shankar, Anne McMunn, James Banks, and Andrew Steptoe (2011) 'Loneliness, social isolation, and behavioral and biological health indicators in older adults.' *Health Psychology*, Vol, 30, No. 4, pp. 377–85.
Leah Doane and Emma Adam (2010) 'Loneliness and Cortisol: Momentary, Day-to-day, and Trait Associations.' *Psychoneuroendocrinology*, Vol. 35, No. 3, pp. 430–441.

Loneliness leaves you stressed, depressed …
Hara Estroff Marano, 'The Dangers of Loneliness', *Psychology Today*, 1 July 2003.
Erin York Cornwell and Linda White (2009) 'Social Disconnectedness, Perceived Isolation, and Health among Older Adults'. *Journal Health and Social Behaviour*, Vol. 50, No.1, pp. 31–48.

social isolation, loneliness and living alone – increase your chance of death, respectively, by 26 per cent, 29 per cent, and 32 per cent.
Julianne Holt-Lunstad et al. (2015) 'Loneliness and Social Isolation as Risk Factors for Mortality: A Meta-Analytic Review.' *Perspectives on Psychological Science 2015*, Vol. 10, No. 2, pp. 227–237.

having better social connections ... makes you 50 per cent more likely to be alive.
Julianne Holt-Lunstad, Timothy Smith, Bradley Layton (2010) 'Social Relationships and Mortality Risk: A Meta-analytic Review.' *PLoS Med*, Vol. 7, No. 7.

loneliness worse than smoking fifteen cigarettes a day, worse than obesity, worse than Type 2 diabetes.
Julianne Holt-Lunstad et al. (2015) 'Loneliness and Social Isolation as Risk Factors for Mortality: A Meta-Analytic Review.' *Perspectives on Psychological Science 2015*, Vol. 10, No. 2, pp. 227–237.
Denis Campbell, 'Loneliness as bad for health as long-term illness, says GPs' chief, *The Guardian*, 12 October 2017.

Three out of four doctors in the UK say they see at least one, and as many as five, lonely people each day.
Source: Campaign to End Loneliness.
Denis Campbell, 'Loneliness as bad for health as long-term illness, says GPs' chief, *The Guardian*, 12 October 2017.

There's No Shame Being Hungry

loneliness plus living alone and social isolation ... are an old person's problem.
Over half (51%) of all people aged 75 and over live alone, according to the ONS (2010). Two fifths all older people (about 3.9 million) say the television is their main company, according to Age UK (2014).

loneliness plus living alone and social isolation ... a young person's problem too.
Sean Coughlan,'Loneliness more likely to affect young people', *BBC.co.uk*, 10 April 2018.
'The Loneliness Experiment', *BBC and Wellcome Foundation*, 2018.
'16–24 year olds are the loneliest age group according to new BBC Radio 4 survey', *BBC.co.uk*, 1 October 2018.

There are 700,000 men, and 1.1 million women in Britain who are lonely.
George Monbiot, 'The age of loneliness is killing us', *The Guardian*, 14 October 2014.

Over 9 million people in the UK – almost a fifth of the population – say they are always or often lonely, but almost two thirds feel uncomfortable admitting to it
'Trapped in a bubble: An investigation into triggers for loneliness in the UK.' *British Red Cross Society and Co-operative Group*, 5 December 2016.

A third of Americans over forty-five say they are 'chronically lonely'
Oscar Anderson and Colette Thayer, 'Loneliness and Social Connections: A National Survey of Adults 45 and Older' (Washington, DC: AARP Research, 2018).

Loneliness ... is just like hunger and thirst and pain.
Tim Adams, 'Interview: John Cacioppo: 'Loneliness is like an iceberg – it goes deeper than we can see', *The Guardian*, 28 February 2016.

UCLA Loneliness Scale.
Dan Russell, Letitia A. Peplau and Carolyn E. Cutrona (1980) 'The Revised UCLA Loneliness Scale: Concurrent and Discriminant Validity Evidence.' *Journal of Personality and Social Psychology*, Vol. 39, No. 3, pp. 472–480.
Dan Russell (1996) 'UCLA Loneliness Scale (Version 3): Reliability, validity, and factor structure.' *Journal of Personality Assessment*, Vol. 66, No. 1, pp. 20–40.

most people who say they're lonely are married or live with others.
Guy Winch, 'Together but Still Lonely', *Psychology Today*, 28 June 2013.

people who have five friends have 20 per cent higher fibrinogen compared to people with twenty-five friends ... around ten fewer friends ... can have the same impact as taking up smoking.
Sarah Knapton, 'Having no friends could be as deadly as smoking, Harvard University finds', *Daily Telegraph*, 24 August 2016.

Living alone doesn't necessarily lead to social isolation ...
Eric Klinenberg, *Going Solo: The Extraordinary Rise and Surprising Appeal of Living Alone* (London: Duckworth, 2014).

'People who live alone tend to spend more time socializing with friends and neighbours than people who are married,' Klinenberg once said. 'Living alone is not an entirely solitary experience. It's generally a quite social one.'
Joseph Stromberg, 'Eric Klinenberg on Going Solo', *Smithsonian Magazine*, February 2012.

How to Achieve the Opposite of Loneliness – According to Science

Even if your doing involves a lot of not-doing.
Bertrand Russell, *In Praise of Idleness* (London: Routledge,1935).

Experiences ... set off a domino line that almost inevitably takes us away from social isolation and feelings of loneliness, and towards the opposite: to meaningful connections and relationships that will help us live longer and happier.
James Wallman, *Stuffocation* (London: Penguin, 2015).
Peter Caprariello, Harry Reis (2012) 'To do with others to have (or to do alone?): The value of experiences over material possessions depends on the involvement of others.' *University of Rochester*, Vol. 104, No. 2.
Cassie Mogilner (2010) 'The Pursuit of Happiness: Time, Money, and Social Connection.' *Psychological Science*, Vol. 21, No. 9, pp. 1348–1354.
Katherine Jacobs Bao and Sonja Lyubomirsky (2014) 'Making Happiness Last: Using the Hedonic Adaptation Prevention Model to Extend the Success of Positive Interventions.' In Parks, A. (Ed.), The handbook of positive interventions. New York: Wiley-Interscience. pp. 1–24.
In particular this:
'People can increase the number of positive events and emotions they experience by engaging in particular activities or by making those activities more social.'

Second, doing something gives you an identity and a sense of belonging.
Gregory Walton and Shannon Brady (2017) 'The Many Questions of Belonging.' *Relevant Processes*, pp. 272–293.

The third reason why experiences are so good for happiness is that if you do something you'll have something interesting to talk about.
Or at least, *something* to talk about, and as we know, that fires up mirror neurons, which creates empathy and connection.
Paul Zak, How 'Stories Change the Brain', *Greater Good Magazine*, 17 December 2013.

Solitude is quite distinct from loneliness
This is summed up very well by: Hara Estroff Marano, 'What Is Solitude?', *Psychology Today*, 1 July 2003.

Hello, Stranger! The Surprising Joy of Talking to People You Don't Know

This is based on Nicholas Epley and Juliana Schroeder (2014) 'Mistakenly Seeking Solitude.' *Journal of Experimental Psychology General*, Vol. 143, No. 5, pp. 1–20.

Malavika Varadan ... TEDx talk, 'Seven Ways to Make a Conversation with Anyone'
Watch it at www.timeandhowtospendit.com/malavika.

5. INTENSITY

Mr Mouse, the Scaredy Cat, and the Rise of the Sufferfests

Source for this section: my own experience, conversations and interviews with Scott and Amber Keneally, articles Scott has written, and Scott's film, *Rise of The Sufferfests* (2016)—still available at www.riseofthesufferfests.com.

Tough Mudder and Tough Guy
www.toughmudder.com and www.toughguy.co.uk

From only 50,000 people doing it in 2009, in the US, where there are good figures available, there are now more than 5 million taking part.
50,000: Amy Donaldson, 'Rise of the Sufferfests' offers exploration of why obstacle course racing is the world's fastest growing sport', *Deseret News*, 30 October 2016.
5.3 million: Haddon Rabb and Jillian Coleby (2018) 'Hurt on the Hill: A Longitudinal Analysis of Obstacle Course Racing Injuries, Orthopaedic.' *Journal of Sports Medicine*, Vol. 6, No. 6.

Meeting Mr Mouse

Hear and see Amber's song at www.timeandhowtospendit.com/amber.

Beep Beep! When a Radical New Approach Signals a Revolution

This section is informed by:

Mihaly Csikszentmihalyi, *Flow: The Psychology of Optimal Experience* (New York: Harper Perennial Modern Classics; 2008).

Reed Larson and Mihaly Csikszentmihalyi (1983) 'The Experience Sampling Method.' In H. T. Reis (Ed.), *New Directions for Methodology of Social and Behavioral Sciences*, Vol. 15, pp. 41–56.

Mihaly Csikszentmihalyi and Judith LeFevre (1989) 'Optimal Experience in Work and Leisure.' *Journal of Personality and Social Psychology,* Vol. 56, No. 5, pp. 815–822.

Csikszentmihalyi was born in 1934 ...
Andrew Cooper, 'The Man Who Found the Flow', *Lions Roar*, 1 September 1998.

the 'remembering self' and the 'experiencing self'
Daniel Kahneman, *Thinking, Fast and Slow* (New York: Penguin, 2011).

Carey Morewedge, 'Utility: Anticipated, Experienced, and Remembered'. In G. Keren and G. Wu (Eds.), *Wiley Blackwell Handbook of Judgment and Decision Making*, pp. 295–330 (Malden, MA: Blackwell Press, 2016).

Richard Walker, John Skowronski and Charles Thompson (2003) 'Life Is Pleasant—and Memory Helps to Keep It That Way!' *Review of General Psychology*, Vol. 7, No. 2, pp. 203–210.

Lorraine was a senior in high school ...
Mihaly Csikszentmihalyi, *Flow and the Foundations of Positive Psychology* (New York: Springer Dordrecht Heidelberg, 2014).

How to be Superman

'group flow' and 'coactive flow'
Charles J. Walker (2010) 'Experiencing flow: Is doing it together better than doing it alone?' *The Journal of Positive Psychology*, Vol. 5, No. 1, pp. 3–11.

Keith Sawyer (2015) 'Group Flow and Group Genius.' *The NAMTA Journal*, Vol. 40, No. 3, pp. 29–52.

Steven Kotler
Find the Flow Genome Project at www.flowgenomeproject.com.

Steven Kotler, *The Rise of Superman: Decoding the science of ultimate human performance* (London: Quercus, 2015).

Herbert Benson
Benson-Henry Institute, www.bensonhenryinstitute.org

Herbert Benson, *The Relaxation Response* (New York: Morrow, 1975).

Herbert Benson, *The Breakout Principle: How to activate the natural trigger that maximizes creativity, productivity, and personal well-being* (New York: Scribner, 2003).

'peak experience'
Abraham Maslow, *Religions, Values, and Peak-experiences* (New York: Viking Press, 1964).

William James called them 'mystical experiences'. See:
William James, *The Varieties of Religious Experience: A Study in human Nature*. (New York: Prometheus Books, 1911).

The Rat People – and the Fake Flow in Your Phone

The story about Darlene comes directly from the Natasha Dow Schüll, *Addiction by Design: machine gambling in Las Vegas* (Princeton: Princeton University Press, 2014).

More than half of Britons – 59 per cent – say they're hooked to their devices. And many of us now spend somewhere between 40 and 60 per cent of our leisure time looking at our screens.
UK Office of Communications: '15m digital detoxers are ditching their device', *Ofcom*, 4 August 2016.

A Superman in the Arena

Its rating on the online movie bible, IMDB, is 8.1 out of 10. On Amazon.com it's 4.4 out of 5. On Apple, 4.7. Ratings as of January 2019.

President Roosevelt was at the Sorbonne in Paris, more than a hundred years ago, when he talked about the 'man in the arena'
The man in the arena is an excerpt from the speech 'Citizenship In A Republic' delivered by Theodore Roosevelt at the Sorbonne, in Paris, France on 23 April, 1910.

Šárka Elias
Watch Šárka play 'I Find My Joy' at www.timeandhowtospendit.com/sarka or visit www.SarkaElias.com

6. EXTRAORDINARY

The New Peak-End Rules

'Dad was a poor Jew from Brooklyn … '
The story of Victoria Grand is based on my experience, my diary from the time, and interviews with Victoria.

Swami Vivekananda Saraswati was and is a great guy. Nowadays, I think he's in Koh Pha Ngan in Thailand.
He is! I looked him up. He founded a yoga centre there called Agama Yoga. Visit him there and at www.agamayoga.com.

Marcelo, Simon, Ellie and Geoff …
I didn't keep up with Marcelo or Simon, but Ellie and Geoff I'm sort of in contact with. Ellie's become a writer. She's at www.elliemarney.com.

The Old Peak-End Rule

A few of the experiments that led to the formation of, and support the usefulness of, the peak-end rule:

Daniel Kahneman, Barbara Fredrickson, Charles Schreiber, and Donald Redelmeier (1993) 'When More Pain Is Preferred to Less: Adding a Better End.' *Psychological Science*, Vol. 4, No. 6, pp. 401–405.
Ziv Carmon and Daniel Kahneman (1995) 'The Experienced Utility of Queuing : Real-Time Affect and Retrospective Evaluations of Simulated Queues.'

Daniel Kahneman and Donald Redelmeier (1996) 'Patients' memories of painful medical treatments: Real-time and retrospective evaluations of two minimally invasive procedures.' *Pain*, Vol. 66, No. 1, pp. 3–8.

... we remember life through 'snapshots'
Daniel Kahneman & Amos Tversky (1999) 'Evaluation by moments: Past and future.' In D. Kahneman & A. Tversky (Eds.), *Choices, values and frames*, pp. 2–23 (New York: Cambridge University Press, 1999).

The New Peak-End Rules

Does the peak-end rule also work for longer experiences? And if it doesn't, how should we think about longer experiences?
Talya Miron-Shatz (2009) 'Evaluating multi-episode events: A boundary condition for the peak-end rule.' *Emotion*, Vol. 9, No. 2, pp. 206–213.
Simon Kemp, Christopher Burt, and Laura Furneaux (2008) 'A test of the Peak-End rule with extended autobiographical events.' *Memory & Cognition*, Vol. 36, No. 1, pp. 132–138.

'Duration neglect'
Barbara Fredrickson and Daniel Kahneman (1993) 'Duration Neglect in Retrospective Evaluations of Affective Episodes.' *Journal of Personality and Social Psychology*, Vol.65, No. 1, pp. 45–55.

... people ... don't remember as accurately as we'd like to think we do ... we dig out a few snapshots ... to make up a movie about what happened.
Daniel Kahneman & Amos Tversky (1999) 'Evaluation by moments: Past and future'. In D. Kahneman & A. Tversky (Eds.), *Choices, values and frames*, pp. 2–23 (New York: Cambridge University Press, 1999).

Trying out new things ... is key for happiness
This is one of the Ten Keys To Happier Living, from UK charity, Action For Happiness (www.actionforhappiness.org).

Variety ... is the 'spice of happiness'.
Kennon Sheldon, Julia Boehm, and Sonja Lyubomirsky (2013) 'Variety is the Spice of Happiness: The Hedonic Adaptation Prevention Model.' *Oxford Handbook of Happiness*, pp. 1–18.
Katherine Jacobs Bao and Sonja Lyubomirsky (2014) 'Making Happiness Last: Using the Hedonic Adaptation Prevention Model to Extend the Success of Positive Interventions.' In Parks, A. (Ed.), *The handbook of positive interventions*, pp. 1–24 (New York: Wiley-Interscience, 2014).

Doing new things helps us get as close as possible to the upper range of happiness available for each of us.
If you try new experiences, you're ever less likely to get bored and avoid getting stuck on the 'hedonic treadmill':
Kennon M. Sheldon and Sonja Lyubomirsky (2012) 'The Challenge of Staying Happier : Testing the Hedonic Adaptation Prevention Model.' *Personality and Social Psychology Bulletin*, Vol. 38, No. 5, pp. 670–680.

New things help people feel more positive ... Just as homes and bank balances are assets that can protect us in times of need, so memories can too.

Gal Zauberman, Rebecca Ratner and B. Kyu Kim (2008) 'Memories as Assets: Strategic Memory Protection in Choice over Time.' *Journal Of Consumer Research,Inc.*, Vol. 35, No. 5, pp. 715–728.

'hedonic treadmill'
Richard Lucas, Christie Napa Scollon and Ed Diener (2006) 'Beyond the Hedonic Treadmill.' *American Psychologist*, Vol. 61, No. 1, pp. 305–314.
James Wallman, *Stuffocation* (London: Penguin, 2015) for why we tend to get bored of material things quicker than experiences.

Trying out new things enables us to build 'experiential CVs'. They expand our sense of self, of who we are and what we can do.
Anat Keinan and Ran Kivetz (2011) 'Productivity Orientation and the Consumption of Collectable Experiences.' *Journal Of Consumer Research*, Vol. 37,No. 6, pp. 935–950.

New release dopamine, which makes us feel good.
Belle Beth Cooper, 'Novelty and the Brain: Why New Things Make Us Feel So Good', *Lifehacker*, 21 May 2013.

They stimulate our minds, make us more creative, and strengthen connections in our brains.
'Rev up your thinking skills by trying something new', *Harvard Health Publishing*, 10 December 2015.

They give us a chance to exercise one of the defining features of being human too, our innate curiosity.
Celeste Kidd and Benjamin Hayden (2015) 'The psychology and neuroscience of curiosity.' *Neuron*, Vol. 88, No.3, pp. 449–460.

awe ...
Dacher Keltner and Jonathan Haidt (2010) 'Approaching awe, a moral, spiritual, and aesthetic emotion.' *Cognition and Emotion*, Vol. 17, No. 2, pp. 297–314.

the anticipating self.
Carey Morewedge (2016) 'Utility: Anticipated, Experienced, and Remembered'. In G. Keren and G. Wu (Eds.), *Wiley Blackwell Handbook of Judgment and Decision Making*, pp. 295–330 (Malden, MA: Blackwell Press, 2016).

us anticipation, which is one of the key reasons why experiences are better than material goods at making us happy: because anticipation is free happiness.
James Wallman. *Stuffocation* (London: Penguin, 2015).
Martha Roberts, 'The joy of anticipation', *Psychologies*, 8 April 2014.

if people treat something quite ordinary as special, they get much more from it.
Colin West, Cassie Mogilner, and Sanford DeVoe, 'How Vacation Increases Happiness' (working paper). Published in Cassie Mogilner Holmes, 'Treat Your Weekend Like a Vacation', *Harvard Business Review*, 31 January 2019.

The Essential Ingredients of the New Peak-End Rules 3: Savouring the End

'explore and exploit'

Meredith Addicott, John Pearson, Maggie Sweitzer, David Barack, and Michael Platt (2017) 'A Primer on Foraging and the Explore/Exploit Trade-Off for Psychiatry Research.' *Neuropsychopharmacology*, Vol. 42, No. 10, pp. 1931–1939.

'savour at the end'
Paul Jose, Bee Lim, and Fred Bryant (2012) 'Does savoring increase happiness? A daily diary study.' *The Journal of Positive Psychology*, Vol. 7, No. 3, pp. 176–187.
Sonja Lyubomirsky, *The How of Happiness: a new approach to getting the life you want* (New York: Penguin Books, 2008).

The Extraordinary Magic in the Ordinary Everyday

To have any chance of being happy ... you have to enjoy ordinary experiences.
Amit Bhattacharjee and Cassie Mogilner (2014) 'Happiness from ordinary and extraordinary experiences.'*Journal of Consumer Research, Inc.*, Vol. 41, No. 1, pp. 1–17.

The best place to find happiness is ... in little everyday pleasures
Paul Jose, Bee Lim & Fred Bryant (2012) 'Does savoring increase happiness? A daily diary study.' *The Journal of Positive Psychology*, Vol. 7, No. 3, pp. 176–187.
Sonja Lyubomirsky, *The How of Happiness: a new approach to getting the life you want* (New York: Penguin Books, 2008).
And rather than spend all your hard-earned cash on one blow-out, extraordinary experience ... you'd be better off spending little and often
Because of adaptation:
Kennon Sheldon and Sonja Lyubomirsky (2012) 'The Challenge of Staying Happier : Testing the Hedonic Adaptation Prevention Model.' *Personality and Social Psychology Bulletin*, Vol. 38, No. 5, pp. 670–680.

if you think of an ordinary experience – in this case, an average weekend – as if it's something special, you get much more out of it.
Colin West, Cassie Mogilner, and Sanford DeVoe, 'How Vacation Increases Happiness' (working paper). Published in Cassie Mogilner Holmes, 'Treat Your Weekend Like a Vacation', *Harvard Business Review*, 31 January 2019.

'the most humdrum experiences'
Mihaly Csikszentmihalyi, *Flow: The Psychology of Optimal Experience* (New York: Harper Perennial Modern Classics, 2008).

'The sacred is in the ordinary ... it is to be found in one's daily life, in one's neighbors, friends, and family, in one's backyard.'
Abraham Maslow, *Religions, Values, and Peak-experiences* (New York: Viking Press, 1964).

How to Make Your Life a Masterpiece

Younger people ... prefer the 'excited happiness' ... As people age, they enjoy 'calm happiness' more ...
Amit Bhattacharjee and Cassie Mogilner (2014) 'Happiness from ordinary and extraordinary experiences.' *Journal of Consumer Research*, Vol. 41, No. 1, pp. 1–17.

Cassie Mogilner, Sepandar Kamvar and Jennifer Aaker (2010) 'The Shifting Meaning of Happiness.' *Social Psychological and Personality Science*, Vol. 2, No. 4, pp. 395–402.
Jennifer Aaker and Sepandar Kamvar (2012) 'How Happiness Affects Choice.' *Journal of Consumer Research*,Vol. 39, No. 2, pp. 429–443.

7. STATUS & SIGNIFICANCE

I'd Like to Thank the Academy ... Wouldn't I?

Robin Williams opened an envelope ...
'Mo'Nique winning Best Supporting Actress', *Oscars Youtube channel*, 12 March 2010. Watch this scene at https://youtu.be/dxxqA4NhQM4.

When it comes to being thanked, the Academy wins hands down, beating God and even Meryl Streep, who's thanked twice as often as God, by some distance.
Fantastic analysis by Nathaniel Rogers and Chris Kirk, 'Meryl Streep Gets Thanked More Than God', *Slate*, 19 February 2014.

Donald Redelmeier ...
Donald Redelmeier and Sheldon Singh (2001) 'Survival in Academy Award–Winning Actors and Actresses.' *American College of Physicians–American Society of Internal Medicine*, Vol. 134, No. 10, pp. 955–962.
I conducted the interview with Redelmeier by email. He (famously) answers with numbered answers. For the sake of flow for the reader—and with Redelmeier's agreement—I've simplified our email correspondence into conversation.

has 'applied scientific rigor to topics that in lesser hands might have been dismissed as quirky and iconoclastic' and 'perhaps the leading debunker of preconceived notions in the medical world'.
Katie Hafneraug, 'Think the Answer's Clear? Look Again', *New York Times*, 30 August 2010.

Jack Palance ... one-handed push-ups
Watch Palance doing one handed press-ups at 'Jack Palance Wins Supporting Actor: 1992 Oscars', Oscars Youtube channel, available at: https://youtu.be/AGxL5AFzzMY.

some other scientists ... decided they'd read it wrong
Marc-Pierre Sylvestre, E Huszti, and James Hanley (2006) 'Do Oscar winners live longer than less successful peers? A reanalysis of the evidence.' *Annals of Internal Medicine*, Vol. 145, No. 5, pp. 361–3.
Marc-Pierre Sylvestre (2007) 'Oscar winners do not live longer.' *Annals of Internal medicine*, Vol. 134, No. 10, pp. 955–962.

The Curious Case of the Status Syndrome

This is based on:

Michael Marmot, *Status Syndrome: How Your Place on the Social Gradient Directly Affects Your Health* (London: Bloomsbury, 2015).
And by interviews with Marmot, conducted by telephone and email in 2018.

a study on the British civil service that would … lead to a startling new understanding of the importance of status on stress, health, happiness and longevity.
Michael Marmot et al. (1991) 'Health inequalities among British civil servants: The Whitehall II study.' *Epidemiology*, Vol 337, Issue No. 8754, pp. 1387–1393.

What's Wrong with Status?

Amartya Sen and the three things they need: control, capabilities and social participation.
Amartya Sen, *Commodities and capabilities* (Oxford: Oxford University Press, 1985).

Five Routes to Higher Status

Transformational Travel Council
www.transformational.travel

'micro-adventures'
Alastair Humphreys, *Microadventures: Local Discoveries for Great Escapes* (London: William Collins, 2014).

'The plots and characters of the popular shows are so repetitive … people report some of the lowest levels of concentration, use of skills, clarity of thought, and feelings of potency when watching television.'
Mihaly Csikszentmihalyi, *Flow: The Psychology of Optimal Experience* (New York: Harper Perennial Modern Classics, 2008).

From a Wooden Shack to the White House: The World's First Female Self-Made Millionaire

This section is based on various sources, including:

Dawn McCall, *Making Their Mark: Black Women Leaders* (Washington: eJournal USA, 2012).
'Wealthiest Negress Dead', *New York Times*, 26 May 1919.
Bundles, A'Lelia, *On Her Own Ground: The Life and Times of Madam C. J. Walker.* (New York: Washington Square Press, 2002).

The Right and the Wrong Sort of Status: Lessons from Two Self-Made Billionaires

The short story of Minecraft is based on various sources, including:

Stephany Nunneley, 'Minecraft has sold over 144 million copies and has 75 million monthly active users', *VG247.com*, 23 January 2018.
Meaghan Lee Callaghan, 'Minecraft Is Now The Second Most Popular Game Ever', *Popular Science*, 2 June 2016
Chris Matyszczyk, 'Billionaire who sold Minecraft to Microsoft is sad and lonely', *CNET*, 30 August 2015.

Aristotle … the traits of the 'good man' is that he will display 'magnificence', by spending large amounts of his wealth on the city where he lives.
Aristotle, *Nicomachean Ethics* (Cambridge: Hackett, trans. by Terence Irwin, 1985).

'Sack Girl'—the story of Oprah Winfrey
Based on various sources, including:

Paul Harris, 'You go, girl', *Observer*, 20 November 2005.

'Oprah Winfrey', InsidePhilanthropy.com
Jen Jones Donatelli, *Oprah Winfrey: Celebrity with Heart* (New Jersey: Enslow Publishers, 2010).

When Halle Berry won an Oscar in 2002, like Mo'Nique, she also thanked Winfrey, calling her 'the best role model any girl can have'.
Halle Berry, 'Acceptance Speech at the 74th Academy Awards, Kodak Theatre, Hollywood', *Academy Awards Acceptance Speech Database, Academy of Motion Picture Arts and Sciences*, 24 March 2002.

Your Mum was Right: It is Better to Give

Elizabeth Dunn and Michael Norton, *Happy Money: The Science of Spending* (New York: Simon & Schuster, 2013).

Now, rather than investigate how people spend their money, they are looking at how people spend, and how they think about spending, their other precious resource: time.
For instance, see:

Cassie Mogilner and Michael Norton (2016) 'Time, money, and happiness.' *Current Opinion in Psychology*, Vol. 10, pp. 12–16.
Jennifer Aaker, Melanie Rudd and Cassie Mogilner (2011) 'If money does not make you happy, consider time.' *Journal of Consumer Psychology* 21, Vo. 21, No. 2, pp. 126–130.
Ashley Whillans, 'Time For Happiness', *Harvard Business Review*, January 2019.

people feel more time poor than ever
Brigid Schulte, *Overwhelmed: Work, Love, and Play When No One Has the Time* (Toronto: Harpercollins Canada, 2015).

In the UK, three out of four Brits now feel overwhelmed.
'Stress: Are we coping?', Mental Health Foundation, May 2018.

Just as spending money on others is a sure strategy for more happiness, so is spending time on others ... giving time to others makes people feel more 'time abundant', as if they have more ... positive happy loop: if you give now, next time you have the chance to give, you will remember the happiness and give more.
Cassie Mogilner, Zoë Chance, and Michael Norton (2012) 'Giving Time Gives You Time', *Psychological Science*, Vol. 23, No. 10, pp. 1233–1238.

CONCLUSION

Eternal Sunshine for Everyone's Minds

You Probably Think this Book is About You

the waste and impact of material goods, both upstream and downstream
Watch the 'Story of Stuff' and read 'Story of Stuff, Referenced and Annotated Script', which contains evidence for the video's statements, at www.storyof-stuff.org.

Note also that flying's footprint has reduced dramatically in recent years, and I believe it'll reduce still further in the years to come.
For instance, consider the 787 Dreamliner, which reduces fuel use and CO_2 emissions by 20–30%; also, Jérôme Bouchard and Fabrice Villaumé, 'New Technology May Help Airlines Cut Fuel Use And Travel Time', *Forbes.com*, 20 July 2018.

Since science has shown that experientialism is better than materialism at making people happy …
James Wallman, *Stuffocation* (London: Penguin, 2015).
Thomas Gilovich, Amit Kumar and Lily Jampol (2014) 'A wonderful life: experiential consumption and the pursuit of happiness.' *Journal of Consumer Psychology*, pp.1–14.
Thomas Gilovich and Amit Kumar (2014) 'We'll Always Have Paris: The Hedonic Payoff from Experiential and Material Investments.' *Advances in Experimental Social Psychology*, Vol. 51, number 1. Pp. 147–187.
Tim Kasser, *The High Price of Materialism* (Cambridge, Massachusetts: MIT Press, 2002).
Tim Kasser (2016) 'Materialistic Values and Goals.' *Annual Review of Psychology*, Vol. 67, No. 1, pp. 489–514.

… research shows that experientialists are more likely to be prosocial, that is, they're more likely to think of others and do things for them too.
Tim Kasser, *The High Price of Materialism* (Cambridge, Massachusetts: MIT Press, 2002) for how materialistic people are not pro-social.
Amit Kumar, Thomas Mann, and Thomas Gilovich (2014), 'Questioning the "I" in Experience: Experiential Purchases Foster Social Connection', in *NA – Advances in Consumer Research*, Volume 42, eds. June Cotte and Stacy Wood, Duluth, MN: Association for Consumer Research, pp. 101–105.
Jesse Walker and Amit Kumar (2016) 'Cultivating Gratitude and Giving Through Experiential Consumption.' *Emotion*, Vol. 16, No. 8, pp. 1126–1136, 1528–3542.

One of the most interesting, and almost always overlooked, aspects of why inequality is bad for societies is that the most important factor that leads to differences in health, happiness and longevity isn't material abundance. It's differences in status.
Richard Wilkinson and Kate Pickett, *The Spirit Level: Why more equal societies almost always do better* (London: Allen Lane, 2009).

when people are asked if they'd swap an experience – a three-star holiday in the Bahamas, say – for a fancier version – like a five-star trip to the Bahamas – they are far less likely to. The answer, so psychologists have figured out, is that their experience was uniquely theirs.
Travis Carter and Thomas Gilovich (2010) 'The Relative Relativity of Material and Experiential Purchases.' *Journal of Personality and Social Psychology*, Vol. 98, No. 1, pp. 146–159.
Travis Carter and Thomas Gilovich (2012) 'I Am What I Do, not What I Have: The Centrality of Experiential Purchases to the Self-Concept.' *Journal of Personality and Social Psychology*, Vol. 102, No. 6, pp. 1304–1317.

poorer people ... currently spend a higher proportion of their income trying to keep up with the arms race of consumerism.

Jennifer Sheehy-Skeffington and Jessica Rea (2017) ' How poverty affects people's decision-making processes.' *Joseph Rowntree Foundation.* pp. 1–79.
Philip Mazzocco, Derek Rucker, Adam Galinsky and Eric Anderson (2012) 'Direct and vicarious conspicuous consumption: Identification with low-status groups increases the desire for high-status goods.' *Journal of Consumer Psychology*, Vol. 22, No. 4, pp. 520–528.
Derek Rucker and Adam Galinsky (2008) 'Desire to Acquire: Powerlessness and Compensatory Consumption.' *Journal of Consumer Research*, Vol. 35, No. 2, pp. 257–267.

societies evolve through a mix of innovation and imitation
Gabriel Tarde, *The Laws of Imitation*, trans. Elsie Clews Parsons (New York: Henry Holt and Company, 1903).
Everett M. Rogers, *Diffusion of Innovations* (New York: Free Press, 1962, fifth edition, 2003).

Diffusion of Innovations diagram
Everett M. Rogers, *Diffusion of Innovations* (New York: Free Press, 1962, fifth edition, 2003).

How to Train Your Elephant

This section is based on various sources, including:

an interview with BJ Fogg in 2018.
Ian Leslie, 'The Scientists Who Make Apps Addictive', *1843 Magazine*, October/November 2016.
Fogg's websites: www.behaviormodel.org. www.tinyhabits.com, www.bjfogg.com
Miguel Helft, 'The Class That Built Apps, and Fortunes', *New York Times*, 7 May 2011.
BJ Fogg, 'Forget big change, start with a tiny habit: BJ Fogg at TEDxFremont', *TEDxFremont*, 5 December 2012 (Available at: www.timeandhowtospendit.com/tedfogg)

'In days gone by this mind of mine used to stray wherever selfish desire or lust or pleasure would lead it ... Today this mind does not stray and is under the harmony of control, even as a wild elephant is controlled by the trainer.'
Jonathan Haidt, *The Happiness Hypothesis: Putting Ancient Wisdom to the Test of Modern Science* (London: Arrow, 2007).

Viva the New Cultural Revolution!

I first came across Warren Susman in Susan Cain, *Quiet: the power of introverts in a world that can't stop talking* (New York: Broadway Paperbacks, 2013).

I was so struck by the idea that I went looking for more. This section is based on that research, including:

Warren Susman, *Culture as History: The Transformation of American Society in the Twentieth Century* (Washington: Smithsonian Inst. Press, 2003).
Robert B. Westbrook (1985) 'Abundant Cultural History: The Legacy of Warren Susman.' *Reviews in American History*, Vol. 13, No. 4. pp. 481–486.

In Memory of Warren I. Susman, 1927–1985: Papers Delivered at Scott Hall, Rutgers, the State University of New Jersey, May 5, 1985. (New Brunswick, N.J.: Rutgers University Press, 1986).

the problem of 'stuffocation' and the rise of the experience economy in the UK as much as in the US.
For instance, in the US:

Sofia Horta e Costa, 'Millennials Are Starting to Change the Stock Market', *Bloomberg*, 1 February 2016.
Blake Morgan, 'NOwnership, No Problem: An Updated Look At Why Millennials Value Experiences Over Owning Things', *Forbes*, 2 January 2019

For instance, in the UK:
Simon Usborne, 'Just do it: the experience economy and how we turned our backs on stuff', *The Guardian*, 13 May 2017.
Leo Lewis and Emma Jacobs, 'How business is capitalising on the millennial Instagram obsession', *The Financial Times*, 13 July 2018.

are more depressed today than ever before
Oliver James, *Affluenza* (London: Vermilion, 2007).
Jean Twenge et al. (2010) 'Birth cohort increases in psychopathology among young Americans, 1938–2007: A cross-temporal meta-analysis of the MMPI.' *Clinical Psychology Review*, Vol. 30, No. 2, pp. 145–154.
Bruce Levine, "How our society breeds anxiety, depression and dysfunction", *Alternet/Salon*, 26 August 2013.

we are the first humans ever to want less, not more
James Wallman, *Stuffocation* (London: Penguin, 2015).

APPENDIX

Experience Intelligence Answers

ExQ:

Correct answers for 1, 2, 3, 4: a
Correct answers for 5, 6, 7, 8, 9, 10: b

To find the reasons why these answers are correct, read the relevant chapters:

1. See *Story, Transformation, Extraordinary* and *Status & Significance.*

2. See *Outside & Offline.*

3. See *Outside & Offline.*

4. See *Relationships.*

5. See *Intensity, Transformation,* and the Self-Determination Theory on page 87.

6. See *Story, Outside & Offline.*

7. See *Intensity,* and the concept of flow in *Extraordinary.*

8. See *Outside & Offline.*

9. See *Extraordinary.*

10. See *Status & Significance.*

ExQ 2:

Correct answers for 3, 4, 6, 7: a
Correct answers for 1, 2, 5, 8, 9, 10: b

To find the reasons why these answers are correct, read the relevant chapters:

1. See *Introduction, Intensity,* and *Status & Significance.*
2. See *Introduction.*
3. See *Outside & Offline.*
4. See *Story.*
5. See *Relationships.*
6. See *Status & Significance.*
7. See *Intensity,* and the concept of flow in *Extraordinary.*
8. See *Intensity.*
9. See *Extraordinary.*
10. See *Extraordinary.*

ACKNOWLEDGEMENTS

Thank you! THANK YOU! Thank you!

To...

... Joel Rickett, for having faith in me and my ideas – again.

... Diana Beaumont, for going on this journey with me, and being a great creative collaborator.

... The rest of the team at Penguin Random House: Lucy, for unfailing patience and being a great collaborator; Jo and Caroline and Patsy, for getting this idea to as many people as possible.

... The people who read early drafts, shared their thoughts on the ideas, and helped me shape the content: Rob Wallman, Alan Wallman, Richard Meier, Carl Kibblewhite, Henri Eliot, Helen Fisher, Andre Kemp, Pete Savage, Hana Manthorpe, Jennifer Lim, Alan Ackers, Helen Lafford, Juliet Le Coz.

... The people who gave me their time and thoughts and expertise and assistance: Tom Gilovich, Joe Pine, Pierre Bismuth, Cassie Mogilner, Clive Williams, Michael Bennett, Amit Kumar, Nir Eyal, BJ Fogg, Adam Alter, Natasha Dow Schüll, Sir Michael Marmot, Kate Lloyd, Tracy Shoolman, George MacKerron, Mark Williamson, Scott and Amber Keneally, Simon Kemp, Donald Redelmeier, David Morris, Brigid Schulte, Ed White, Hayley Shepherd, Flip Ryan, Deirdre McCloskey, Yoshifumi Miyazaki, Yoshi Kanehara, Danny Bowman, Victoria Grand, Jonah Berger, Dan Keeley, Michael Bennett.

... The scientists whose thinking, research, and hard work have provided the ingredients that, once distilled, would become this book's checklist: from Daniel Kahneman to Juliana Schroeder, Edward Deci, Sonja Lyubomirsky, Ann Masten, and all the others whose work is mentioned in the end notes.

... The people who supported Stuffocation, because the existence of *this* book is based on the success of *that* book: Nick Perry, Andy Gibson, Mark Tanzer, Ian Carrington, Victoria Grand, Sarah Oliver, Laura Atkinson, Julia Hartz and Terra Carmichael and the team at Eventbrite, David Hieatt and his team at the Do Lectures, Mark Williamson, Yvonne Cox, Anna Cofone, Sophie Taylor, Tom Hodgkinson, April Hutchison, Nelleke and Minouk van Lindonk, Pam Roderick, Chris Evans, Steve Wright, Claus Sendlinger, Christian Malcher, Serdar Kutucu, Henning Schaub, Dina Gundzya, Bobbi MacCaughan.

... Heini Davies, for fantastic, intelligent, sweeping research. And Nikita Skvortsof and Robelyn Amores for great research too.

... Thiru and Raj Raj-manickam, the best parents-in-law a man could have, for your support in general, and loaning me your house to write in.

... The people who looked after me in The Hampshire Hog, The Thatched House, the De La Warr Pavilion, and Punta Prima—especially Lydia, Juliet, and Jose.

... Susan Herbert, Davina MacKail, Nizami Cummins, Ewa Kolodziejska, Wendy Mandy, Lynn Jackson, Rita Hraiz, Logan Murray, Chris Coleridge—for inspiring and supporting my journey to here.

... The people who always support me, especially when things aren't working out... friends in need are friends indeed :-): Rob Wallman, Edwin Blanchard, Ben Pollard, Fiona Lay, Philipp Schwalber, Marc Jones.

… My Mum and Dad, of course. And their partners, Ian and Marilyn.

… Indy-May and Woody, because you two are the most amazing people I've ever had the luck to know. You inspire me with your energy, and giggling, and games, and tree-climbing, and bicycling, and swimming, and how you make even just jumping into the water or hanging out around the house an event that feels special and fun and magical.

… Tizz, for being a sounding board, an idea-generator, and a tricksy, difficult questioner who pushed me and believed in me; and for being a pretty terrific friend, lover, and wife.

… YOU, the person who bought this book. I think these ideas are pretty exciting, especially because they're less 'my' ideas, and much more my distillation and curation of what smart, hard-working scientists have discovered. These ideas are scientifically proven to lead to more happiness. How great is that! They've made my and my family's life more enjoyable, and I hope they do the same for you.

James
January 2019

For more inspiration and information on the latest experiences that tick the boxes of the STORIES checklist and are worth your time, check out:

www.timeandhowtospendit.com.

Share how you're using the STORIES checklist to have richer, happier days with me and the 'Time and How to Spend It' community!

Use @jameswallman when you post on Twitter or Instagram.

Email me at james.wallman@gmail.com with TIME AND HOW TO SPEND IT or STORIES in the title.

Use Facebook.com/timeandhowtospendit

INDEX